**Dark E~~**

**Book**

Scarab

by

**K. M. Ashman**

Copyright K. M. Ashman – January 2025

All rights are reserved. No part of this publication may be reproduced, stored, or transmitted in any form or by any means without prior written permission of the copyright owner. All characters depicted within this publication are fictitious, and any resemblance to any real person, living or dead, is entirely coincidental.

----

## Also by K. M. Ashman

### The Exploratores
Dark Eagle
The Hidden
Veteranus
Scarab
The Wraith
Silures
Panthera

### Seeds of Empire
Seeds of Empire
Rise of the eagle
Fields of Glory

### The Brotherhood
Templar Steel
Templar Stone
Templar Blood
Templar Fury
Templar Glory
Templar Legacy
Templar Loyalty

### The India Summers Mysteries
The Vestal Conspiracies
The Treasures of Suleiman
The Mummies of the Reich
The Tomb Builders

### The Roman Chronicles

The Fall of Britannia
The Rise of Caratacus
The Wrath of Boudicca

**The Medieval Sagas**
Blood of the Cross
In Shadows of Kings
Sword of Liberty
Ring of Steel

**The Blood of Kings**
A Land Divided
A Wounded Realm
Rebellion's Forge
The Warrior Princess
The Blade Bearer

**The Road to Hastings**
The Challenges of a King
The Promises of a King
The Fate of a King

**The Otherworld Series**
The Legacy Protocol
The Seventh God
The Last Citadel
Savage Eden
Vampire

## Character Names

### The Occultum

| | |
|---|---|
| Seneca | Roman Tribune |
| Marcus | Roman Centurion |
| Brennus | Batavian Auxiliary |
| Sica | Turkish Assassin |
| Falco | Ex Gladiator |
| Talorcan | Belgic Guide |
| Cassius | Exploratore |

### Other Roman Characters

| | |
|---|---|
| Veteranus | Retired Exploratore Veteran |
| Decimus | Retired Explorator Veteran |
| Raven | Traitorous Ex-member of the Occultum |
| Lepidus | Senator in charge of the Occultum |
| Postumus | Governor of Egypt |
| Tullus | Optio at the fort in Pselchis |

**Egypt**

**Circa 43AD**

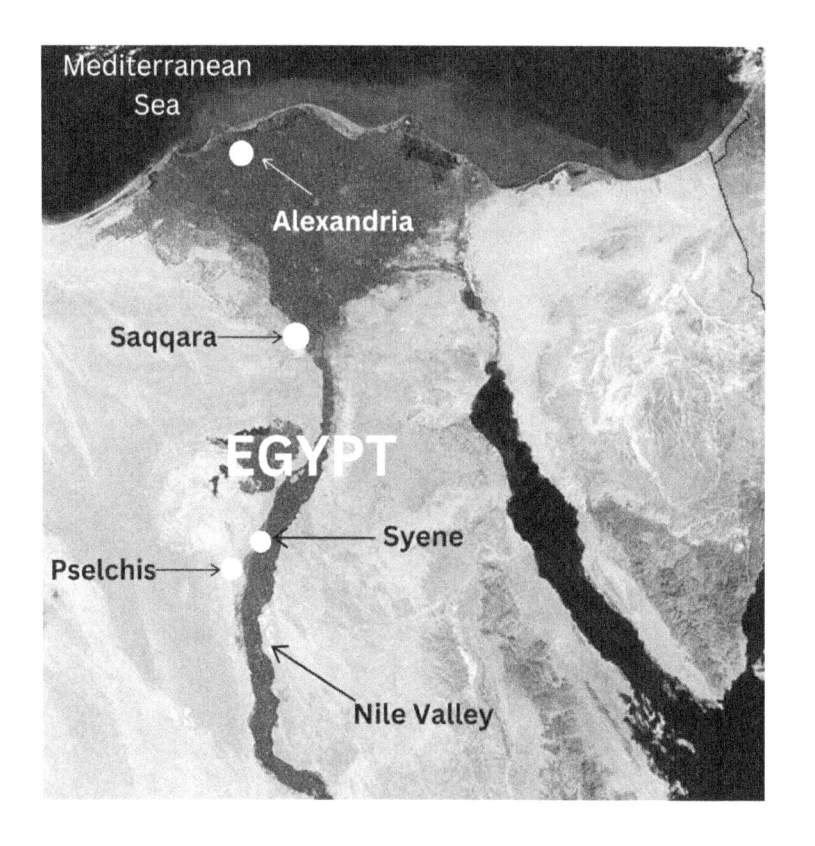

# Prologue

## Alexandria – AD 43

The capital of Egypt, Alexandria, unfurled along the shimmering blue expanse of the Mediterranean like a mosaic of marble and ambition. Founded by Alexander the Great, it had grown into one of the greatest cities of the ancient world, a place where the monumental collided with the ephemeral. It was here that Rome's dominion over Egypt was most tangible, yet Alexandria maintained a soul of its own, neither fully Roman nor wholly Egyptian, but something in between.

The city's famed harbours bustled with activity as the grain fleets prepared for departure. Merchants shouted in a cacophony of tongues, Latin mingling with Greek, Aramaic, and the fluid cadences of the Nile's native dialects. Masts rose like a forest of pines from the docks, their sails painted with the emblems of trading houses from across the empire. The salt-laden air carried the scent of spices from Arabia, the tang of freshly caught fish, and the earthy undertones of grain being loaded by the ton.

At the heart of the city stood the Great Lighthouse, the Pharos of Alexandria, its white stone tower glinting in the afternoon sun. A marvel of engineering, it guided ships safely through the treacherous waters of the delta, its flames visible for miles. Sailors whispered that the gods themselves watched over the beacon, ensuring the city's prosperity.

The streets of Alexandria radiated outward from the Canopic Way, a grand boulevard lined with colonnades and bustling with life. Roman soldiers patrolled in tight formations, their polished Lorica Segmentata catching the light, while citizens darted between them, their robes flaring in the breeze. Public baths and marketplaces teemed with humanity, a mix of merchants, scholars, labourers, and beggars, all jostling for space and shouting to be heard above the din.

The cultural heart of the city lay further inland: the Library of Alexandria, or what remained of it. Though much of the collection had been lost in earlier fires, scholars still roamed its echoing halls, poring over scrolls and debating philosophy in quiet alcoves. The library symbolized the city's enduring hunger for knowledge, a beacon of intellect even under Rome's yoke.

Yet the true power in Alexandria resided in the Roman governor's palace, a sprawling complex overlooking the harbour. The governor's residence was a fortress of bureaucracy, its marble halls crowded with scribes and officials managing the empire's lifeblood: the grain shipments destined for Rome. Statues of Caesar Augustus and the reigning emperor, Claudius, stood sentinel over the entrance, reminders of who truly ruled here.

Despite the Roman presence, Egypt's ancient soul thrummed just beneath the surface. The temples of Isis and Serapis remained hubs of devotion, their incense-laden courtyards filled with petitioners seeking the gods' favour. Priests in flowing robes moved with quiet purpose, their chants mingling with the cries of street vendors and the distant calls of gulls.

To the east of the city, the Nile stretched in all its majesty, a ribbon of life winding through the desert. From its fertile banks came the wealth that sustained Alexandria and, by extension, Rome itself. It was said that whoever controlled the Nile controlled the fate of empires, a truth etched into the very stones of the city.

As the sun dipped toward the horizon, Alexandria came alive with a different kind of energy. The wealthy reclined in their villas, hosting feasts where wine flowed like water and the strains of lyres and flutes filled the air. In the darker corners of the city, shadows flickered as merchants struck clandestine deals and whispered of uprisings that never came to fruition.

It was a city of contrasts: wealth and poverty, Roman

order and Egyptian mysticism, the ancient and the modern. It stood as both the jewel of the empire and the stinking underbelly of Rome's opulence, its undeniable beauty masking the struggles of the poor simmering beneath.

    And it was here that the fires of rebellion kindled, a weak yet growing flame of hope, and fear, and anticipation, as those that navigated the streets of power with such ease, colluded with the men of the dark. The time was getting near and soon the tyrannical yoke of Roman oppression would be cast aside, and the country of Aegyptus returned to the true leaders of the people, the old gods. To Ra, Osiris and Isis, and to Horus, Anubis and Thoth, each important deities in the pantheon of Egyptian gods, and each waiting patiently to be restored to the greatness they had enjoyed for millennia. The time was coming, and there was nothing the Romans could do about it.

----

## Chapter One

## The Mare Nostrum – AD 43

The grain ship Fortuna, its hull laden with precious cargo, creaked and groaned as it cut through the rolling swells of the Mediterranean. Its oaken timbers, bleached and cracked from years of salt and sun, carried the lifeblood of Rome: Alexandrian grain, destined to feed the hungry masses clamouring for their daily bread. The square sail, patched in places but still serviceable, bellied under a steady easterly breeze, while the rhythmic plunge of long, sturdy oars beneath her reinforced hull kept her true on her course toward Ostia.

The ship's master, a wiry Greek named Demetrios, stood at the stern with one hand on the tiller and the other shading his eyes against the glare of the late afternoon sun. His sharp gaze swept the horizon, but his thoughts lingered on the dangers that plagued these waters. Pirates were no longer the only menace; rumours of ships vanishing without trace or found adrift with no crew had spread fear among the Mediterranean's mariners.

High above, the lookout perched precariously in the swaying crow's nest let out a sudden cry of alarm.

'Smoke, my lord. To the east!'

Demetrios stiffened, his head snapping up to where the man pointed. Against the vivid blue of the sky, a distant dark plume curled and twisted, an ominous smudge rising from the shimmering expanse of the sea. The crew, hardened sailors and slaves alike turned their faces to the horizon with unease. They were in the middle of the sea, and there should be no smoke. Demetrios turned to his first mate, a burly Thracian named Aros.

'Change course,' he said quietly, 'let's see what burns.'

The Fortuna angled toward the smoke, her oars carving the waves with precision. As they drew closer, the source of the smoke revealed itself, a galley, its once-proud form now blackened and crippled, wallowing in the swell. Flames licked hungrily at the remnants of its scorched sails, but the fires along its deck seemed to have subsided, leaving only charred wreckage and tendrils of smoke that stung the nostrils as the grain ship approached.

Demetrios swore under his breath. The vessel was unmistakably Roman, its sturdy construction and reinforced hull marking it as a war galley. Scars along the prow spoke of battles fought and won, and its bronze ram, shaped like a snarling wolf, glinted dully in the fading light. But there was no sign of life aboard, no frantic figures battling the flames, no desperate cries for aid. Only the groan of wood and the crackle of dying embers.

'By the gods,' Aros muttered as they neared. 'What could've done this?'

Demetrios said nothing, his hand tightening on the tiller.

'Hold steady,' he ordered the rowers. 'Wait until the fire's out before we get any closer.'

The crew obeyed, their eyes fixed on the smouldering wreck. The Fortuna circled warily, the oarsmen straining against the currents to keep her at a safe distance, until the only evidence of the blaze was a scorched tangle of rigging hanging limply from the mast. Finally, Demetrios gave the order to approach.

'Ready grappling hooks,' he called. 'And stay sharp, whatever did this might still be nearby.'

The rowers brought the Fortuna alongside the crippled galley with practiced skill, their oars folding like wings as the two ships kissed gently in the swell. Hooks flew and lines tightened, drawing the vessels together as Aros and a small team scrambled aboard the galley, their footsteps kicking up the ash on the scorched deck.

The scene that met them was one of desolation. Blackened timbers jutted skyward like broken bones, and the acrid stench of smoke and charred flesh hung heavy in the air.

Demetrios' unease deepened as he watched his men search the ruined vessel. The sea was calm, the horizon empty. Yet the feeling of being watched lingered, a prickling at the base of his neck. Something was wrong. Something terrible had happened here.

Aros and his team advanced cautiously across the galley's deck, their sandals crunching on charred splinters and scorched debris. The faint creak of timbers and the rhythmic slap of the waves were the only sounds, an eerie counterpoint to the grisly tableau that greeted them.

The bodies of Roman mariners lay scattered everywhere, but something was wrong. Aros had seen dead men before, hundreds of them, and had even taken part in several battles, but he had never seen anything like this. The bodies, their expressions now frozen in death, did not show rage, or terror, or fury. There were no broken bones, or torn clothing or scattered weapons, there was nothing but dead men who had seemingly just laid down and died.

'Keep your nerve,' Aros growled. 'Whatever happened here, it's done. Focus on finding anything useful, or anyone still alive.'

The men nodded reluctantly, spreading out to search, their makeshift weapons clutched tightly as though they might ward off whatever horrors had visited the galley.

Demetrios watched from the Fortuna, his lean frame taut with tension. His knuckles whitened on the tiller as he shouted across the narrowing gap between the ships.

'What do you see, Aros?'

'Death,' came the grim reply. Aros knelt by a corpse, rolling it over with care. His grimace deepened as he inspected the man's wounds, a single slice to throat, opening his jugular.

The search yielded little beyond the grim evidence of slaughter. The ship's stores had been raided; amphorae lay shattered, their contents spilled and wasted. Personal belongings were scattered and trampled, but some crates of military supplies, javelins and spare shields, remained untouched, as though the attackers cared only for speed.

'Anything of value?' Demetrios called again. He felt the eyes of his own crew upon him, their unease mirroring his own. Mariners who plied the grain routes were accustomed to danger - storms, pirates, and reefs, but this was something else entirely.

Aros stood slowly, scanning the deck one last time.

'Nothing alive, Captain,' he said, louder now. 'And no sign of what killed them, only that they all died the same way.'

A sense of dread settled over the grain ship's crew as the team returned to the railing. Their faces were pale, their movements quick and nervous as they swung back onto the Fortuna.

'We've seen enough,' Aros said grimly as he climbed aboard. 'Whoever, or whatever, did this is gone, but their handiwork speaks for itself.'

Demetrios nodded sharply, his gaze fixed on the dark stains that marked his men's sandals. He didn't need to ask for more details. He had seen the terror in their eyes.

'All oars to the water,' he barked. 'We leave this place now. Ready the sail.'

The crew scrambled to obey, their movements fuelled by desperation. But as the Fortuna turned away from the ruined galley, Demetrios couldn't shake the sensation of unseen eyes still watching, lurking just beyond the horizon.

----

As the Fortuna reached a distance from the crippled galley, the crew worked in uneasy silence, their eyes darting to the horizon as though expecting an unseen enemy to appear. At the stern, Demetrios remained at his post, one hand still gripping the tiller while his other rested on the pommel of the small dagger at his belt, a pitiful comfort against the kind of menace that could slaughter an entire Roman war galley's crew.

Aros approached, his broad shoulders hunched and his weathered face grim. The stench of smoke and blood still clung to his tunic, and his steps felt heavy with the weight of what he had seen. He climbed the few steps to the captain's platform and stood there for a moment, watching the smoking wreck recede into the distance before speaking.

'What is it, Aros?' said Demetrios, 'spit it out.'

'They were all dead, captain,' said Aros. 'Every last one of them. No sign of a fight. No enemy bodies. No scattered weapons or signs of a struggle. Just… dead men lying in pools of their own blood. It's as if they didn't even fight back, they just stood there and… let it happen.'

'That's impossible,' said the captain. 'A Roman galley's crew is disciplined, trained to fight and die on their feet if need be. Even if they were caught by surprise, they wouldn't go down without a struggle.'

'Exactly,' Aros agreed. 'But this… this wasn't natural. It felt wrong. Like something otherworldly.'

Demetrios cast a sharp glance at his first mate.

'Watch your tongue, Aros,' he snapped. 'We're sailors, not storytellers. Don't let superstition infect the men.'

'I'm not trying to scare them,' Aros said, holding the captain's gaze. 'But you saw their faces when we came back aboard. They felt it too, the wrongness of it. Something terrible happened on that ship, and we're fools if we don't take it seriously.'

'Double the watch tonight,' said the captain. 'No one sleeps more than four hours, and I want two men at every station. If they see anything at all, they sound the alarm.'

Aros nodded and turned to carry out the order, but Demetrios stopped him with a hand on his arm.

'And Aros,' he said, 'keep the men calm. We've got a long journey ahead, and I don't need them jumping at shadows.'

The first mate gave a grim smile.

'Aye, Captain. Though I'll wager it's not shadows they fear.'

As Aros descended to the deck, Demetrios stayed where he was, his gaze lingering on the distant plume of smoke. He couldn't shake the gnawing feeling in his gut, a sense that they had stumbled into something far beyond their understanding. And he for one wanted to get as far as he possibly could away from it.

----

## Chapter Two

## Egypt

The moon hung low over the desert, its pale light glinting off the shifting sands as the Nubian raiding party crept toward the Egyptian border town. They moved like shadows, their bodies swathed in dark cloth that blended seamlessly with the dunes.

Their leader, Abasi, a wiry man with eyes like a hawk, signalled with a sharp flick of his fingers, and the group came to a halt. They crouched in the lee of a jagged outcrop, the town now visible in the shallow valley below. Its low, mud-brick walls were dark against the sands, and the faint outlines of storage silos stood silhouetted against the horizon.

Abasi scanned the scene carefully. The Romans, he knew, kept a fort not far from here. The patrols were sporadic but deadly, the legionaries well-armed and ruthless. A single misstep, a clumsy sound, an errant glint of metal, could bring them down in force.

His fellow tribesmen looked to him with total trust and obedience. He had been their leader for many years, ever since his father had been killed by a desert lion, and he had proved a good chieftain, in good times and in bad. These were the latter, a time of fear and of desperation. Hunger drove them, but they were desert men, accustomed to patience. Any food obtained from the village before them could feed their people for weeks, perhaps longer… if they succeeded.

Abasi gave the signal to advance, and they continued down the slope towards the Egyptian village. The approach was slow, deliberate. Bare feet slid noiselessly over the cool sand, careful to avoid the crunch of loose stones or the brittle snap of dried grass. Abasi paused at the edge of the town, raising a hand again to halt his men. The silence struck him first, a deep, unnatural stillness. No dogs barked, no muffled voices murmured from within the homes, no faint snatches of song or laughter broke the night.

His brow furrowed. Something wasn't right. The villagers here were poor but lively and their evenings were usually filled with the sounds of life. He exchanged a glance with the man closest to him, a hulking fighter named Kamalu, who shrugged uneasily.

Cautiously, Abasi motioned them forward. They slipped into the town like shadows, the silence deepening as they entered the narrow streets, the air thick with an almost oppressive stillness.

The first house they passed had its door ajar, swinging slightly in the faint breeze. Abasi peered inside but found no sign of life, no sleeping bodies, no evidence of hurried departure. A clay jar lay shattered on the floor, its contents spilled and congealed.

They pressed on, skirting the central square where a well stood dark and unused. The granaries loomed ahead, their thick wooden doors reinforced to protect the grain from thieves and rodents. To the Nubians' surprise, the doors were unbarred.

Kamalu stepped forward, his bulk moving with surprising grace as he eased the door open. Inside, sacks of grain were piled high, untouched. The men exchanged wary glances, this was too easy.

'Take what we can and leave,' whispered Abasi.

They moved quickly now, each man hefting as many sacks as he could carry. The grain was heavy, its weight a blessed burden on their starving shoulders. Still, the eerie emptiness of the town gnawed at them. Abasi's instincts screamed a warning, but he pushed it aside. They needed to get back to the desert before the Romans found them.

As they retreated, the silence became oppressive. The town seemed to watch them, its shadowed alleys and abandoned homes exuding an unnatural stillness and by the time they reached the outskirts, even Kamalu, normally unshakable, kept glancing over his shoulder.

They retreated back up the hill, moving swiftly and silently, the town disappearing into the darkness behind them. No alarms had been raised, no shouts of pursuit followed them. It was almost as if no one had been there to notice their presence at all.

----

Abasi led his men deeper into the dunes, their burdens growing heavier with each step. The desert was a fickle ally, its cold night air biting at their skin while the sand shifted treacherously underfoot. The village was behind them now, swallowed by the endless sea of darkness, but its silence clung to their thoughts like a persistent shadow.

The group moved with a grim determination, their silence a tacit acknowledgment of the unease none dared voice. Then, cutting through the stillness, came a sound, a sharp yip, followed by the low growl of a scavenger. Abasi stopped abruptly, raising his hand. The men froze, their breathing shallow as they listened.

More cries followed, the unmistakable squabbling of jackals. The noise grew, rising and falling in a chaotic symphony that seemed to come from just over the next rise. Kamalu stepped up beside Abasi.

'Jackals,' he muttered. 'There must be something dead nearby.'

'It's worth a look,' said Kamalu, 'there may be some meat we can salvage.'

Abasi nodded, his face impassive. Meat was always hard to come by, even scavenged meat. With a bit of luck, it could be the leg of an antelope, or even a head, all meat was good.

'Let's go,' he said, and the men followed him off the well-beaten track.

The jackals' cries grew louder as they neared, their savage

squabbles echoing off unseen rock faces. The dunes gave way to harder ground, the sand thinning to reveal patches of cracked earth and jagged stones. As they crested the next rise, the clouds above shifted, peeling back from the moon to flood the landscape with pale light, and what they saw stopped them cold.

A vast natural bowl lay before them, its sloping sides leading down to a blackened pit where the remains of a fire still smouldered. Around it, littered in chaotic disarray, were the bodies, hundreds of them, men, women, children, their lifeless forms sprawled across the ground like discarded dolls. The moonlight caught on twisted limbs, gaping wounds, and the dull sheen of blood that had long since dried.

The smell hit them next, a sickening stench of decay and charred flesh that clawed its way into their nostrils and turned their stomachs. Several of the men gagged, one doubling over to retch into the sand.

Abasi forced himself to breathe shallowly, his hand tightening on the hilt of his curved blade. He scanned the scene, his sharp eyes picking out the details: the torn clothes, the scattered belongings, the sheer, unrelenting scale of the carnage. These were no soldiers; the dead wore the simple garments of villagers.

Among the corpses moved the jackals. Dozens of them, their thin, mangy bodies darting between the dead, ripping into the flesh with gleaming teeth. They snarled and snapped at each other, their bloodied muzzles glistening in the moonlight.

Kamalu cursed under his breath.

'What in all the hells is this?' he whispered.

Abasi didn't answer. He stepped forward, scanning the ground for any signs of movement among the bodies. There was none.

'We shouldn't be here, Abasi,' said one of the younger men behind him. 'This is… this is cursed ground.'

Abasi straightened and looked over at him.

'Curses don't kill hundreds of people,' he said, though the words felt hollow even to his own ears. 'We don't leave without understanding what happened here.'

Kamalu looked at him sharply.

'And if it happens to us?'

Abasi's gaze hardened.

'If we don't understand this, it might. Keep your wits about you. We'll make it quick.'

The men reluctantly spread out, keeping close enough to hear each other over the squabbling of the jackals. Abasi descended toward the fire, his every step calculated, his senses straining for any sign of danger. As he neared the center of the bowl, the heat from the embers prickled his skin, though the fire was long dead. Around it lay more bodies, arranged in a haphazard circle, as though they had fallen while fleeing.

At the edge of the fire pit, he stopped and knelt, gently turning over the body of a baby. His heart missed a beat at the sight of her injuries, and he said a silent prayer, begging for a safe journey for her spirit on her journey to the afterlife.

He straightened slowly, his mind racing. It would have taken many men to do this, and it would not have been quick, but what scared him the most was the fact that there were no signs of any sort of struggle. Some of the men gathered around and stared down at the baby.

'We take what we've seen back to the others,' he said finally, the dread coiling in his gut.

The men nodded, their faces pale as they retreated from the bowl and, as they ascended the rise, the jackals paused in their feasting to watch them, their yellow eyes glinting in the moonlight.

----

## Chapter Three

### Alexandria

The long shadows cast by the braziers danced against the marble walls of the governor's palace, illuminating its grandeur with a flickering, golden light. Gaius Julius Postumus sat at the head of an ebony table so vast that it seemed to consume the room. The edges of the table were inlaid with ivory, a gleaming contrast to the dark wood, while the carved legs curled into lion's paws. Behind him, the towering window framed Alexandria's great harbour, its waters silvered by moonlight. Masts swayed lazily in the breeze, and the distant cry of a gull carried faintly through the silence.

Postumus was not a man of grand gestures. His power, as Rome's prefect of Egypt, was spoken in quiet commands, enforced by legions, and felt across the empire in the grain that fed its hungry masses. Yet tonight, he looked troubled. His sharp eyes, deep-set beneath a furrowed brow, rested on the long scroll unfurled before him. A half-empty goblet of Falernian wine sat untouched at his elbow, its aroma mingling with the faint scent of incense wafting from the corners of the room.

Standing nearby, his chief aide, Lucius Marcellinus shifted uncomfortably. The Roman administrator was a man tired by the demands of empire. His thinning hair was slicked back, but sweat still glistened on his brow, betraying the strain of recent weeks. In his hands, he clutched yet another report, one of many that had passed across this room in an endless tide of bad news.

'Another shortfall,' said Postumus, his words slicing through the silence. 'First Memphis, then Hermopolis, and now Crocodilopolis.' He leaned back, his gaze piercing. 'These governors test the patience of the empire, Lucius.'

The aide hesitated, then stepped forward, unrolling the scroll he carried.

'Excellency,' he began carefully, 'the reports from the nomes are... consistent. The Nile's flooding has been erratic this year. In some regions, the waters never reached the fields. In others, entire villages were swept away. Panehesy, the governor of the Crocodilopolis nome, claims his stores were...'

'Panehesy?' Postumus interrupted. He leaned forward, his hands resting on the table's edge. 'That name has crossed my desk far too often. Every year, there is some excuse. A failed harvest, bandits, flooding. Yet the grain quotas are not negotiable. Do you think the mobs in Rome will accept a barren Nile as an explanation when they riot for their bread?'

'No, Excellency,' replied Lucius, 'but Panehesy is not alone in this. Other governors report similar struggles. Even the nome of Antaeopolis, which has never failed us before, sent only half its usual stores.'

Postumus leaned back, his gaze narrowing as he considered the scrolls scattered before him. The flickering torchlight deepened the lines on his face, making him look older than his forty years.

'This is not the first time I've heard such claims,' he said quietly. 'But this... this is worse. Every week, another nome falls short. And it is not just the grain. The roads are less safe, merchants speak of bandits growing bold, and priests whisper of unrest among the peasants. Tell me, Lucius, are we losing control?'

The aide straightened, though his expression remained grim.

'No, Excellency. The legions hold the garrisons, and the grain routes remain open. But there are... murmurs. The old gods of Egypt have always stirred unrest amongst the people, and with famine comes desperation.'

Postumus's mouth curled into a faint sneer.

'The old gods,' he said, the words heavy with disdain. 'Let them pray to Ra and Osiris all they like. It will not fill their bellies. The Nile's favour is fickle, Lucius, but Rome's is not. These governors will deliver their quotas, or they will face consequences.'

Lucius hesitated, then inclined his head.

'Panehesy will be here shortly, Excellency. He is one of the last to respond to your summons.'

'And he is late,' Postumus said coldly. 'This is not a council of equals, Lucius. The governors of Egypt's nomes are servants of Rome, just as the grain fields are Rome's property. If Panehesy thinks he can shirk his duty because he bows to his precious Isis and not the emperor, he is mistaken.'

The bronze doors at the far end of the hall groaned suddenly, their weight reverberating through the chamber as they swung open. Postumus turned his gaze toward them, his expression unreadable. Beyond the threshold, the flickering torches revealed the figure of Panehesy.

The Egyptian governor stepped hesitantly into the room, his sandaled feet making faint echoes on the polished marble floor. He wore the robes of his station, their gold embroidery catching the light, but his face betrayed his unease. His features were proud, his skin weathered by years under the desert sun, but his eyes darted nervously between the towering statues of Augustus and Isis that flanked the entrance, as though measuring his allegiances.

Postumus remained seated, his presence commanding even in stillness. He let the silence stretch as Panehesy began his slow, deliberate walk across the expanse of the hall. The Roman guards stationed along the walls stood motionless, their polished armour glinting in the torchlight, while the ever-watchful Lucius stepped back into the shadows, his sharp eyes fixed on the approaching figure.

Panehesy's steps faltered slightly as he neared the table, his unease palpable in the cavernous room. Postumus let his gaze rest on the Egyptian governor, unblinking, the weight of his authority filling the silence like a thundercloud. Finally, Panehesy stopped several paces from the table and inclined his head in a shallow bow.

'Excellency,' he said, 'I am at your service.'

Postumus did not reply immediately. Instead, he regarded the man with a cool, calculating look, as though weighing every word that would follow. The brazier flames flickered, and the oppressive silence returned, broken only by the distant murmur of Alexandria beyond the palace walls.

Panehesy's shallow bow lingered a moment longer before he straightened, his fingers twitching nervously at his sides. His dark eyes flicked between the seated governor and the shadowed columns behind him, as though seeking an escape that didn't exist. Postumus, seated like a marble statue at the head of the table, did not gesture for him to sit. Instead, he stared at Panehesy with a gaze that might have turned lesser men to stone.

'Well?' he said eventually, 'I summoned you hours ago, Panehesy. Why do you keep me waiting? I hope it is because your mules are weighed down by so many sacks of grain, they are even slower than usual?'

Panehesy stiffened, his lips tightening, though he dared not show his anger.

'No, Excellency,' he said. 'The journey was long, and I thought it prudent to ensure my reports were complete before I appeared before you.'

'Prudent,' Postumus echoed. He leaned back in his chair, the rich crimson of his cloak pooling around him. 'Very well, then. Let us hear your report. Explain to me, Panehesy, why yet another nome under your administration has failed to deliver what is owed to Rome.'

Panehesy swallowed hard and clasped his hands before him.

'Excellency, the grain is there,' he began, 'the fields are full, but… I cannot get it in, not in time.'

Postumus's eyes narrowed, but he said nothing, allowing Panehesy to continue.

'The floodwaters receded late this year,' Panehesy explained, his words tumbling out now, as if he could will his sincerity to bridge the chasm between them. 'The fields ripened, but the workers… they stayed away. By the time I could gather enough hands, the grain had begun to wither under the sun.'

'You let the grain rot in the fields,' Postumus said coldly, his words more an accusation than a question. 'What good are full fields if the granaries are empty? Do you think Rome cares for your excuses?'

Panehesy's hands tightened into fists, the tension in his posture betraying his desperation.

'I tried everything, Excellency. I increased the payment for labourers. I sent my officials to every village, to every hut. I promised rewards, food, protection for their families. When that failed, I turned to harsher measures, threats, beatings. I conscripted anyone I could find. And yet…'

'And yet you failed,' Postumus finished. 'These are your lands, Panehesy. Your workers. If they do not obey, it is because they do not fear you enough.'

Panehesy's face flushed with frustration.

'Excellency, it is not fear of me they lack. They are just more afraid of something else. Something… beyond my reach.'

Postumus raised an eyebrow.

'What nonsense is this? Bandits? Raiders? Speak plainly.'

'It is not men they fear, Excellency,' replied Panehesy. 'It is the old gods.'

Postumus leaned forward, his gaze turning icier.

'The old gods,' he said slowly. 'Do not waste my time with such superstitions, Panehesy. Isis and Osiris are nothing but stone and myth. These workers are peasants, they eat, they work, they sleep. They fear empty bellies more than their gods.'

Panehesy's expression twisted, his frustration spilling through.

'Excellency, with respect, you do not understand. These people would rather starve than anger the gods. They whisper of curses, of omens. They say the floods came late because the gods were displeased. That to disturb the fields at the wrong time is to invite their wrath. I have seen it with my own eyes, men collapsing in fear at the edge of the fields, refusing to set foot on the soil. I cannot force them if they believe they are already doomed.'

Postumus slammed his hand down on the table, the sound echoing sharply through the hall. Panehesy flinched, his shoulders drawing tight.

'Then make them believe otherwise!' he shouted, 'show them what happens when Rome is displeased! Drag their priests into the fields if you must and make an example of them. Burn their temples if that is what it takes to remind them who rules here but do something. This is not acceptable.'

Panehesy shook his head, his face creased with worry.

'It is no good, Excellency. I have tried. I have arrested their leaders, beaten their elders, even destroyed their offerings but it only hardens their resolve. They would rather face Rome's punishments than anger the gods. They believe that their suffering is temporary, but the wrath of the gods is eternal.'

The tension in the room was suffocating, and Postumus stared at Panehesy intensely trying to assess whether his words any fragment of truth or were simply excuses.

'And what do you believe, Panehesy?' he asked finally. 'Do you also fear the wrath of Isis and Osiris? Is that just an excuse why you come to me with your failures instead of solutions?'

Panehesy straightened.

'I serve Rome, Excellency. My fears are irrelevant. But the workers... the workers serve their gods before all else. You may have the power to break their bodies, but not their faith.'

Postumus said nothing for a long moment. The brazier flames flickered, casting long shadows across the governor's face, and the tension in the room stretched taut, ready to snap.

'Enough,' he snapped eventually. 'You have failed to deliver what is owed to Rome, and I do not have the luxury of tolerating failure. Rome demands grain and grain it will have. If you cannot compel your people to work, then I will send the legions to your precious fields and administer Rome's punishment myself. Do you imagine your villagers will still cower before their gods when they see and feel Roman steel? When their homes burn, and their livestock are slaughtered?'

Panehesy stiffened. He looked like a man caught in a storm, buffeted on all sides, yet unable to find shelter.

'Excellency,' he began, 'I will do all I can. But threats alone will not...'

'You will do more,' shouted Postumus, rising from his chair. His crimson cloak swirled as he stepped forward. 'You will gather the grain. You will remind your people that it is not Isis or Osiris who holds power here, it is Rome. Fail me again, Panehesy, and I swear it is you that will feel the physical pain of failure.'

Panehesy's shoulders slumped slightly, defeat creeping into his posture. He inclined his head, his tone resigned.

'Yes, Excellency,' he said quietly and without another word, he turned on his heel and walked toward the great bronze doors. His sandaled feet echoed hollowly in the vast chamber, each step heavy with despair. As the doors groaned shut behind him, the silence returned, oppressive and cold.

Postumus remained standing, his gaze fixed on the closed doors for a long moment before he exhaled sharply and turned to his aide.

'The same old excuses,' he muttered, 'floods, famine, and now this nonsense about the old gods. How many times have we heard it?'

'Too many, Excellency,' replied Lucius, stepping. His thin face bore the weary expression of a man who had no good answers. 'Every report is the same. The grain rots in the fields because no one will harvest it and no amount of coin, threats, or violence has made a difference.'

Postumus moved to the window. The harbour lay beneath him, the faint lights of Alexandria flickering like distant stars.

'What is it, Lucius?' he asked after a pause. 'What makes these fools so afraid? I've dealt with unrest before, rebellions, uprisings, but this is something else. They speak of the gods, but no one can tell me what it is they fear most. Is it Isis? Osiris? Some obscure deity buried under the sands?'

Lucius hesitated, his hands fidgeting with the edge of his scroll.

'I don't know, Excellency. Perhaps it's all of them, or none. They speak in riddles. Omens, wrath, a curse on the Nile. But no one will say more, as if even naming their fears would bring ruin.'

Postumus stared out into the night.

'It is a mystery,' he said finally. 'And it is one we cannot afford to let linger. The emperor will not accept riddles, nor will I. Have you sent the message I dictated to Rome two months ago?'

'I have, Excellency,' Lucius, replied, straightening. 'And I received a reply just this morning.'

Postumus turned sharply, his interest piqued.

'And?'

Lucius fumbled briefly with his papers, his fingers finding the right scroll. He unrolled it carefully and scanned the contents.

'The Senate is aware of the situation,' he said. 'The reply

states that something is being put in place to investigate. Reinforcements, perhaps, or a delegation. It's not specific.'

Postumus frowned.

'Who sent the reply?'

Lucius squinted at the bottom of the scroll.

'It was signed by a senator, Excellency. A man by the name of... Quintus Marcius Lepidus.'

Postumus's expression darkened, his brow furrowing.

'Lepidus?' he repeated, his tone both sceptical and intrigued. 'I do not know the name.'

'Nor I,' Lucius admitted, his tone hesitant. 'But the message bore the imperial seal so whatever this Lepidus is planning, it comes with the emperor's blessing.'

Postumus nodded slowly, his gaze distant.

'Very well,' he said. 'For now, we will do what we can but if Rome does not act swiftly, Egypt will descend into chaos.

----

## Chapter Four

### Aquae Tarbellicae

Falco and Sica stepped into the warmth of the Hornless Bull, their travel-stained cloaks swirling around their boots as the heavy wooden door shut behind them. The familiar scent of roasting meat, spiced wine, and the faint tang of ale hung in the air, mingling with the low murmur of voices from the clustered patrons. Aquae Tarbellicae was far from the bustling cities of Gaul, but the taberna was always lively, a crossroads for travellers, traders, and those who sought refuge from the weather…and the overbearing gaze of anyone official.

Falco slowly adjusted the strap of his pack, his wounds still a dull ache despite weeks of recovery. His dark eyes scanned the room, and he smiled warmly as he caught sight of the woman they'd come to find, Marcia. She stood behind the counter, pouring a foaming cup of ale, her sharp features framed by dark hair tied loosely at the nape of her neck. She noticed them immediately, her lips twitching into a faint smirk. Marcia had owned the Hornless Bull for many years and the men of the Occultum, both past and present, treated it as their home, knowing that, not only were they were safe from betrayal, but Marcia's vast net of informants were always able to keep them one step ahead of any danger.

'Falco, Sica.' Her voice carried above the hum of the crowd as she waved them over. 'Come, we've been expecting you. What took you so long?'

'Blame the Celts,' Falco replied with a crooked grin, shrugging off his pack and heading toward the counter. 'Is Decimus here?'

Marcia shook her head.

'Not yet. I'll send for him in a moment, but first…' She

gestured toward the back of the taberna, 'let me get you settled.'

Without waiting for a response, she led them through the narrow passage behind the bar and into a small, dimly lit room. A sturdy oak table dominated the space, its surface scarred by years of use. A platter of roasted cheese, crusty bread, and a jug of red wine waited, the sight enough to make Falco's stomach tighten with hunger.

'Sit,' she said briskly, pouring them each a cup of wine. 'There'll be hot food coming soon but, in the meantime, this should ease the worst of your hunger.'

Falco eased into a chair with a muffled groan, his body protesting the movement. He took a long sip of the wine, savouring its warmth before setting the cup down with a satisfied sigh. Sica remained standing, watching the door.

'Relax, Sica,' said Marcia, her tone lightly mocking. 'You know you're safe here.'

'Safe is an illusion,' Sica replied, though he finally took a seat and leaned out for a cup of wine.

Falco reached for the bread, tearing off a piece and chewing thoughtfully.

'She hasn't changed,' he said, once she had left the room. 'Still as sharp and as beautiful as ever.'

A short time later, the door creaked open and Decimus entered, his broad frame filling the doorway. His grizzled features were weathered by years of service, his grey-streaked hair pulled back in a rough knot. Despite his semi-retirement, he still carried himself with the quiet confidence of a man who had seen too much to be easily rattled.

'Falco, Sica,' he said as he crossed the room to clasp their forearms in greeting. 'It's good to see you both alive. Where are the others?'

'I suspect they are on their way,' said Falco, 'but we came on ahead.'

Decimus settled into a chair, pouring himself a cup of wine.

'Well, you two are here,' he said, 'so at least we can make a start.'

'We didn't have much choice,' said Sica. 'What is this about? Why have we been called here?'

Decimus set his cup down carefully.

'Let's just say... Lepidus is worried. And when Lepidus worries, it's never good news.' He hesitated for a moment, as if weighing his next words, before continuing. 'It seems that Rome has serious problems in Egypt and needs the Occultum to find out what is going on.'

Falco's brow furrowed as he tore off another piece of bread, chewing slowly.

'The whole Occultum? That's ambitious, considering we don't even know if Seneca and the others are still alive.'

'We don't,' said Decimus, ' but for now, we'll make do with what we have.'

'So, what's the problem?' asked Sica.

'Grain,' said Decimus simply. 'Rome has been losing grain ships in the Mare Nostrum, and those that do make it to Ostia aren't carrying nearly enough. The people are hungry, and bread riots are breaking out in the streets. Unrest and is brewing and you know as well as I, that when the people hunger, they'll turn on anyone... senators, the legions, even the emperor.'

'And why is that our problem?' asked Falco. 'We're not grain merchants.'

'Because Rome believes the problem starts in Egypt,' replied Decimus. 'There are whispers of a rebellion brewing, hidden in the shadows, supported by corrupt Egyptian officials. Ships are disappearing, quotas aren't being met, and no one knows exactly why. If Egypt revolts, or if its officials conspire against Rome, the empire's grain supply collapses, and if that happens, Rome itself falls into chaos.'

Sica frowned.

'If Rome suspects a rebellion, why not use the legions? That's what they're for.'

Decimus shook his head.

'The legions are stretched thin. The southern borders are bleeding men against the Numidians and those stationed in Alexandria and Cairo are in no condition to be sent south. Many of them are… unwell.'

'What do you men unwell,' asked Falco?'

Decimus hesitated, his hand tightening around his cup.

'Men are seeing things, claiming they've seen the old gods of Egypt with their own eyes. Osiris, Anubis, even Ra. They've begun worshipping them, abandoning their oaths to Rome. It's not just a handful, either. Whole barracks are infected with this… madness, and the governor is struggling to keep what peace remains.'

The room fell silent, the weight of Decimus's words sinking in. The faint hum of voices from the main room of the taberna seemed distant, swallowed by the oppressive tension.

'The legions are the backbone of Rome,' Decimus continued. 'If they falter, if they fall to superstition and fear, the enemies at our borders will sense the weakness and strike. Egypt is already surrounded, Numidians to the south, raiders in the east, and now internal threats as well.'

Sica's brow furrowed as he stared at Decimus.

'And what are we supposed to do about it?' he asked. We're not soldiers anymore nor are we medici. We can't fight an invisible rebellion or cure men of their delusions.'

'No one's asking us to fight,' Decimus replied. 'Lepidus doesn't need swords, he needs eyes and ears. We've been tasked with infiltrating various organizations in Egypt, including the legions and the government offices. Our orders are to stay undercover and listen. Find out what's happening and who is behind this. We're to gather information, nothing more.'

Falco scoffed, leaning back in his chair and taking a swig of wine.

'There's no way I'm joining a legion again, Decimus. My days of marching under Rome's banner are long gone.'

'You don't have to,' replied Decimus, a small smile tugging at the corner of his lips. 'I have something else in mind for you. There's a ludus in Alexandria, a damn good one, run by a man I trust. Your skills would make you a star there. As a freedman, you'd be free to come and go as you pleased, mingling with the upper levels of society, the same upper levels who are obsessed with gladiatorial competitions. Lepidus suspects that this whole thing is being orchestrated by the wealthy and that could be our way in. They'll talk, Falco, and if you are successful in the arena, you will be there amongst them to listen.'

Falco's expression shifted, the frown replaced by a glint of interest.

'A ludus, you say. It's been a while since I've put on a real show. They haven't seen anything like me yet.' He sat back, a cocky grin spreading across his face as he took another long drink of wine. 'I'll do it. Let's see what the high and mighty in Alexandria have to say when they're watching me leave their champions bleeding in the sand.'

Sica leaned forward, resting his elbows on the table, and fixed Decimus with a hard stare.

'And what about me?' he asked. 'You've got Falco prancing around with a sword, charming senators with blood and guts. What's my role in this grand plan?'

'You, my Syrian friend, will be delving into the underbelly of Alexandria. The back streets, the alleys, the places where the lantern light barely reaches. The people who thrive in the shadows, smugglers, thieves, sellers of secrets. The kind of people who make their living by less-than-honourable means.'

Sica raised an eyebrow.

'And why do you think I'll fit in so well with that lot?'

Decimus chuckled.

'Because you are that lot, Sica. Don't play coy. You've spent more time in the underworld than most of them. You know the language, the rules, and how to get what you want without getting a knife in the ribs. You'll fit right in, better than the rest of us, at least.'

Sica leaned back, rubbing his jaw thoughtfully.

'Fair enough,' he said, a flicker of interest in his expression. 'Loose tongues tend to wag in the backstreets, and people will sell their own mothers for the right price. I can work with that.'

Decimus nodded, his tone turning serious again.

'Good. When Seneca gets here, his focus will be the governor. If this rebellion is being supported by Roman officials, that's where we'll find the trail. And Marcus will join one of the legions He'll keep his ears open and report back on whatever he learns. The rest of the Occultum will also be stationed in Alexandria but will keep a low profile until ready to act if needed.

'Under whose command?' asked Falco.

'Mine,' said Decimus.

Falco let out a low whistle, setting his cup down.

'You? Back on the front line? I thought you'd retired, old man. Living the quiet life, enjoying the comforts of a soft bed and good wine.'

Decimus snorted, a bitter edge to his laugh.

'Retirement isn't all it's cracked up to be, Falco. Civilian life is... dull. Endless days of nothing, and besides...' He paused, his expression hardening as he looked down into his cup. 'My woman left me.'

Falco blinked, caught off guard by the sudden turn in

tone.

'Left you? Why?'

Decimus swirled the wine in his cup.

'Because I got stupid drunk and beat a man half to death just for looking at her. She said she couldn't forgive me for that. And, honestly, I don't blame her.'

The room fell quiet for a moment, the weight of Decimus's confession settling between them. Falco broke the silence with a dry chuckle.

'Well, it sounds like you're back where you belong then, Decimus. Among men who'll also beat someone to within an inch of their life and call it a good day's work. But if you're leading this, you'd better keep up. I'd hate to carry you when things get messy.'

Decimus raised his cup in a mock toast, his smirk matching Falco's.

'Don't worry about me, Falco. Just worry about keeping yourself alive in that ludus. They might have loved you in the arenas of Rome, but until you prove otherwise, the crowds of Alexandria will see you as just another sword-swinging brute.'

Falco raised his own cup, his grin widening.

'You are right,' he said. 'They haven't seen anything like me yet.' He leaned back in his chair. 'When do we go?'

'We'll wait a few weeks,' said Decimus, 'perhaps a month and see if the rest turn up.'

'And in the meantime,' said Falco. 'We enjoy free wine, good food, and a bit of... local entertainment?' He raised his eyebrows suggestively, his grin widening.

Decimus snorted, shaking his head.

'I should have known your mind would wander there, Falco. No, we'll be using the time wisely. I've already made arrangements.'

'Arrangements?' asked Falco. 'What sort of arrangements.'

'I've met a man here in Aquae Tarbellicae,' said Decimus.

35

'A trader who spent years in Egypt. He speaks the language fluently and has agreed to teach us the basics. All of us. A month of hard learning should get us at least able to hold a conversation.'

Falco's expression shifted from confusion to outright horror.

'You want me to learn Egyptian? Have you lost your mind, Decimus? I can barely speak Gallic, and now you want me jabbering about hieroglyphs and pyramids?'

Sica, sitting across from him, smirked over the rim of his wine cup. The subtle curve of his lips didn't escape Falco, who shot him a sharp look.

'What's so funny?' he growled, narrowing his eyes. 'You'll have to do it too. You'll be just as miserable as me.'

Sica set his cup down and leaned back in his chair, a picture of calm amusement.

'Not quite,' he said casually, 'I'm already fluent.'

The words landed like a slap. Falco's jaw dropped as his hands fell to the table.

'You're what?' he barked.

'Fluent,' Sica repeated, savouring the word as if it were fine wine. 'I spent a long time in Egypt many years ago. Although, I have to say, it isn't easy, and it will be a pure joy to watch you struggle.'

Falco's face reddened, and he clenched his fists on the table.

'You think this is funny, don't you?'

Sica nodded, unashamed.

'Very funny.'

'You smug little…

'Falco, stop whining,' interrupted Decimus. You'll pick it up fast enough. And if you don't, well, just grunt and wave a sword. You're good at that.'

Falco groaned, sinking into his chair and muttering curses

under his breath. Sica smirked again, earning another glare from Falco, though the big man said no more.

Their discussion was cut short as the door creaked open, and two servants entered, carrying trays laden with steaming dishes. The rich aroma of spices and roasted meat filled the room, and all three men turned to watch as the food was placed before them. One tray held spiced lentils and roasted vegetables, another a platter of skewered meats glistening with juices.

The last servant entered, carrying a plate stacked with thick, perfectly seared steaks and the sight was enough to make Falco sit up straight, his earlier annoyance vanishing in an instant.

'Now that is what I've been waiting for,' he declared, eyeing the steaks hungrily. He leaned forward, counting them with exaggerated care. 'Twelve steaks, that's two each for you two and eight for me.'

'Eight steaks?' gasped Decimus, 'you're joking.'

Falco tore his gaze away from the food long enough to look at him seriously.

'Not joking. If I'm going to fight in the arenas again, I need to rebuild my muscle. You don't win by looking like a half-starved Celt.'

'You don't win by eating yourself into a stupor, either,' replied Decimus.'

Falco ignored him, already reaching for one of the steaks.

'Fine. Three each for you two, six for me. Fair deal.' Without waiting for their agreement, he grabbed a steak with his bare hands and tore into it, his teeth ripping through the tender meat with the enthusiasm of a starving wolf.

Sica and Decimus exchanged a glance, shaking their heads with bemusement.

'You're an animal, Falco,' said Sica with a sigh.

'And proud of it,' Falco replied around a mouthful of steak, juice dripping down his chin. He gestured vaguely with the hunk of meat in his hand. 'You'd better dig in before I finish the rest.'

Decimus chuckled, leaning back in his chair.

'A month here is going to be interesting with you around, Falco. That much, I'm sure of.'

The three of them settled into the meal, the weight of the earlier discussion momentarily lifted by the warmth of the food and the companionship of old friends. For now, at least, they had the luxury of laughter and full bellies, but all of them knew that life had a way of changing very quickly and it could be a long time before they experienced such luxuries again.

----

## Chapter Five

### Saqqara

    The desert was a canvas of shifting shadows under the full moon, its pale light spilling across the jagged teeth of the rocky escarpment that loomed like a sentinel over the lifeless plain. Silence reigned, heavy and oppressive, broken only by the occasional hiss of shifting sands or the distant cry of a night bird.

    Sprawled between the mass of rocks and dust stretched a sprawling graveyard, a labyrinth of ancient tombs and mastabas, carved into the sandstone. Their facades, weathered by millennia of desert winds, bore faded hieroglyphs and crumbling statues of forgotten gods. Some entrances were sealed, their heavy stone doors still intact, while others gaped open like yawning mouths, their interiors swallowed by shadow. Sand spilled into these violated sanctuaries, mingling with the debris of broken burial jars and the splintered remains of wooden sarcophagi.

    A lone jackal emerged from the darkness, its thin frame and patchy coat betraying the harshness of its existence. It moved with a cautious, almost reverent tread, weaving between the tombs as though wary of disturbing the slumber of those who rested within. Its yellow eyes glinted like twin coins under the moonlight, reflecting an intelligence that seemed out of place in the stillness of this ancient necropolis. For a moment, the creature stood motionless, a silhouette against the pale sands, before it slunk away, disappearing into the deeper shadows of the graveyard.

    The ruins lay still once more, bathed in the cold light of the moon. The silence of the Saqqara necropolis was absolute, broken only by the occasional whisper of wind weaving its way through the scattered ruins. The vast expanse seemed untouched by time, a frozen tableau of forgotten grandeur and desolation, until eventually, from the eastern edge of the graveyard, a hooded figure appeared, cutting a ghostly silhouette against the pale sands. His gait was slow and purposeful, as he made his way carefully through the labyrinth of tombs, as though this place, with its crumbling tombs and faded hieroglyphs, was a path well-trodden.

The man's steps were soundless, his sandals stirring no more than a whisper of sand as he passed a toppled obelisk and a broken statue of Osiris. He glanced neither left nor right, his attention fixed ahead, on the escarpment that loomed over him like a watchful guardian. The ruins of Saqqara stretched out above him, mystical and brooding, but he seemed unconcerned with their ancient splendour. His destination lay elsewhere.

He reached the base of the escarpment, its sheer rock face rising like a wall before him. To any observer, the cliff appeared unbroken, smooth and featureless save for the occasional jagged crevice or weathered indentation. Yet the figure continued toward it without hesitation and when he was within touching distance, he stopped. For a moment, he stood motionless, a part of the shadowed landscape. Then, as if the night itself swallowed him, he disappeared.

Minutes passed and then, from the same direction, another figure appeared. This one was shorter, cloaked in a similar dark garment, his strides brisk and confident. He walked the same path through the maze of tombs, his movements eerily similar, his gaze fixed on the escarpment. Like the first, he reached the base of the cliff and vanished into the rock face, leaving no trace behind.

And so it continued. One by one, they appeared from different directions, each figure cloaked and faceless, each taking the same silent journey toward the escarpment, and all disappearing into the same blank expanse of stone, the crag consuming them as if they had never existed. To any watchers it would have seemed magical, but there were none, except perhaps, the ghosts of millennia who remained unconcerned of the ways of the living.

For a moment, the desert returned to its quiet dominion. The sands shimmered under the moonlight, the ruins standing as eternal witnesses to secrets untold. Then, a final figure emerged.

He was taller than the rest, his bearing commanding even at a distance. He moved with deliberate slowness, his hood drawn low, concealing his features. The ruins seemed to close in around him as he passed, the air growing heavier, seemingly charged with an unspoken energy. Unlike the others, his gaze swept the necropolis as he walked, lingering on the broken tombs and jagged ruins as though committing them to memory.

When he reached the escarpment, he stopped short, his head tilting slightly. He did not step forward into the invisible threshold as the others had. Instead, he turned back to stare the way he had come, checking he had not been followed until finally, when he was satisfied he was alone, the ominous looming crag, complete with its millennia of ancient secrets, swallowed him whole and he disappeared into the cleft, his figure melting into the shadowed trail beyond.

----

Just over a hundred leagues away, perched on the eastern bank of the Nile, the Temple of Coptos, for many generations a testament to ancient devotion, now, reflected nothing but Roman might. Once a sacred site dedicated to Min, the god of fertility and the desert's vast expanse, it had been repurposed by the empire into a well-fortified outpost and here, at the edge of the Nile's fertile embrace and the desert's unforgiving wilderness, Rome's grip on the region was absolute.

Though weathered by centuries of wind and sun, the temple's stone pylons still loomed over the surrounding terrain, carved with faded hieroglyphs that whispered of gods long forgotten. Columns rose from its heart, their surfaces adorned with worn reliefs depicting ancient rituals, but these once-sacred halls, nestled amidst the cliffs and dunes of the Eastern Desert, now served a far more practical purpose.

The Romans had claimed the temple as their own, transforming it into a fortified camp. The perimeter, once lined with sacred sphinxes and procession routes, was now encircled with sharpened stakes and rocky defences. Watchtowers towered above the desert at strategic points, and sentries patrolled with practiced discipline, their helmets catching the moonlight as their boots crunched softly against stone and sand.

Inside, the temple was a strange fusion of ancient grandeur and Roman pragmatism. The central hall, where priests had once offered incense and offerings to Min, now housed the command centre. A massive stone altar, still bearing faint carvings of deities and prayers, had been converted into a tactical table and maps of the Nile and its surrounding territories lay spread across its surface, secured by small weights. Two legionaries stood guard near the altar, their spears held upright as their watchful eyes swept the chamber as a Centurion leaned over the maps, murmuring instructions to his Optio.

The adjacent chambers, once sanctuaries of divine rituals, now served as quarters for the soldiers. The walls, still adorned with faded depictions of divine processions, contrasting sharply with the rows of simple cots, armour racks, and supply chests. Discipline remained the lifeblood of the camp and despite the ancient surroundings, the soldiers of Coptos knew better than to relax their vigilance.

Rome's reach in this region was ironclad, its presence unchallenged by the local population. The nearby villages paid their tributes in grain and labour without question, their inhabitants cowed by the sheer might of the empire. Patrols along the Nile reinforced this subjugation, their steady rhythm a reminder to all who dared dream of rebellion.

And yet, the temple itself exuded a quiet unease. Whispers of strange occurrences rippled through the ranks. Some men spoke of hearing faint chants late at night, their origin impossible to pinpoint. Others claimed to see shadows moving in the corners of their vision, only for the darkness to yield nothing when they turned. Superstitions grew in hushed tones, but any soldier caught spreading them was swiftly disciplined. Yet, for all their faith in Rome's gods and their fear of the punishment administered by their Centurions, the soldiers couldn't ignore the weight of the temple's ancient presence.

----

In a secluded chamber near the rear of the temple, where the walls depicted the underworld's journey, a young recruit shifted uneasily in his cot. His dreams were troubled, filled with visions of sandstorms and dark figures emerging from the desert. He awoke with a sharp intake of breath, his heart pounding in his chest. Around him, his comrades remained undisturbed, their steady breaths the only sound in the room.

Tiberius had never truly been accepted by the veterans. They laughed at his frail build, mocked his inability to keep pace on marches, and sneered when his hands trembled during training. His nickname, Ovicula, little sheep, was spat at him with derision and although the isolation suited him, it gnawed at his already fragile sense of belonging.

The room was filled with the low hum of sleeping men: the gentle snores, the rustle of blankets, the faint creak of the wooden cots. The oppressive heat pressed against his chest like a weight, and his restless mind churned.

He stared at the ceiling, where faint outlines of ancient carvings flickered in the light of a single oil lamp. The shapes danced and twisted in ways his weary eyes struggled to follow, and then it came, a sharp, unnatural pressure exploded in his skull, as if an iron spike had been driven into the base of his neck.

Tiberius sat bolt upright, gasping, his heart hammering in his chest. Sweat soaked his thin blanket, clinging to his skin. His vision blurred, the edges of the room dissolving into an indistinct haze. The air seemed to grow thicker, heavy with an energy that crackled against his skin.

His breath came shallow, panicked. He rubbed his eyes, trying to clear them, but the haze deepened. A faint sound tickled his ears, at first a whisper, like wind scraping against stone. It grew louder, more guttural, alien. Words, or something like them, churned in the air around him, filling his head with a language he didn't understand but instinctively feared.

'What... what is this?' he croaked. His body felt... strange, his limbs heavy and sluggish. He swung his legs off the bunk and stood, but his knees buckled. He staggered, his hand catching the edge of a crate to keep him from collapsing entirely. The room pitched and rolled like the deck of a ship in a storm, and he stumbled forward, his movements jerky and unnatural.

Tiberius blinked, trying to focus, and then he saw them. Shapes forming in the corners of the room, emerging from the shadows, monstrous and towering. One had the head of a jackal, its eyes burning with golden fire, another, a falcon, its curved beak sharp and glinting. They didn't move, not exactly, but their presence filled the room, suffocating him with a primal, incomprehensible dread.

'No...' he muttered, clutching his head as if to squeeze the visions from his mind. The whispers grew into a cacophony, the words stabbing into his thoughts like blades. He staggered toward the others, desperate to wake someone, anyone. He reached the nearest cot and reached out, his hand trembling as it landed on a shoulder. The flesh beneath his fingers was cold, unnaturally cold.

Tiberius blinked, his vision sharpening for a brief moment. The Decurion, their leader, lay sprawled on his back. His eyes were wide and staring, his mouth frozen in a rictus of terror. A dark, gleaming pool of blood surrounded his head, soaking into the cot and dripping onto the floor. His throat had been slit, the wound clean and precise, the edges dark against his pale skin.

Tiberius stumbled back, his foot sliding in the sticky blood. He fell hard, the air driven from his lungs as he hit the floor. Gasping, he tried to crawl away, his palms leaving red smears on the ancient stone. He turned his head and saw them, all of them. The rest of the soldiers in the chamber. Every one of them was dead.

They lay in their bunks, their bodies twisted and pale, their throats bearing the same gruesome wound as the Decurion. The expressions on their faces were the same: mouths open in silent screams, eyes wide with terror. The stench of blood filled the chamber, thick and metallic, and Tiberius gagged, bile rising in his throat. His hands trembled as he tried to push himself away from the carnage, but his legs refused to obey.

The figures in the shadows moved closer now, no longer content to stay in the periphery. The jackal-headed god towered over him, its golden eyes piercing into his soul. The falcon screeched, its cry silent but deafening in Tiberius's mind. The hieroglyphs on the walls glowed faintly, their ancient carvings coming to life, writhing and shifting like serpents. The air pulsed with energy, and Tiberius clutched his head, his fingers digging into his scalp.

'Get out... get out of my head!' he screamed. But the gods would not relent. Their cries grew louder, their presence heavier, until it felt as though the very walls were pressing in on him. He stumbled to his feet, his limbs moving without coordination, and ran, blindly, instinctively, toward the exit.

He didn't make it far. His foot caught on the edge of a cot, and he pitched forward, crashing to the ground.

From the corridor came the sound of boots, running, pounding against the stone floor. Torchlight spilled into the chamber, casting flickering shadows across the carnage the voices of the soldiers panicking, confused.

'By the gods,' shouted one, 'what's going on in here?'

Tiberius turned toward them, but his mind was already fracturing. The faces of his comrades twisted into monstrous forms, their features warped and inhuman. The jackal-headed god loomed closer, its golden eyes burning with divine rage, and the falcon's scream tore through what remained of Tiberius's sanity. He opened his mouth to speak, but no words came, and the last thing he saw before the darkness claimed him, was Anubis's hand, outstretched, as if reaching into his very soul.

----

## Chapter Six

### The Docks in Alexandria

The Port of Alexandria was alive with the chaotic hum of activity, a cacophony of sounds and scents that greeted every new arrival. The ship groaned as it docked, its ropes pulled taut by sweating labourers who barked orders in a mix of Greek and Egyptian. The sun hung high, blazing down upon the sprawling harbour, where countless vessels bobbed on the glittering waters of the Mediterranean, triremes, grain barges, merchant ships from distant ports, their sails emblazoned with symbols from every corner of the empire.

Among the throng disembarking was Falco, towering and unmistakable even amidst the crowd. His shoulders were hunched slightly, the stiffness in his movements betraying the two arrow wounds he was still recovering from. Yet his immense frame carried him forward with a determination that suggested the pain was merely an inconvenience. Beside him was Sica, his dark eyes scanning everything and everyone, his hands twitching slightly at his sides as though they itched to be holding a blade.

The two men paused as they stepped off the gangplank, the full force of Alexandria's port washing over them. The air was thick with the mingling smells of salt, tar, fish, spices, and sweat. Merchants shouted over one another in a jumble of languages, from Greek to Coptic to Latin, hawking everything from baskets of pomegranates to bolts of dyed silk. Donkeys brayed, sailors argued, and the heavy creak of cartwheels on stone underscored it all.

Falco stretched his back carefully, wincing at the pull of his wounds, but a grin tugged at the corner of his lips.

'Hades, this place is alive,' he said. 'Makes the Forum in Rome look like a temple.'

Sica's gaze darted about, absorbing the swirling activity with something bordering on familiarity. He inhaled deeply, the mingling scents triggering a flood of memories, sharp and vivid, of another time, another life. His expression remained guarded, but the way he lingered on the sounds and smells betrayed his thoughts.

'Egypt always feels like home,' he said, 'even after all these years. It's not Syria, but... it's close enough. The colours, the noise, the heat... Rome has none of this.' He gestured to the dockworkers, their dark skin glistening with sweat as they hauled crates and amphorae, their laughter punctuating the shouts of merchants. 'Even the people remind me of the streets I grew up on. It's chaos, but it's living. Rome is too... cold.'

Falco said nothing. He leaned against a stone wall, resting his back, and allowed himself to soak in the energy of the docks.

'Stay here,' Sica said suddenly and melted into the crowd, heading toward the dockside market.

Falco settled back and let his gaze wander. The market sprawled along the edge of the port, a maze of makeshift stalls and canvas awnings that created patches of shade beneath the merciless sun. The scents of exotic spices filled the air, cinnamon, cumin, and saffron mingling with the sharper tang of vinegar and brine from barrels of salted fish. Traders called out in loud, musical voices, their accents thick with the dialects of the region.

To his left, a woman in a linen dress balanced a towering basket of figs on her head, her children trailing behind her with smaller loads. A bearded merchant waved swatches of vibrant blue and red fabric, extolling their beauty to a cluster of wide-eyed onlookers and across the way, a burly man carved chunks of meat from a hanging carcass, his blade moving with practiced precision. The meat was skewered and grilled over open flames, the aroma drawing a steady line of customers.

Falco watched it all with fascination. The life here was

infectious, unlike the disciplined order of Rome or the grim monotony of a military camp. The Egyptians spoke with their hands as much as their voices, their gestures animated, their laughter bold and unrestrained. Even the animals seemed louder, the braying of donkeys and the squawking of chickens competing with the merchants' calls.

It wasn't long before Sica returned, moving through the crowd with his usual furtive grace. He carried a small bundle wrapped in coarse linen, and in his hands was a scrap of parchment with some writing upon it.

Falco's eyes narrowed as the Syrian approached.

'What's that?' he asked, nodding toward the bundle.

'A thawb for you,' said Sica. 'Put it on.'

Falco stared in surprise.

'You've bought me a gift,' he said humbly. 'I am touched.'

'It's not a gift,' snapped Sica. 'The contact Decimus gave back in Gaul has a stall in the market selling thawbs and there were many people there watching me. I needed to buy something to get close enough to ask him questions.'

'What did you find out?'

'Nothing much but he furnished me with an address where we can lay up until the others arrive.' He held up the piece of parchment with the address written upon it.

'It's a start,' said Falco. 'Let's move before the sun cooks me alive.'

Sica smirked, adjusting the bundle under his arm.

'You've faced down all sorts of gladiators in the arenas across Rome, killed men of all statures and abilities across Gaul, Germania and Britannia, yet you're undone by a little sun. Truly, the gods are cruel.'

Falco grunted.

'Mock all you want. Let's see you take two arrows to the back without so much as a murmur of pain.'

Sica shook his head at the monstrous exaggeration. Falco took every opportunity he could to repeat how he took the two arrows just to save his comrades and how he had suffered in heroic silence ever since. Again, an exaggeration, but that was Falco all over and everyone who knew him loved him for it.

----

They walked together through the maze of streets leading away from the docks, the chaos of the market gradually giving way to the stone buildings of the town.

The streets narrowed as they moved deeper into the city's back alleys, the cobbled paths slick with something Falco preferred not to identify. The din of the markets faded behind them, replaced by the muffled sounds of daily life, the wail of a child, the creak of a cart, and the distant clatter of pots. Shadows stretched long in the fading light, and the air grew heavy with the scent of damp stone and rotting refuse. Sica spoke quietly to a few of the older men sitting on doorsteps as they passed, showing them the address, and soon one nodded and took him to a door set back in an alleyway.

Sica negotiated a price, and, with the deal done, the man led them into a dingy courtyard surrounded by crumbling buildings. A single olive tree stood forlorn in the center, its gnarled branches spreading like skeletal fingers over a patch of barren soil. The walls around them bore the scars of time, cracked plaster, faded murals, and graffiti scrawled in Greek and Egyptian.

'Here,' the landlord rasped, gesturing with a bony hand to a narrow staircase leading to an upper level. The wooden steps were warped and weathered, each one groaning under the old man's weight as he climbed.

At the top of the stairs, he fumbled with a giant rusting key before pushing open a creaking door. He handed Sica two stubby candles and a lit lantern, its flame flickering weakly against the darkness.

'There's a well at the end of the street,' he muttered. 'Clean enough for drinking. Keep your business to yourselves. No trouble, or you're out.' Without waiting for a reply, he shuffled back down the steps, disappearing into the courtyard's shadows as though he'd never been there.

Sica stepped inside, holding the lantern high. The two rooms beyond were cramped and oppressive, the air heavy with the stench of mildew and human filth. Shuttered windows lined one wall, their wood warped and stained, though mercifully intact. Two ancient cots sat against opposite walls, their horsehair mattresses lumpy and threadbare and a battered pisspot stood in one corner, the smell wafting from it enough to make Falco catch his breath.

'Gods, this is vile,' muttered Falco looking around.

Sica set the lantern on a rickety table, its glow casting long, flickering shadows across the room. He took a deep breath, his expression unreadable.

'It's perfect,' he said finally.

'Perfect?' Falco snorted, gesturing to the pisspot with exaggerated disgust. 'The only thing perfect about this place is how quickly I'll be leaving to join the ludus. Then you lot can have this little piece of Hades all to yourselves.'

Sica crossed over to one of the cot, testing it with a firm press of his hand. The mattress barely gave, its stuffing compressed into something resembling stone over the years. He nodded approvingly.

'No one will notice us here,' he said simply. 'It's quiet. Forgotten. People like us don't attract attention in a place like this.'

Falco sighed, tossing his pack onto the other cot with a resigned grunt.

'If I catch anything in this hole, you're paying for the healer.'

Sica set the candles on the table beside the lantern.

'I'll pay for the pyre, too, if it comes to that.'

Falco shot him a look but said nothing, settling onto his cot with a groan. The coarse horsehair pricked at his skin, and the odour of countless unwashed bodies clung to the fabric. Still, the mattress held his weight, and after days of travel, he finally closed his eyes to try and get some sleep.

Sica moved to the shuttered window and eased it open a crack, letting in a faint breeze that carried with it the smells of the city. He stood there for a moment, his sharp eyes scanning the courtyard below, before shutting it again and turning back to the room.

'This will do,' he said. 'For now.'

----

Back in the rear room of the Hornless Bull in Aquae Tarbellicae, the faint glow of a single oil lamp once again cast long shadows across the walls as the remaining members of the Occultum gathered to discuss their plans.

Seneca sat at the head of the table, while Cassius and Marcus sat along one side. All had arrived a day or so earlier, missing Falco and Sica by only a few days.

Decimus was also in attendance and had briefly explained what had happened so far but refused to go into more detail until their handler arrived, Senator Lepidus.

'Falco and Sica,' Marcus said quietly, his deep voice rumbling through the space. 'If they're in Alexandria already, they'll have their work cut out for them. Falco has a way of attracting attention, whether he means to or not.'

'Sica will keep him in line,' said Cassius, 'or at least try. Of course, there is also a high probability that they end up tearing each other apart before they find anything useful.'

'They'll manage,' said Seneca. 'Sica knows the shadows better than most, and Falco... well, let's just say his kind of flair might serve us better than we think. A gladiator can get close to certain circles where soldiers cannot.'

The door creaked open, and the room fell silent. Lepidus entered, his dusty cloak a far cry from the elegant robes he wore in the Senate.

'Lepidus,' Seneca said, rising from his seat. 'It is good to see you again.' He walked forward and took the forearm of the Senator in his grip, greeting him as both mentor and friend. 'Come, I'll get you some wine.'

Lepidus inclined his head in acknowledgment, settling into a chair with a sigh. He took a sip of the wine, before setting the cup down with deliberate care. He looked around the room, meeting each man's eyes in turn before speaking.

'Thank you for waiting,' he said, 'I'll get straight to the point. You men are here because Egypt teeters on the brink of chaos, and if it falls, so does Rome. It's as simple as that.' He leaned forward, clasping his hands on the table. 'The grain shipments have been erratic, fewer and smaller with each passing month. Some never arrive at all. The emperor's stores in Rome are dangerously low, and the people are beginning to notice. Bread riots are already breaking out in the Forum.'

Cassius frowned.

'Has the Nile failed?'

'No,' said Lepidus, shaking his head. 'The Nile flooded as expected. The fields were fertile, but many have gone unharvested. Of the grain that was collected, much has not reached the granaries or the ships. Nomes are falling short of their quotas, their governors offering excuses ranging from worker shortages to fears of divine wrath. And then there are the stories.'

'Stories?'

Lepidus's gaze darkened.

'The legions whisper of demons in the desert. Monsters that haunt the night and slaughter patrols without a sound. The

Roman navy speaks of spirits that prowl the decks of ships, striking crews dead in their sleep. Even our governors claim to hear strange things, chants in forgotten tongues, shadows moving where no man should tread.'

'Superstitions spread fast,' said Decimus from his position by the door. 'Men fear what they can't explain.'

Lepidus nodded.

'True. But these superstitions are having real consequences. Patrols are shrinking or not being carried out at all. Sailors refuse to take certain routes, and entire barracks are plagued by strange visions and nightmares. Discipline is faltering and our enemies to the south, the Nubians, the desert raiders, they sense weakness. Even as we speak, they're testing us, probing the borders for cracks.'

'I hear you sent Falco and Sica ahead,' said Marcus.

'I have,' Lepidus replied. 'They've been tasked with establishing themselves in Alexandria in advance of your arrival. They'll establish a base from where you can operate. Once done, Falco will take a position in one of the city's most renowned ludi while Sica will work the city's underbelly to gather intelligence.'

'And us?' Seneca asked.

'You'll dig deeper,' replied Lepidus. 'We have heard a rumour that something is happening at the highest levels, but we have no idea of who or what. The Occultum's strength has always been its ability to operate in shadows, so you'll infiltrate Egypt's most critical institutions, its legions, its government, its temples. Find out what's causing this chaos. Is it rebellion? Corruption? Something else? Whatever the truth, uncover it and send word to me as soon as you can.'

'And if it's worse than we fear?' Cassius asked quietly.

Lepidus's gaze hardened.

'If it's worse, then you stop it. By any means necessary but whatever happens, Egypt must not fall.'

The room fell silent again, the weight of the task settling over the men like a tangible force. Outside, the murmur of the tavern seemed far away, as though the world itself were holding its breath.

'It is certainly a strange assignment,' said Decimus eventually, 'but I see no reason why we can't get to the bottom of it. When do we go?'

'As soon as you are able,' said Lepidus.' I will furnish Seneca with official documents to gain access to the governor in Alexandria, and Marcus will be posted to Legio III Cyrenaica on the southern border, in the guise of a recovering Centurion. The rest of you will join Sica and make enquiries of your own. Focus on the temples and the priests. They seem to be quite quiet about this situation and that is not like them at all.'

'Is there anything else you can tell us,' asked Seneca, 'some direction or clue as to what to look for?'

'Not really,' said, Lepidus, 'though strangely enough, it seems that many of our men on the front line have developed an unnatural fear of beetles.

'Beetles?' repeated Seneca.

'Yes, and for some reason they all seem to be obsessed with one type in particular.'

'Which one?' asked Seneca.

'The dung beetle,' said Lepidus. 'Also known by the Egyptians as the Scarab.'

----

## Chapter Seven

## Britannia

The sound of the dripping water was gone. Veteranus stirred, his mind dragging itself up from the suffocating depths of confusion and haze. He could feel it again, the maddening fog that dulled his senses and distorted his thoughts, a remnant of the potions forced upon him by the druids on Mona. The familiar weight of chains on his wrists and the unyielding cold of the cavern floor lingered in his memories, so deeply ingrained that he expected to feel them now. But he didn't. Something was different.

He lay still, his instincts urging caution even as his thoughts clawed at clarity. The air was warmer, softer somehow, lacking the damp chill that had pervaded his prison. His body, which had grown accustomed to constant aches, was cradled in something far more forgiving than jagged rock. A faint, earthy scent lingered around him, peat, wood smoke, and something animalistic, perhaps wool.

It took a monumental effort, but he finally cracked his eyes open. The dim light around him was no longer the eerie, green glow of leaf-filtered light through a hole in a cavern roof, instead, it was the familiar warm light of many candles, set into niches built into the stone walls surrounding him, and a thatched roof replaced the cold cavern ceiling above.

For a long moment, he simply stared, the sight alien and incomprehensible to his fogged mind. His fingers twitched, brushing against something soft. Looking down, he realized he was covered in sheepskin blankets, their warmth enveloping him in a way that seemed impossible. His body sank into a bed of straw and wool, a crude construction but infinitely more comfortable than anything he had known in weeks.

The realization hit him slowly, like ripples spreading

across a pond. He wasn't in the cavern. He wasn't on the damp, freezing stone floor that had been his world since his capture. He was somewhere else.

A wave of unease followed the discovery, piercing through the lingering fog in his mind. The lethargy from the druids' potions still gripped him, but his pulse quickened. He pushed himself up onto his elbows, his muscles protesting after long disuse, and his gaze swept the room.

The hut was small and plain, its walls built of un-mortared stone. A single wooden door stood closed, and the room's only furnishings were a rough stool, a battered table, and the bed he now occupied. In the corner sat a bowl of water and a loaf of bread, its crust dark and coarse. A faint wisp of smoke curled from a low hearth, filling the space with warmth and the faint scent of smouldering peat.

Confusion gnawed at him as he struggled to piece together how he had come to be here. The last clear memory he could summon was of Mordred's voice in the cavern, echoing with words of bloodlines and destiny. Beyond that, everything blurred into a haze of whispered chants and the oppressive weight of drug-fuelled sleep.

His head swam as he tried to think. Was this another manipulation of the druids, a trick to make him let his guard down? The warmth of the blankets and the softness of the bed offered comfort, but it felt wrong. He had been a prisoner for so long, stripped of any luxury, any solace. Why now?

His fists clenched at the edge of the blanket as he fought to gather his scattered thoughts. He was free from the cavern, but at what cost, and, more urgently, where was he?

A sound came from outside, a faint scrape of movement, a shift of weight on loose stone. Someone was near. Veteranus pushed himself back up the bed, his shoulders pressing against the cool stone wall as his eyes remained fixed on the door.

For weeks, the only constants in his life had been cruelty and manipulation. The druids on Mona had made certain of that, breaking him down piece by piece, using his body as a canvas for pain and his mind as a playground for confusion.

He could still feel the pain of countless beatings, the fists and clubs of masked men and women who seemed to enjoy the sport of his suffering. The bruises were fading but the memory remained vivid, etched into his psyche. He had been promised release more times than he could count, each pledge a cruel jest that left him tethered to hope before it was ripped away.

They had tormented him with food, parading platters laden with roasted meats, fresh bread, and ripe fruit in front of his starving eyes. The aroma alone had driven him to madness, his stomach twisting in agony as he reached out for a morsel, only for it to be snatched away at the last moment.

And then there was the water, so many buckets of freezing water thrown over him that he had lost count, the shock of the cold stealing his breath and leaving him gasping like a beached fish. When he wasn't soaked, he was scorched, the heat from braziers placed so close that his skin blistered, his senses overwhelmed by the unbearable dance of firelight.

Yet through it all, his mind had not been his own. The drug they had administered so liberally, whether through drink, food, or smoke, had rendered him a prisoner within his own thoughts. His memories of the past weeks were an indistinct blur, his every emotion dulled, every flicker of resistance smothered beneath a haze of dreamlike wonder and confusion.

And now, even though the cavern was gone, the scars of his captivity lingered. He did not trust the warmth of the sheepskin blankets or the quiet comfort of the stone hut. To him, this was merely another cruel game.

His eyes darted to the door. It was closed, but the scrape of movement he had heard moments ago filled him with a familiar dread. Someone was out there, watching, waiting. The druids had done this before , letting him believe he was alone, letting him think he had a chance to gather his wits, only to burst in with a new form of torment.

The loaf of bread on the table caught his eye, and his stomach growled painfully. But he did not move to take it. He knew better. Hunger, thirst, comfort, none of it could be trusted. The moment he reached out, they would take it away again, laughing as his desperation played into their hands.

He shifted against the wall, his muscles coiled, every nerve in his body braced for the worst. Whatever awaited him beyond that door, it would be no kindness. The druids had made sure he expected nothing else.

The creak of the wooden door opening sent a jolt through his body. His heart hammered in his chest, the thrum of panic and expectation tightening his throat. A man stepped into the hut, his broad frame filling the doorway and momentarily blocking the light that spilled in from outside.

He was a typical Celtic warrior: tall, muscular, and proud. His long hair, tied back in a simple knot, revealed sharp features and piercing eyes that seemed to measure Veteranus in an instant. Yet there was something different about this man. Unlike the others, the druids cloaked in robes and shrouded in an air of mysticism, this one wore no such attire. His clothing was practical, more like that of a hunter than that of a warrior. He bore no overt symbols of druidic authority, no charms or painted marks that spoke of the rituals Veteranus had come to dread.

Two young women followed behind him, both in plain garments. One carried a steaming bucket of hot water, its heat fogging the air between them, while the other held a neat pile of folded woollen hand cloths and a small pot of ash mixed with lavender oil. Their faces were calm but guarded, their eyes flicking to the man as if awaiting silent instructions. The man's gaze settled on Veteranus, unflinching and commanding and the room seemed to shrink under his presence.

'They are here to help you,' he said. 'You will be cleaned and when it's done, you will be given fresh clothing and fed.' He paused, his tone darkening. 'If you hurt them, threaten them, or make them afraid, I will take you back to the cavern and you will live out the rest of your days enduring every pain and deprivation you've already suffered, only worse.'

Veteranus stared at him, his body tense and unmoving. The words carried an air of finality, as if the man had already decided what would happen if he refused. Yet there was no cruelty in his tone, only unyielding resolve.

He shifted his gaze to the women. They looked at him nervously, the one with the bucket gripping its handle tightly, the other clutching the cloths and soap to her chest like a shield.

Still, Veteranus hesitated. The warmth of the hut, the promise of cleanliness and food, it all felt like another ploy, another way to torment him when he allowed himself to hope. He fought the urge to lash out, to test the reality of this scene, but his body ached with exhaustion, and the smell of the soap stirred something deep within, a memory of better days. Finally, he gave a slow, reluctant nod.

The man stepped aside, motioning for the women to proceed, his watchful eyes never leaving Veteranus. The women approached cautiously, their nervous glances flicking between Veteranus and the man still watching from the doorway. When they reached the bedside, they hesitated for a moment before one of them took hold of the edge of the woollen blanket. She pulled it back slowly, revealing Veteranus's naked, grime-covered body.

The air in the room grew heavier with the scent of sweat, filth, and faint herbs from the steaming bucket. Veteranus didn't flinch or react, his tired, bloodshot eyes fixed on the man by the door. He didn't know what to expect. His mind, still sluggish and hazy, struggled to reconcile this sudden shift from the cruelty of the cavern to the strange, almost clinical attention he was receiving now.

The women worked with quiet efficiency, their discomfort clear but their hands steady. Using rough wool cloths dipped in the steaming water, they began to wash him, starting with his face and neck before moving to his arms and shoulders. His chest, back, and legs followed, and the water quickly darkened as it peeled away weeks of dirt, sweat, and blood from his battered skin.

Veteranus barely moved, his silence unnerving but deliberate. He didn't speak, didn't resist, and didn't acknowledge the women. His gaze remained locked on the man in the doorway, who watched the proceedings with an impassive face, his arms crossed over his broad chest.

When the women began to wash his hair, they had to work carefully, their fingers untangling the knotted strands before they dragged a comb through the matted mess. The comb snagged painfully, pulling at his scalp, but Veteranus made no sound, his muscles rigid with tension.

After they had combed his hair free of knots, one of the women retrieved a small clay pot from her bundle. She scooped out a thick, fragrant oil and worked it into his hair, massaging it into his scalp with surprising care. The sharp scent of herbs filled the air, masking the remnants of the filth they had just scrubbed away. When they were done, they tied his hair back, neatly and tightly, in the same manner as the man by the door.

The entire time, Veteranus's mind churned, his thoughts sluggish and fragmented. What was this? A kindness before another cruelty? A trick to disarm him? Or was it something else entirely?

When the women finally stepped back, their task complete, the man straightened and gave a single command.

'Stand.'

Veteranus hesitated for a moment before obeying, his stiff and aching limbs protesting as he pushed himself upright. He swayed slightly, unsteady on his feet, but caught himself. The room seemed smaller now, the cold of the stone floor biting at his soles.

As the women gathered the sodden blankets and filthy cloths, another entered, carrying a folded set of clothing, simple leggings and a tunic. She placed them on the stool before stepping back and bowing her head slightly.

Veteranus glanced at the clean garments, then back at the man by the door. For the first time, he spoke, his voice rough and cracked from disuse.

'What now?'

The man's piercing gaze met his, steady and unflinching.

'Now you dress.' He nodded at the bread still on the table. 'Eat some of that for now and tonight, we will share hot food.'

Veteranus stared for a long moment, his mind still caught in the haze of uncertainty, before finally nodding, his hands twitching at his sides. For the first time in weeks, he felt clean. But it did nothing to wash away his doubt.

The man turned to follow the women out of the hut but as he reached the doorway, Veteranus spoke again.

'Wait,' he rasped, the word scraping against his throat. The man paused, one hand on the doorframe, his broad shoulders stiffening slightly. 'You are not like the others, who are you. What's your name?'

The man stood motionless for a moment, the silence stretching uncomfortably. Slowly, he turned his head, just enough for his profile to catch the dim light of the hut. His eyes, sharp and dark, met Veteranus's with an intensity that sent a shiver down his spine.

'My real name,' he said evenly, his voice as calm as it was cold, 'would mean nothing to you.' He lingered, letting the weight of his words settle before a faint, humourless smile tugged at his lips. 'But my other name… that one, you might know.'

The room seemed to hold its breath as the man turned fully, stepping back into the threshold. His gaze bore into Veteranus like a blade as he spoke the single word that froze the air between them.

'My name,' he said, 'is Raven,' and without another word, he turned and strode out into the fading light, slamming the door behind him.

----

## Chapter Eight

## Alexandria

Sica and Falco made their way through the busy streets of Alexandria, heading towards the arena at the edge of the city. Falco, towering over the crowd, stomped through it with a scowl etched deep into his face, a loose-fitting thawb swishing awkwardly around his legs as he walked. Purchased by Sica at the docks, the garment was far too light for his liking, the thin fabric doing little to hide his broad frame. The plain, neutral colour made it clear it wasn't the attire of a wealthy man, neither did it suit a brute accustomed to leather armour or a gladiator's harness.

'I look like a bloody idiot,' Falco grumbled, 'this thing's too loose. Makes me feel like I'm walking around naked.'

'You stood out too much before.,' said Sica. 'With this, you'll look like a dockhand or a common trader, someone not worth a second glance.' He moved through the crowd with an ease that Falco envied, his smaller stature allowing him to weave between the throng with barely a pause.

Falco shot him a glare, his frustration mounting.

'I don't see you wearing one.'

'I don't need to,' Sica said without breaking stride. 'I already blend in.'

Falco let out a growl of annoyance, the sound drawing wary glances from a pair of passersby. He caught their stares and glared back, causing them to quickly look away.

'I don't see the point. A man my size isn't going to blend in no matter what I'm wearing.'

'No, but you won't scream 'trouble' from a hundred paces, either,' Sica said, throwing a quick look over his shoulder. 'And in a city like this, that's enough to keep us alive a little longer.'

Falco muttered something under his breath and adjusted

the thawb again, but he stopped complaining. Sica was right, much as he hated to admit it. Alexandria's backstreets were a dangerous maze of potential threats, and they couldn't afford to draw attention. Not yet, at least.

They continued through the bustling city, the arena finally coming into view ahead. Its towering wooden walls rising above the surrounding buildings, a monument to Roman power and spectacle. Attached to one side, just as Sica had described, was the ludus, its stout structure as imposing as the arena itself.

'Finally,' Falco muttered, his frustration ebbing as a new energy surged within him. The promise of a fight, of proving himself, was enough to distract him from the awkward robe.

The pair crossed the courtyard leading to the ludus, the hum of training and the clash of metal audible even from outside. At the entrance, Falco looked up at the massive wooden doors, their iron studs gleaming in the sunlight.

'This is it, then?' he said, his earlier irritation replaced with anticipation.

Sica nodded, his hand already raising to knock.

'This is it. Keep that temper of yours in check and let me do the talking.' He rapped on the door and took a step backwards. Moments later, it creaked open and a slave appeared, his thin frame and downcast eyes speaking of years of servitude.

'We are here to see your master,' said Sica, 'he is expecting us.'

The slave nodded and stepped aside, gesturing for them to enter. Falco ducked his head slightly as they passed through, his size forcing him to squeeze through the narrow doorway.

Inside, they were led to a small waiting room, its barren stone walls devoid of decoration or comfort. A pair of worn wooden benches lined the room, but neither man sat. The oppressive silence stretched as they waited, the sounds of training from beyond the walls growing faint.

Falco's patience frayed with each passing minute.

'This place smells like piss,' he muttered, pacing the room.

'Relax,' Sica said, leaning against the wall. 'It's a ludus, not a palace. And besides, it won't matter once you're in the ring.'

Before Falco could respond, the door opened, and a grizzled man stepped through. His scarred face was a testament to countless battles, his expression sharp and appraising as he looked them over.

'I am Julius, the lanista of this ludus,' he said. 'I understand from your message you want to do business?'

Sica straightened, speaking with unusual confidence.

'I do. My name is Sica, 'and I'm the manager of the best gladiator you'll ever see,' he nodded toward Falco. 'We're here to offer his services to your ludus.'

The man's sceptical gaze shifted to Falco, narrowing as he took in the towering figure and the thawb draped awkwardly over him.

'Best gladiator, is he?' the man said, his tone thick with doubt. 'They all say that. How much?'

'No cost,' Sica replied smoothly. 'Your house keeps all the prize money. We'll earn more than enough from wagers on his matches. A fair deal, wouldn't you agree?'

The master rubbed his chin, his eyes never leaving Falco.

'A good offer, I'll admit. But I've heard big claims before, and they rarely deliver. He looks the part, I'll give you that, but I don't take anyone without seeing them fight first.'

Falco grinned, stepping forward as he shrugged off the thawb, letting it fall to the floor. Beneath it, his muscled frame seemed carved from stone, the scars of past battles serving as silent proof of his experience.

'You want to see me fight?' he said, 'fine. Bring me someone worth the effort.'

The master's lips curled into a faint, knowing smile, his

scepticism giving way to intrigue.

'What are these,' he asked, pointing at the two healing wounds on Falco's chest.

'Battle wounds,' said Falco, 'earned saving the lives of many against a barbarian hoard in Britannia. Don't worry about those, I hardly feel them anymore.'

Julius glanced at Sica who was biting his tongue to avoid responding to Falco's annoying arrogance.

'He certainly loves himself,' he said, 'and I am willing to give him a run. But not until those wounds are healed.'

'Understood,' said Sica, 'but I want him admitted to your Ludus in the meantime. It's like trying to drag a giant camel through the streets and I have business to attend.'

Falco shot Sica an annoyed glance at the insult but kept his mouth shut. He knew the mission was just too important.

'I'm happy to do that,' said Julius, 'but you pay for his rations until his first fight. After that, assuming he is as good as he thinks he is, I will pick up any costs.'

'Agreed,' said Sica and they sealed the deal by grasping each other's wrists.

Minutes later, he walked out of the Ludus, leaving Falco behind regaling Julius with his many stories of his time in the arenas of Rome. Sica smiled at the thought, already feeling sorry for the men who would have to listen to his incessant boasting day after day.

Once he was back in the city, he headed back towards the poorer areas. After all, he had his own work to do.

----

## Chapter Nine

## Egypt

Weeks later, under the relentless Egyptian sun, a new detachment of legionaries disembarked from a fleet of ships moored along the Nile's southern reaches. Dispatched from Rome, their mission was to reinforce the depleted ranks of Legio III Cyrenaica, strained by ongoing skirmishes with the Blemmyes, nomadic raiders from the Eastern Desert who had long harassed the empire's southern borders.

Among the fresh arrivals was Marcus, once more clad in the full regalia of a Centurion. The weight of the armour and the familiar scent of oiled leather and metal were both comforting and confining, evoking memories of a life he had thought left behind. His time with the Occultum had been a departure from the rigid discipline of the legions, immersing him in shadows and secrets far removed from the structured chaos of military life.

Yet, he understood the necessity of his presence here. This assignment was temporary, a means to an end, and soon he would return to the clandestine operations that had become his true calling.

Despite his initial unease, the rhythms of legionary life quickly enveloped him. Commands barked in Latin, the synchronized march of hobnailed sandals on packed earth, the ritual of setting up camp, all of it was ingrained in his muscle memory. He found himself slipping back into the role that had defined most of his adult life, issuing orders with authority, inspecting gear with a critical eye, and drilling the men with a precision that brooked no dissent.

The men already respected him, recognizing a seasoned leader who had walked the same paths of war and hardship. In their eyes, he was a Centurion through and through, his past affiliations with the Occultum hidden beneath the veneer of military decorum. For now, Marcus embraced the familiarity of legionary life, even as his thoughts lingered on the missions that awaited him beyond the horizon.

The journey from the Nile to Syene, albeit fairly short, was a far cry from the rigid discipline he had once been accustomed to. The fresh recruits were eager but untested, their march awkward despite his efforts to instil order. As they approached Syene, the sprawling fort and its surrounding settlement came into view, a bastion of Roman authority on the southernmost edge of the empire's heartland.

The fort was imposing, its stone walls towering over the city, with sentries pacing along the battlements. Beyond the fort, Syene itself bustled with activity, traders haggling in the markets, fishermen transporting their catches from the Nile, and locals scurrying under the watchful eyes of Roman patrols. It was a city of contrasts, where Roman discipline met the chaotic vibrancy of Nubian and Egyptian life.

Marcus halted the column outside the holding camp, a temporary staging ground just outside the city walls. He barked commands, his voice carrying over the din of the recruits' shuffling boots and clinking gear. Supplies were inventoried, tents were assigned, and watches established and by nightfall, the men were settled, their chatter quiet as they rested in the shadow of the Syene garrison. Marcus, however, spent the evening speaking with the local officers, gleaning what he could about the situation further south. Reports of skirmishes with Blemmyes raiding parties and whispered rumours of strange occurrences beyond the frontier only deepened his resolve.

The following morning, Marcus stood in the pale light of dawn as a Tribune arrived from the fort, his ornate armour gleaming as he dismounted from his horse.

'Centurion,' he said.

'My lord,' Marcus replied, snapping a salute.

The Tribune handed over a scroll bearing the seal of the governor of Egypt.

'Orders. Your detachment is to reboard the ships immediately and proceed south. You are being deployed to Pselchis, the empire's southernmost post. The situation there is tenuous, and reinforcements are critical.'

Marcus accepted the scroll with a nod, though the weight of the assignment settled heavily on his shoulders. Pselchis. The name alone carried a reputation for danger. It was a remote outpost, isolated and exposed, where supplies were scarce, and the threat of raiders, constant. It was also a place where secrets lingered, whispers of things that did not belong in the world of mortals.

'Understood,' he said.

The Tribune's sharp gaze lingered on Marcus for a moment longer.

'Have we met before,' he asked eventually.

Marcus's heart missed a beat. The last thing he needed was to be identified as a man who had once been accused of cowardice.

'I don't think so, my lord,' he replied. 'I have been deployed in Germania for many years.'

'So, why are you here?'

'I returned to Rome wounded but when healed, it seemed they needed experienced men here, so here I am.'

'Interesting,' said the Tribune. 'I could have sworn I had seen you before.' He turned and strode away, leaving Marcus staring after him. It had been close, too close but he had gotten away with it. He turned away to organize his men's departure and saw a battle-scarred legionary marching towards him carrying a sarcina.

'Centurio,' said the soldier, coming to a halt. 'My name is

Optio Tullus, and I have been assigned to your command.'

Marcus stared at the man, instantly recognising the mannerisms and stature of a man used to war. He nodded in approval.

'Good to have you, Optio,' he said, 'let's get the men back to the boats.'

----

Hours later, the detachment once more boarded the Nile ships and the oars dipped into the slow-moving water, propelling them southward against the current. Marcus stood at the prow, his eyes fixed on the horizon. Beyond lay Pselchis, a posting that most would dread but one he knew he had to face.

The distant banks of the Nile slid past, the greenery giving way to the harsh, golden expanse of the desert. The journey ahead was perilous, but Marcus had made peace with danger long ago. For now, he steeled himself for what awaited at the empire's edge.

----

Inside the governor's palace many leagues to the north in Alexandria, Postumus, sat at his sprawling ebony desk, his sharp features furrowed in concentration. Before him lay stacks of scrolls and wax tablets, the weight of their contents etched into his expression.

Across from him, stood his aide, holding a small slate, and reading aloud the latest figures from the nomes. His voice was flat, the monotony of bad news having dulled even his usually brisk demeanour.

'The quotas from Crocodilopolis remain short, Excellency,' said Lucius with a sigh. 'Panehesy sent another missive claiming disruptions in the labour force. The grain from Thebes is delayed again, likely due to the raids reported in Upper Egypt, and Antaeopolis has sent only half its usual share.'

Postumus leaned back in his chair, rubbing his temple as frustration coursed through him.

'And these disruptions,' he said coldly, 'how much of it is incompetence, and how much is genuine?'

Before Lucius could respond, a soft knock echoed through the chamber, and the heavy wooden door creaked open. A servant entered, bowing low.

'Excellency,' said the servant, keeping his gaze downcast. 'A visitor has arrived. He says he comes from Rome.'

Postumus arched an eyebrow, exchanging a glance with Lucius

'From Rome? Who?'

'He carries credentials, Excellency. He is waiting in the atrium.'

Postumus gestured impatiently.

'Well, bring him in. Let's see what this visitor wants.'

The servant bowed again and disappeared. Postumus adjusted his crimson cloak, straightening in his chair as Lucius stood to one side, his slate held at the ready.

Moments later, the door swung open again, and the visitor stepped inside. He was young, mid-thirties, perhaps, with sharp eyes that betrayed a confidence beyond his years. He wore the polished armour and scarlet cloak of a Tribune, the eagle-topped insignia on his chest gleaming in the soft light. He approached the desk and saluted crisply.

'Excellency,' he said, his voice smooth and precise. 'Tribune Gaius Octavius Seneca sent by Senator Lepidus to offer whatever assistance you require in meeting your grain quotas.'

Postumus studied the young man with a sceptical eye, his silence stretching uncomfortably. Finally, he leaned back, steepling his fingers.

'A Tribune,' he said slowly. 'Sent by Lepidus. How interesting.'

Seneca held his composure, though he could sense the faint edge of derision in the governor's tone. Postumus gestured to the stack of scrolls before him.

'Tell me, Tribune, what exactly does a man like you imagine you can do to assist with this mess?'

Seneca met his gaze without flinching.

'I have been fully briefed, excellency, and while I may not be able to help with the actual numbers, I have certain experience in, shall we say, resolving problems that may lie beneath the surface. If you grant me your support and patience, I may be able to establish what, if anything is going on behind the scenes that is contributing to this mess.' He nodded towards the table.'

'And how do you intend to do that?' asked Postumus.

'I am not at liberty to say,' said Seneca, 'but I can share the fact that I am not alone and already have men deployed across Egypt to see what they can find out.'

'Interesting,' said Postumus. 'I sent a message asking for another five thousand men to force the labour into working harder, and they send one man with wild ideas of rooting out some fanciful conspiracy theories. Sometimes I worry that the Senate do not occupy the same world as the rest of us.' He stared at Seneca again before beathing deeply and letting out a worried sigh. 'Very well. You may stay here at the palace and have whatever resources you may require, but be aware, Tribune, I have too much on my plate to play the dutiful host.' He turned to his aide. 'Lucius, have the servants prepare quarters and arrange an extra place for the evening meal. Tribune Seneca will be joining us.'

The aide bowed and moved toward the door, issuing quiet instructions to a waiting servant.

Postumus's gaze returned to Seneca.

'You've had a long journey, Tribune. I suspect you're eager for some rest. The servants will take you to your quarters, and later we will dine together. Then we can discuss Egypt and Rome in greater detail.'

Seneca nodded.

'As you wish, Excellency.'

Postumus waved him off, and Seneca turned to follow the servant out of the room.

As the door closed behind them, Postumus leaned back in his chair once more, his expression thoughtful.

'Well?' he said to Lucius.

The aide shrugged.

'He's young. But if Lepidus sent him, he must be capable.'

Postumus grunted.

'We'll see.' Then, with a wave of his hand, he gestured to the scrolls again. 'Let's finish what we can before it gets too hot. I am of a mind to get some rest myself.'

Outside, Seneca followed the servant down the wide, marble-lined corridors of the palace. He had achieved the first aim but that had been the easy part. Now all he had to do was try to find out if everything was as it seemed, and he had no idea how to begin.

----

## Chapter Ten

### The Governor's Palace

The dining room was a testament to the fusion of Roman authority and Egyptian grandeur. The walls were adorned with vibrant frescoes depicting both Roman triumphs and scenes of the Nile's eternal majesty, reeds swaying in the breeze, ibis birds perched along the riverbanks, and gods in their resplendent forms. The ceiling was painted in deep blue, dotted with stars, mimicking the night sky over Alexandria.

At the center of the room, an intricately laid table stood under the glow of bronze oil lamps, their light flickering off gold and silver plates, goblets adorned with etched patterns, and bowls brimming with exotic fruits.

Seneca paused as he stepped inside, his gaze sweeping over the scene. The room was alive with conversation, soft laughter, and the gentle clink of goblets. Groups of Roman officials, Egyptian nobles, and finely dressed courtiers stood in clusters, their postures relaxed but their eyes keen.

Near an open window overlooking the sprawling city, Postumus stood with a small group. His crimson cloak caught the light as he gestured animatedly, clearly holding court. Beside him, a stunning young woman leaned lightly on the windowsill, her flowing gown of sheer Egyptian linen accentuating her beauty. Her dark eyes sparkled with intelligence as she laughed at something Postumus said. To the other side, a Roman officer, a legatus, judging by the embossed insignia on his armour, listened with a polite smile, sipping from a crystal goblet.

As Seneca entered, Postumus's sharp eyes caught his movement. His expression brightened, and he waved him over with a broad, welcoming gesture.

'Ah, Tribune Seneca,' he called, his voice carrying easily

over the hum of conversation. 'Come, join us!'

The nearby guests turned their heads briefly to glance at the newcomer before returning to their conversations. Seneca made his way across the room, his boots silent against the polished marble floor. Postumus extended a hand as Seneca approached, clasping his forearm in a gesture of camaraderie.

'You've met me in my austere office, Tribune,' he said, 'but now you will see how we really do things in Alexandria.'

Seneca allowed himself a small smile.

'An impressive display, Excellency. I see why Rome values Egypt so highly.'

Postumus chuckled and gestured to the others.

'Allow me to introduce you. This is Lady Callista, a true gem of Alexandria.' The young woman gave a slight, graceful nod, her gaze lingering on Seneca with mild curiosity.

'And this,' Postumus continued, motioning to the officer, 'is Legatus Decius Valerianus, commander of Legio XXII Deiotariana, stationed here in Alexandria.'

The legatus extended his hand, his grip firm.

'Welcome to our corner of the empire, Tribune,' he said with a faint smile. 'I hear you've come to help us whip these troublesome nomes into shape.'

'I'll do what I can,' Seneca replied diplomatically.

Postumus clapped him on the shoulder.

'Good, good. But tonight is not for work. Tonight, you eat, drink, and enjoy the best of what Alexandria has to offer.' The governor motioned to a nearby servant, who handed Seneca a goblet of wine. Taking it with a nod, Seneca sipped the sweet, spiced liquid, his eyes flicking to the table. Whatever lay ahead for him in Egypt, it was clear that for this evening, at least, he was expected to play his part in Alexandria's carefully curated image of opulence and control.

----

The dinner was a feast worthy of Alexandria's wealth and influence, a showcase of the empire's reach and the city's place as its jewel in the desert. Servants moved with practiced precision, bringing out platters heaped with roasted lamb, spiced fish wrapped in fig leaves, and bowls of honey-glazed fruits. Amphorae of wine, both Roman and Egyptian, were poured freely into goblets of crystal and silver, and the table itself was a vision of extravagance, strewn with garlands of fresh flowers and illuminated by golden candelabras that cast a warm glow over the gathered guests.

Seneca found himself seated beside Lady Callista, whose presence was as captivating as the lavish surroundings. Her emerald-green eyes sparkled in the soft light, framed by kohl-lined lashes and accentuated with the shimmering gold dust of her eyeshadow. Her braided hair was adorned with delicate ornaments that gleamed like the treasures of a Pharaoh's tomb, and her scent, a blend of myrrh and lotus, was intoxicating.

As the evening unfolded, their conversation flowed effortlessly. Callista's voice was light and melodic, her laughter brightening the air around them like sunlight breaking through clouds. She asked about Rome, her questions curious and intelligent, probing into the political intrigue of the Senate and the life of its soldiers.

'And what of you, Tribune?' she asked, resting her chin lightly on her hand as she gazed at him. 'What brings you so far from the heart of the empire? Surely Rome's finest are not sent south without cause.'

Seneca smiled, deftly sidestepping the question.

'Egypt has its challenges, as I'm sure you're aware. My role is simply to lend support where it's needed.'

Her lips curved into a teasing smile.

'You're far too modest, Seneca. But I see I won't pry the truth from you so easily.'

He chuckled, shifting the conversation with practiced ease.

'And you, Lady Callista? It seems you've mastered both the charms of Egyptian culture and the sophistication of Rome. How does one manage such a perfect balance?'

Callista's laughter was soft and genuine.

'It's not so difficult when you've spent your life navigating both worlds. Alexandria has a way of drawing the best from East and West, though I must confess my heart belongs more to the Nile than to the Tiber.'

As they spoke, the other guests engaged in spirited discussions about the pressing issues of the day. Postumus led a conversation about the grain quotas, his tone veering between exasperation and calculated charm as he explained the difficulties of wringing compliance from the nomes.

'The people cling to their gods and their old ways,' he said, gesturing with his goblet. 'It's a constant battle to remind them that Rome, not Isis or Osiris, is their true master.'

Legatus Decius chimed in, his tone pragmatic.

'The raids from the south don't help. Every time the Blemmyes strike, it emboldens the nomes to shirk their duties. They see weakness where there is none.'

Callista glanced at Seneca.

'Conversation in Egypt is always about politics or war,' she said with a sigh. 'Sometimes both.'

Seneca smirked.

'Rome is no different. The only difference is the gods they blame for their misfortunes.'

Callista laughed again, the sound drawing the attention of nearby diners. Her natural grace and beauty made her the centrepiece of the room, but she seemed entirely at ease, as though it was her rightful place.

As the servants brought out a final round of sweet pastries and dates, Callista leaned closer to Seneca, her voice dropping slightly.

'You're an enigma, Tribune. But I like enigmas. They make the world a far a more interesting place.'

Seneca held her gaze, her mesmerizing green eyes holding him captive for a moment longer than he intended.

'And I imagine you make this corner of the world far more interesting, Lady Callista.'

Her smile deepened, and the conversation moved on, flowing seamlessly into lighter topics. Yet as the evening progressed, Seneca couldn't shake the feeling that beneath her charm and beauty lay a sharp mind, one that might see far more than she let on.

----

Eventually, the delightful evening came to an end and as the dinner guests gradually took their leave, Seneca found himself lingering near Lady Callista, her presence a magnetic pull he could not resist. As the last of the company departed, she turned to him with a soft smile, her green eyes gleaming in the lamplight.

'Tribune,' she said, her voice lilting, 'the night is too beautiful to waste. Would you join me for a walk in the gardens?'

Seneca hesitated only a moment before nodding.

'It would be my honour, Lady Callista.'

She led the way through the palace corridors and out into the sprawling grounds, the night air cool against the lingering warmth of the day. The gardens were a marvel, a fusion of Roman symmetry and Egyptian elegance. Manicured hedges framed pathways that wound among towering palm trees, vibrant blooms of lotus and hibiscus, and statues of both Roman and Egyptian deities. The soft glow of lanterns illuminated the marble paths, casting flickering shadows on the intricate carvings of sphinxes and imperial eagles.

Their conversation remained light at first, filled with laughter and playful jabs. Callista's wit was as sharp as her beauty, and Seneca found himself relaxing in her presence, his duties momentarily forgotten.

'You seem enchanted, Tribune,' Callista said teasingly as they paused near a reflecting pool adorned with golden lilies.

'Enchanted,' Seneca admitted, glancing at her before letting his gaze sweep upward to the heavens. 'And not just by the gardens. The stars here… they're brighter than I've ever seen.'

Callista followed his gaze, a soft smile playing on her lips.

'Egypt's skies have a way of reminding us how small we are, yet how connected we are to the divine.'

As they continued walking, the conversation drifted toward the gods of Egypt. Callista spoke with a reverence that surprised Seneca, her voice weaving a tapestry of myth and devotion. She told him of Osiris, the god of the afterlife, and his resurrection by Isis, of Anubis, the jackal-headed protector of the dead, who guided souls to the scales of judgment, and of Ra, who traversed the heavens by day and the underworld by night, bringing balance to the world.

'These gods,' Callista said softly, her fingers brushing against the petal of a night-blooming flower, 'are not merely stories to us. They are woven into the fabric of our land. The Nile rises and falls with their will, the sun rises because Ra wills it so. Even now, under Roman rule, they persist.'

Seneca listened, enthralled by the passion in her voice. Though he had heard of the Egyptian gods, he had never considered them in such a light.

'And do you believe,' he asked cautiously, 'that they still hold power in a world ruled by Rome?'

Callista smiled, a knowing gleam in her eyes.

'Power comes in many forms, Tribune. Rome's power is visible, its legions, its roads, its laws. But Egypt's power… it is quiet, eternal, and far older than Rome will ever be.'

They walked on, the gardens growing quieter as the hour

grew late. The stars above seemed to watch over them, their light reflecting off the polished stones and the rippling waters of fountains.

Finally, they returned to the palace steps, where their paths would part. Callista turned to him, her expression softer now, her voice low.

'You've made this evening most enjoyable, Seneca. I hope we'll have more opportunities to talk.'

'As do I,' Seneca said, his voice sincere.

She leaned forward and pressed a soft kiss to his cheek. As she pulled back, her emerald eyes lingered on his, the faintest hint of a smile on her lips.

'Perhaps soon, we'll grow even closer,' she murmured, her words hanging in the air like the scent of her perfume. Before he could respond, she turned and glided away into the shadows of the palace, her figure disappearing beyond the lanterns' reach.

For a moment, Seneca stood frozen, his hand drifting to his cheek where her lips had been. His mind raced, trying to understand her meaning, but her intentions remained as enigmatic as her beauty.

Finally, with a deep breath, he turned and made his way to his quarters. As he entered the dimly lit room and closed the door behind him, the lingering scent of myrrh seemed to follow, a reminder of her presence and though he had faced countless challenges as a soldier and an agent of the Occultum, none felt as disarming as the spell Lady Callista had cast over him.

----

Several hours later, Seneca woke with a start, his breath coming in ragged gasps as he sat upright in the luxurious bed. His body was drenched in sweat, the damp sheets clinging to him like a second skin. His chest heaved as he tried to shake off the lingering terror of the nightmare that had dragged him from sleep.

The dream had been unlike anything he'd ever

experienced. In it, he had been lost in a swirling, shifting landscape where the familiar blurred into the grotesque. Egyptian gods loomed above him, their forms imposing and sinister. Isis, her once-protective gaze cold and accusing, towered over him. Ra, his sun disk burning like a relentless inferno, scorched the ground beneath his feet. But it was Anubis, the jackal-headed god, who had struck the deepest chord of terror.

In the dream, Anubis had seized him, dragging him toward the gaping maw of the underworld. The stench of decay had choked him, and unseen voices whispered threats and curses in a language he could not understand.

He swung his legs over the side of the bed and sat for a moment, his hands trembling slightly as he dragged them down his face. The room was silent save for the distant hum of life outside the palace, the soft morning light filtering through the shuttered windows, bringing with it the promise of a new day.

Determined to shake the dream, he rose and padded across the cool marble floor toward the far side of the room. There, a wide basin of water awaited him, the servants having quietly prepared it sometime before dawn. The water was tepid, its surface still and inviting.

Seneca plunged his hands into the basin, the coolness grounding him. He splashed water onto his face, scrubbing away the sweat and the vestiges of the nightmare. For a moment, he leaned heavily on the edge of the basin, his head bowed, droplets falling from his face into the water below.

He straightened, dragging a hand through his damp hair. The dream still clung to him, but there was work to be done, and it was already late. The governor would expect him, and there was no time to dwell on the phantoms of the night.

----

## Chapter Eleven

## The Southern Borders of Egypt

The Nile shimmered in the distance as Marcus led his contingent of recruits along the dusty trail toward the fortress at Pselchis, the southernmost bastion of Roman Egypt's defences. Its location, perched on a rocky outcrop half a league inland, was strategic but fraught with peril. From here, the legions monitored the restless frontier, keeping a wary eye on the Nubian lands to the south. Raiding parties, particularly from the Blemmyes, were a constant threat, testing Roman vigilance with their swift and brutal strikes.

The fortress itself came into view, its weathered timber walls a stark contrast to the imposing stone edifices Marcus had known in Rome and many of the northern provinces. The fort's position on the rocky rise gave it a commanding view of the surrounding plains, the nearby Nile, and the vital nileometer at the base of the outcrop. This ancient well, maintained by generations of priests before Rome's arrival, served a dual purpose. It provided a steady supply of filtered water and allowed the garrison to monitor the Nile's levels, a critical task in a land where the river's rise and fall dictated survival.

As the column drew nearer, Marcus's experienced eyes scanned the fortifications, and his unease deepened. The wooden walls, though practical in their haste to construct, were ill-suited to withstand the test of time or determined enemies. Timber supports sagged, their surfaces splintered and faded under the relentless desert sun and large sections appeared hastily patched or simply left to deteriorate.

'Not exactly the jewel of the empire,' Marcus muttered.

'It certainly is not,' the Optio replied, his voice tinged with the same unease that gnawed at Marcus.

When they passed through the gates, the true nature of the fort's decline became starkly apparent. The air inside the walls was heavy with neglect. Gone were the sharp cries of Centurions drilling their men, the clang of swords striking shields, or the rhythmic tramp of hobnailed boots on packed earth. Instead, an oppressive silence reigned, punctuated only by the occasional creak of wood and the low murmur of dishevelled soldiers lounging in the shade.

Several legionaries sat slumped against the walls, their armour dulled by neglect and their tunics stained with the grime of disuse. They regarded the arriving recruits with listless gazes, some showing faint derision, others a flicker of sympathy. The parade ground was a barren stretch of dust, its surface marred with long-neglected grooves. Training dummies leaned drunkenly, their straw guts spilling out, unrepaired.

Marcus's jaw tightened as he took in the scene. This was not the Roman discipline he had known. Pselchis, the first line of defence against the Blemmyes and the watchtower of the empire's southern border, had become a shadow of what it should have been.

Marcus turned to his Optio.

'Establish a camp against the far walls. I'm not having our men mingling with this lot until I know who's running this fort, and what in Hades has happened to it.'

'Yes Centurio,' Tullus replied, snapping a salute before moving off to relay the orders. His barked commands broke the eerie stillness, the recruits scrambling to comply.

Marcus remained where he was, his sharp eyes sweeping the fort. A smithy sat silent, its forge long cold. The barracks, their doors ajar, revealed interiors cluttered with discarded gear and forgotten duties. The sentry towers, manned by soldiers with slouched postures, betrayed no sense of vigilance.

Nearby, a legionary caught Marcus's attention. The man

leaned against a splintered post, his tunic hanging loose over his gaunt frame. His helmet sat askew, and he regarded Marcus with a mix of indifference and lazy amusement. Raising a hand in a lacklustre salute, the soldier muttered something inaudible before turning his gaze away.

The Centurion in Marcus burned to march over and demand answers, to bark commands until the garrison remembered what it meant to serve Rome. But he resisted the impulse. His previous service in the legions had taught him that dysfunction like this ran deep, born not of mere laziness but of something far more insidious. He strode toward the guard, immediately noticing his sunken eyes, ringed with dark patches, betraying an obvious lack of sleep. His beard was unkempt, and his hair hung far too long for a soldier of Rome.

'Who commands this fort?' he demanded.

The guard hesitated, licking his dry lips before replying.

'Tribune Tullius Acastus, Centurio, but he is suffering from the sickness.'

'What sickness?'

The guard shifted uneasily.

'We know not, Centurio. Many have fallen to the same thing. A slave woman tends to him.'

Marcus exhaled sharply, irritation flickering into disbelief.

'And the Pilus Prior? The garrison must have someone in command.'

The guard hesitated again, glancing at the ground before answering.

'The Pilus Prior… he's dead, my lord, as is the Optio. Both died weeks ago, haunted by the visions.'

'So, who is in charge here?'

The guard's voice lowered as if the very walls might hear.

'No one, Centurio. You're the first authority we've seen since the Tribune fell ill.'

Marcus muttered a curse under his breath as he looked around. His men, having set their packs down in a loose formation, moved toward a water barrel near the gate.

'Take me to the Tribune,' he said. 'Now.'

The guard turned toward one of the few intact huts within the fort. Marcus followed, his sharp eyes scanning the surroundings. The disarray was worse than he'd imagined. Equipment lay scattered in the dust, tents sagged under poor maintenance and soldiers moved aimlessly, lacking purpose or direction.

The guard stopped at a doorway and gestured inside. Marcus ducked through the low entrance, his broad frame casting a shadow over the room. The air inside was heavy with the scent of sweat and sickness. A young man, pale and drenched in sweat, lay writhing on a cot. His tunic clung to his thin frame, and his lips moved in incoherent murmurs.

A slave woman knelt beside him, her dark hair falling over her shoulders as she wrung out a cloth in a bowl of tepid water. She dabbed the Tribune's forehead, her face a mask of quiet concentration. Marcus stepped closer, his boots scraping against the stone floor.

'Tribune Acastus,' he said firmly, hoping the sound might penetrate the haze of fever.

The young man's head turned slightly, his glazed eyes flickering open for a brief moment before falling shut again. The slave woman looked up, her eyes wide with a mix of fear and hope.

'He's too weak to answer, my lord,' she said softly.

Marcus stared at the young officer for a moment longer, then exhaled slowly. There was no help to be had here. He turned and left the hut, stepping back into the glaring sun.

From his new vantage point, he scanned the fort again. The small barrack block and the number of tents suggested only a few hundred men, far short of a full cohort. The garrison's disorganization was evident in every corner. Men lounged idly, some sleeping in the shade while others sat in small groups, gambling with dice or drinking from waterskins. It was a far cry from the disciplined camps Marcus had known throughout his career. Clenching his fists, he sought out the signal tower, where the garrison's cornicen sat dozing next to his curved horn. Marcus stomped toward him, the man jolting awake as the Centurion's shadow loomed.

'You,' he shouted, 'at first light tomorrow, you will sound the muster. Every man in this fort, without exception, will report to the parade ground. Is that understood?' Any missing will have a ten-league forced march in the noon sun. Understood?'

'Yes, Centurio.' said the Cornicen, 'at first light.'

'With full marching kit,' added Marcus before striding back toward the far wall where his recruits were pitching their tents in neat, orderly rows, a stark contrast to the rest of the fort.

As the sun dipped below the horizon, Marcus stood silently near his men, watching the garrison settle into the uneasy quiet of night. The weight of his task pressed heavily on his shoulders. What he had envisioned as a temporary assignment had become something far greater. The fort was broken, its men demoralized, its command structure in ruins. If this was the state of Rome's frontier defences, it was no wonder the Blemmyes saw an opportunity and Marcus knew that if he didn't act decisively, the empire's southernmost post would collapse entirely.

As the first stars appeared in the vast desert sky, Marcus exhaled slowly. He had his own mission to consider but before he could even begin to give it any attention, there was work to do. Tomorrow, that work would begin, and he would remind these men, along with his own recruits, what it meant to wear the eagle of Rome.

----

## Chapter Twelve

## Alexandria

The Alexandria sun blazed overhead, beating down on the training grounds of the ludus, where the sounds of grunts, shouts, and clashing wood filled the air. Falco, his body glistening with sweat, attacked the training dummies with relentless precision. His movements were fluid yet powerful, each strike of the wooden sword landing with a satisfying crack against the battered target.

His muscles, once softened by weeks of recovery, had regained their hardened definition, and the rhythm of his strikes, the ferocity of his stance, and the sheer focus in his eyes drew the attention of those watching.

Standing near the edge of the training area, Julius observed with crossed arms. His face betrayed no emotion, but his sharp gaze missed nothing. Beside him, one of the trainers, a grizzled man with a thick beard and a limp, nodded approvingly.

'Not bad,' the trainer said, spitting into the dirt. 'He's got speed and the power. Looks like those wounds didn't slow him down much.'

'He's got potential,' Julius admitted. 'But his opponent is just wood and straw. The true test is when it's flesh and blood.'

The trainer grunted, his weathered face breaking into a smirk.

'Easy enough to fix that.' Without waiting for a response, the trainer limped forward, raising his voice to cut through the cacophony of the yard.

'Falco! Enough with the dummies. Let's see if you can handle something that fights back.'

Falco lowered his sword, turning to face the man. His chest heaved with exertion, but his expression remained calm. He gave a short nod, acknowledging the challenge.

'Tiber!' the trainer barked, summoning one of the seasoned fighters.

From the shade of the yard, a massive figure emerged. Tiber, a veteran gladiator with a torso crisscrossed with scars, grinned wickedly as he strode forward. His body was a testament to countless battles, his muscles thick and corded, his presence imposing. The trainer pointed at the two men.

'Wooden swords. Fight to submission. No rules.'

Tiber's grin widened as he grabbed a wooden sword from the rack. He hefted it, testing its weight with practiced ease before turning to face Falco.

'No rules, eh?' he drawled, 'this might actually be fun.'

Falco's face remained unreadable as he stepped into the circle that was quickly forming, the other gladiators abandoning their own training to watch the spectacle.

The air grew taut with anticipation as the two men squared off, circling one another like predators assessing their prey.

The trainer chuckled, crossing his own arms as he stood beside him.

'Think your new boy's ready for this?'

'We'll find out soon enough,' Julius said quietly.

The circle of gladiators pressed tighter, their collective anticipation palpable as Falco and Tiber squared off. The sun beat down relentlessly, but neither man seemed to notice, their focus entirely on each other.

Tiber was the first to strike, lunging with his wooden sword in a powerful overhead swing. Falco sidestepped smoothly, the move deceptively light for a man of his size. He responded with a quick jab aimed at Tiber's midsection, but the veteran deflected it with ease. Each man was testing the other, taking mental note of their opponent's weaknesses and strengths but as their confidence increased, so did the intensity.

Blow followed blow, each as hard as each other and each deflected with skill and aggression, swords cracking against each other with fierce concentration. Falco's movements were precise, his footwork measured, but he fought with a noticeable restraint. His breathing grew heavier, and a flicker of discomfort crossed his face as his old wounds began to burn under the strain.

Tiber, ever the opportunist, noticed the faint grimace and the slight falter in Falco's step.

'You're slowing down, Roman,' he taunted, launching a rapid series of strikes that forced Falco to retreat.

The crowd murmured, sensing the shift in momentum. Tiber was relentless, his sword a blur as he aimed for Falco's ribs, shoulders, and legs. Falco parried each blow, but the effort was taking its toll, his movements losing their earlier fluidity.

Tiber snarled, his confidence swelling. He swung low, aiming for Falco's knees, but the big man jumped back just in time. The movement cost him, a sharp pain shooting through his chest where one of the arrow wounds had only recently healed.

Sensing weakness, Tiber redoubled his efforts, his strikes growing wild yet effective. Falco's back was to the edge of the circle now, his opponents' advantage clear. The crowd roared, some cheering for Tiber, others urging Falco to rally.

And then, when it seemed the tide had turned irrevocably, Falco's eyes narrowed. He shifted his stance, the weight of his sword shifting subtly in his grip. Tiber, already drunk on his near victory, barely registered the change before it was too late.

Falco feinted high, drawing Tiber's sword up for a block and in the same motion, Falco spun, his massive frame moving with a grace that seemed impossible. He ducked low under Tiber's swing and twisted behind him in a single fluid motion. Before Tiber could react, Falco's wooden sword pressed firmly against his throat from behind, his other arm locking the man in place.

The crowd erupted in a mix of gasps and cheers. For such

a large man, Falco's tactics had been nothing short of extraordinary. Tiber stood frozen, his chest heaving, a grudging respect flickering in his eyes as he realized he had been outmatched.

Julius raised his voice, cutting through the noise.
'Enough!'
Falco released Tiber, stepping back and lowering his sword. Tiber rubbed his throat and gave Falco a sharp nod, acknowledging the skill of his opponent.
'Go and get some food,' barked Julius. 'We'll pick this up later. Move!'
The gladiators dispersed reluctantly, their voices buzzing with admiration for Falco's display. Some clapped him on the shoulder as they passed, others simply nodded in respect.
As the yard cleared, Julius and the trainer lingered near the edge of the training ground, their voices low.
'Impressive,' the trainer admitted, scratching his beard. 'For a man his size, that was... unexpected.'
Julius nodded, his gaze lingering on Falco as he wiped sweat from his face and took a drink from a water skin.
'He's more than muscle. He's got instincts, timing. Tiber's no slouch, and he handled him easily.'
The trainer tilted his head.
'What are you thinking?'
Julius's lips curled into a calculating smile.
'He's not just a fighter. He's a spectacle. That spin? That finish? The crowd will eat it up. And the bets...' He trailed off, his eyes gleaming with ambition. 'We'll make a fortune.'
The trainer chuckled, shaking his head.
'Just don't get ahead of yourself, Julius. Let him settle in first.'
Julius smirked.
'Oh, I'll give him time. But soon, very soon, we're going to

see just how much gold he's worth. Send a message to his sponsor. Tell him I want to see him as soon as possible.'

The trainer nodded and both men walked back toward the ludus, leaving Falco standing in the yard, oblivious to the schemes already forming in his new master's mind.

----

The following morning, Sica arrived at the Ludus and was shown through to the training arena where gladiators sparred, and trainers barked orders. The smell of sweat and leather filled the air, mingling with the faint tang of sand and blood.

Julius stood near the observation platform, his sharp eyes fixed on a group of trainees. He barely turned when Sica approached, but his voice carried authority, nonetheless.

'Ah, Sica. Good. I was hoping you'd come quickly.'

'What's this about?' asked Sica.

Julius turned, gesturing toward the training grounds, where Falco was sparring with one of the junior fighters. Even from this distance, Falco's movements were precise and powerful, each swing of his training sword echoing with intent.

'He's almost ready,' he said simply.

Sica raised an eyebrow.

'For what?'

Julius allowed a rare smile to cross his face.

'There's a tournament in two weeks. An allcomers challenge. Modest prize money, nothing grand, but it's the perfect re-entry for your gladiator. He'll face anyone who thinks they can beat the fighters of this ludus.'

Sica considered the proposal, his brow furrowing.

'Falco could take a dozen of these men at once. This doesn't seem like much of a challenge.'

'That's precisely the point,' Julius replied, his voice lowering conspiratorially. 'It's a way to introduce him back into the arena without too much risk. Let him feel the sand beneath his feet again, hear the roar of the crowd. He'll need that before we take on the bigger events.'

Sica nodded slowly.

'Alright. I'll talk to him.' He turned to leave but stopped when Julius called him back.

'One more thing,' said, his tone suddenly sharper.

Sica hesitated, sensing something unusual.

'What is it?'

'When he fights,' said Julius, 'I want him to lose.'

Sica froze, staring at him in disbelief.

'Lose? Why in the name of the gods would you want him to lose?'

'I have my reasons, but I don't just want him not just lose, I want him to appear clumsy, inexperienced. Slow, even. He'll throw the fights, not once, but three times. Let them see a gladiator who's untested, unimpressive. Someone who doesn't look like a threat.'

Sica's eyes narrowed.

'Why?'

Julius smiled thinly, his gaze calculating.

'The real tournament, the one we're aiming for, is one month away. The entire province will be watching. The governors, the merchants, the gamblers, they'll all be there. Falco is an impressive man, and his stature and skills will be easily remembered. If he displays what he is truly capable of in these lesser tournaments, his odds of winning in the larger one will be cut. However, if he fights like a green recruit now, no one will see him coming when he shows his true skill. The odds will be stacked against him, and when he wins, we'll all walk away with a fortune.'

Sica stared before shaking his head slowly.

'He's not a man who throws fights. And even if I convince him, what about his reputation? He's a gladiator, not an actor.'

Julius's expression hardened.

'You'll convince him. Tell him about the bigger prize. A few fake losses won't hurt him in the long run, not when he's crowned the champion of the greatest tournament Alexandria has seen in years.'

Sica's hesitation was evident, but he couldn't deny the logic. They needed Falco to explode into the consciousness of the higher echelons of Alexandrian hierarchy and this could be the perfect opportunity. He exhaled slowly.

'I'll talk to him,' he said, 'but I can't promise anything.'

'That's all I ask,' said Julius. 'This is a once in a lifetime opportunity, Sica. Don't let it slip away.'

Sica turned and walked toward the training grounds, his mind already racing. Convincing Falco would be no small task, but if they could pull this off, they could achieve the aim they had come here for in the first place. The rich and powerful loved mingling with gladiator champions all across the empire and if Falco could impress them with a magnificent triumph, doors would be opened. Doors that would provide access to the richest, most powerful, and by association, the most corrupt members of Alexandrian society. And that was exactly where he needed to be.

Still, as he watched Falco dismantle another sparring partner with ease, he wondered how the giant, skilful, self-opinionated oaf of a man would take to the idea of pretending to be something he wasn't.

It was a conversation he wasn't looking forward to.

----

## Chapter Thirteen

## Britannia

The days passed slowly for Veteranus, each one blending into the next with little to mark the passage of time. His world had shrunk to the confines of the stone hut, a space that had become both sanctuary and prison. The small comforts afforded him, regular meals, clean water for bathing, and a second set of clothing that fit far better than the first, were unexpected luxuries. The hunter's tunic and leggings felt familiar, a far cry from the ill-fitting rags he had initially been given. He almost felt like himself again as he pulled them on each morning, though the lingering ache in his head reminded him he was far from free.

Every day, the same two women attended to him, bringing food, water, and ensuring the room remained clean. He tried repeatedly to speak with them, to ask questions, but their language was foreign, their expressions apologetic as they shook their heads in response. The one word that bridged the divide was 'Raven.' Whenever he said it, their expressions would change subtly, sometimes wary, sometimes sympathetic, but it always ended the same: no answer, no explanation, and no sign of the man himself.

The pain in his head was becoming a growing concern. Each morning, it greeted him like a hammer blow, a relentless throb that clouded his thoughts and left him irritable despite the care he received. His frustration mounted until one morning, as the women tended to his room, he managed to communicate his distress through gestures and broken phrases. He pointed to his head and grimaced, miming the pain.

The next day, one of the women returned carrying a small vial of white liquid. She offered it to him with an encouraging nod, her expression calm but insistent. Veteranus hesitated. He had no illusions about what the vial contained, it was a drug, probably the same one that had caused him so many visions and long days of unconsciousness, but the pounding in his skull was unbearable, and as the dose was far smaller than he had received before, he decided it was worth the risk. And besides, he was growing desperate.

Finally, decision made, he took the vial and lifted it to his lips, the sharp, familiar scent tickling his nose as he drank. He grimaced as he swallowed, before setting the empty vial aside. Moments passed, and then the effects began. The throbbing in his head receded, like the tide retreating from a battered shore. In its place came a profound sense of calm, a soothing balm for his frayed nerves. His breathing slowed, his muscles loosened, and for the first time in weeks, he felt… whole.

He knew the feeling was artificial, the result of whatever concoction he had consumed. Yet the relief was undeniable, and he couldn't deny the allure of that pain-free peace.

Days passed, and slowly, his strength returned. He began pacing the confines of his room, his stride growing more confident with each passing day. The food was plain but nourishing, the water clean and cool, and though the hut remained a prison, it was no longer a place of suffering. Each day he looked forward to the little vial of comfort brought by the women, almost tearing it from their hands and downing it in one, welcoming the relief like an old friend.

Finally, when he accepted that his fate was not going to change any time soon, the door creaked open again and a familiar silhouette filled the doorway. Raven. The man's dark eyes locked onto his, unreadable and piercing. The air between them seemed to thicken, the moment stretching taut with unspoken tension. Veteranus felt his pulse quicken as he straightened, his mind racing. Questions, accusations, demands, all jostled for position in his throat, but none made it past his lips. He simply stared, his fists clenching instinctively at his sides.

For a moment, neither man spoke, then, without warning, Raven raised a hand and motioned for Veteranus to follow. With only a brief hesitation, Veteranus stepped forward and as he passed through the doorway, the brilliance of the midday sun struck him like a physical force, and he instinctively raised a hand to shield his eyes. For weeks, he had been confined to the dim interior of the hut, and the stark contrast left him momentarily disoriented.

Blinking against the glare, he looked around, his mind racing with assumptions. Surely, he would find himself amidst some elaborate religious or military compound, the kind of spiritual enclave he'd imagined when he first saw the druids. But as his vision adjusted, what he saw instead shocked him.

The village was... ordinary. Thatched huts with smoke curling from their chimneys were scattered across a wide clearing. Women worked at looms or tended to bubbling cauldrons over open fires. Men hauled firewood, repaired tools, and tended livestock while children darted between them, their laughter a stark contrast to the eerie silence he'd grown accustomed to in captivity.

Raven watched him for a moment, an unreadable expression flickering across his face. Then, with a curt nod, he turned and began walking. Veteranus followed, and they moved through the village, the sounds of life enveloping him, the bleating of goats, the rhythmic clanging of a blacksmith's hammer, the hum of conversation. It was a place of activity and vitality, a far cry from the oppressive dread of his confinement.

A small child, no older than six, darted toward him with a bright smile, clutching a shiny red apple in her tiny hands. She held it out to him without a word. Veteranus blinked, caught off guard by the simple kindness. He knelt slightly and took the apple, offering a faint smile.

'Thank you,' he said, his voice rough but genuine. The girl

giggled and dashed away, disappearing among the other children. Further along, a woman approached, her expression warm. She held a clay flask and extended it toward him.

'For me?' he asked, gesturing to himself in surprise. The woman nodded, her soft smile unwavering. He accepted the flask and uncorked it, taking a cautious sip. The water that touched his lips was shockingly cool, its sweetness unlike any he had tasted before. It refreshed him to his core, and for a moment, he closed his eyes to savour the sensation.

'Thank you,' he said, returning the flask. The woman inclined her head and walked away, leaving him to marvel at the unexpected hospitality.

Their path wound toward the village center, where a large, imposing structure dominated the clearing. The longhouse stood tall and proud, its wooden beams dark with age but sturdy. Smoke curled from a hole in the roof, and the faint murmur of voices could be heard from within. Veteranus recognized it immediately. The central longhouse, similar to so many other Celtic villages he had encountered across Gaul and Germania. A place of leadership, feasting, and decision-making. The sight stirred something within him, a strange mixture of familiarity and unease.

Veteranus hesitated and turned to look back at the bustling village once more. The warmth of its people and the vibrancy of its life contrasted so sharply with the shadowy dread that had consumed him for weeks, and the foreboding menace that seemed to emanate from the longhouse like a crawling mist.

'By now,' Raven said, 'I would imagine it has become clear to you that it is Mordred and his people who are the true leaders of this land. Your comrades have fought against him and witnessed both his strength and mercy. And you, Veteranus… you've talked long into the night with him, experiencing the visions and history of these lands. You have also suffered, both mentally and physically but Mordred's power is not rooted in fear or deceit. It is rooted in understanding, of the land, its people, and the forces that have shaped this world for millennia. He wields the old ways because they are real, because they matter, and because power is not about brute strength, it is about timing, patience, and the will to act when the moment is right. Mordred does not need to prove himself to you or anyone else. His time will come, and when it does, Britannia will rise as it was always meant to be, free of Roman chains.' He gestured toward the longhouse. 'Go. He is waiting.'

Veteranus hesitated, his heart pounding as he stepped toward the doorway. Each step felt heavier than the last, the weight of Raven's words pressing against his resolve. Whatever lay beyond, he knew his life would never be the same. He took a deep breath, steadying himself, his mind churning with uncertainty.

As he reached the doorway the guards stepped aside without a word, and, as the door creaked shut behind him, his eyes adjusted to the dim light, his breath catching in his throat.

The chamber was vast, far larger than he'd anticipated. The air was clean and scented with incense, and massive wooden beams arched overhead, their surfaces carved with intricate runes and symbols that seemed to shimmer faintly in the flickering light of dozens of torches.

But it was not the structure, the carvings, or the many statues and emblems all around the walls of the druid's hall that shocked him to the core. It was the sight of the feared Mordred, seated in the center of the hall on the floor… playing and laughing with three small children.

----

## Chapter Fourteen

## Pselchis

The next morning, Marcus stood in the shadow of the fort's crumbling walls, tapping his Vitis, the vine stick that signified his rank and authority, against his leg as he surveyed the two groups assembled on the dusty parade ground.

On one side stood the garrison's existing legionaries, their formation haphazard and their appearance a poor reflection of Rome's martial standards. Their equipment, though functional, bore the tarnish of neglect, and their postures betrayed a complacency Marcus could barely stomach. Opposite them stood the newly arrived recruits, their armour gleaming in the morning sun, weapons polished and ranks straight and disciplined. The contrast was striking.

Marcus inhaled deeply, the sharp desert air biting at his lungs. If this garrison was to function as a fighting force, drastic changes were needed, and fast. Striding purposefully along their ranks, he scrutinized each man in turn, his gaze sharp enough to draw beads of sweat even in the cool of the morning. Some of the legionaries looked away as he passed, their eyes betraying the fear of being singled out. Finally, Marcus stopped in front of one soldier, a man whose hair hung long and untamed beneath his helmet.

'You,' Marcus barked, pointing his vitis at the man. 'Step forward.'

The soldier hesitated, his eyes darting nervously toward his comrades before stepping out of formation.

'Optio Tullus,' called Marcus, 'it seems some of these men want to grow their hair in the manner of a woman. Show them what is acceptable.

The Optio stepped forward. retrieving a pair of crude iron shears from a satchel at his side and after casting aside the soldier's helmet, began cutting. The shears hacked through the hair unevenly, leaving him with a rough, patchy scalp and though the result was far from neat, the message was unmistakable.

Marcus turned back to the ranks.

'By tomorrow morning,' he said, his voice carrying across the yard, 'every man here will be short-haired, bathed, and with gleaming armour and weapons. Failure to comply will result in you being staked in the desert sun for a day without water.'

A murmur of dissent rippled through the ranks and Marcus's eyes narrowed. He immediately marched toward the source of the grumbling, a heavy-set legionary whose lips were still moving in protest. Without hesitation, Marcus raised his vine-stick and struck the man hard across the side of his head, the sharp crack of the impact silencing the murmurs instantly. The soldier staggered backward and fell to the ground, gasping for breath.

'Get him out of my sight,' Marcus said coldly. 'He will be the first to feel the sun on his back.'

Two nearby soldiers hesitated before stepping forward to haul their comrade to his feet and out of the ranks. Marcus's glare swept across the remaining men.

'I will not tolerate dissent,' he called. 'You are legionaries of Rome, not a rabble of brigands. If you cannot act as such, you will not survive under my command. Your standards disgrace this fort, this empire, and yourselves.' His eyes flicked to the garrison's water skins, slung over their shoulders. 'Empty them,' he ordered curtly.

The men exchanged uneasy glances, reluctant to obey. Marcus's vine-stick snapped against his open palm and one by one, the legionaries uncorked their water skins and tipped them out onto the thirsty ground. Marcus waited until the last drop had fallen before issuing his next command.

'I don't know what has gone on here yet, but it is clear that you have forgotten the discipline it takes to be a soldier of Rome. So perhaps we should remind ourselves, starting with the basics. We will now march to the Nile and be back here by noon. Any man who fails to return in time will not eat until tomorrow.' He turned sharply, his eyes falling on the recruits. 'New blood, you will lead. Show these men what discipline looks like.'

The recruits snapped to attention, their ranks tightening as they moved to the front of the column. Marcus walked to the gates of the fort, signalling the guards to open them, revealing the vast desert beyond. He turned back to the garrison one final time.

'This is your chance to show me you are not a lost cause. *Advance!*'

The recruits began to move, their march steady and precise as they led the way out of the fort. Behind them, the dishevelled garrison followed reluctantly, their steps dragging but compliant under Marcus's steely gaze.

----

Marcus strode alongside the column carrying exactly the same equipment as the men, his vine-stick tapping against his leg with each step.

The recruits held their formation admirably, their shields aligned and their movements steady. Their training showed in every disciplined stride, and though sweat beaded on their brows, their resolve remained unbroken. Behind them, the garrison soldiers were a stark contrast. Their ranks wavered, their steps uneven, and their faces grew more haggard with every step they took.

'Straighten those lines!' barked Marcus. 'You are legionaries, not a pack of wandering goats!'

Optio Tullus moved up and down the struggling ranks, his sharp eye catching every faltering step.

'Keep moving!' he shouted, 'the Nile isn't coming to you!'

He stopped beside a soldier whose pace was lagging. 'Are your feet broken, or is that just your spirit dragging you down?'

The man gritted his teeth and pushed forward, his muscles burning as the heat of the day grew more oppressive. Some men faltered under the weight of their gear, stumbling as the relentless sun bore down on them. Others clenched their jaws, spurred on by Marcus's cold glare and Tullus's cutting remarks.

A few, however, began to show signs of what Marcus had hoped for. Their steps grew more purposeful, their postures stiffened, and their shields no longer sagged in their grips. Determination fuelled by anger replaced their earlier lethargy, though their breaths came hard and fast in the sweltering heat.

When the Nile finally came into view, its glistening waters snaking through the parched landscape, a murmur of relief rippled through the ranks. The thought of plunging their heads into the cool water or drinking deeply from its life-giving flow spurred a brief surge of energy. But Marcus had other plans and as they reached the river's edge, he turned sharply and raised his vitis.

'Halt!' he ordered, his voice cutting through the groans of relief. 'Form a single line!'

The men stared at him in disbelief, their parched throats aching for water. A few began to step toward the river, but Marcus's glare stopped them in their tracks.

'Did I give you permission to drink?' he demanded. 'Back in line. Now.'

Grumbling under their breaths, the men shuffled into formation as Marcus gestured to the recruits.

'Each of you will take your waterskins and give two mouthfuls to every man in this garrison. Not a drop more.'

The recruits moved through the ranks, offering measured sips to each soldier. Some men drank greedily, their eyes closing in momentary relief, while others muttered curses under their breath, clearly unsatisfied. Marcus watched the process with a steely gaze, ensuring no one dared disobey his orders.

'You may think you're done,' he said, 'but this is only the halfway mark. In battle, you could go days without water, so this is good training. The good thing is, back at the fort, the water in the well is colder and cleaner and you can drink your fill there. So, the sooner we get back the better.'

The groans of protest were immediate, but Marcus silenced them with a sharp gesture.

'Form up! Recruits at the front. Move!'

The march back began at an even faster pace, Marcus himself setting the rhythm with his measured strides. The heat was now oppressive, and the soldiers' tunics clung to their sweat-soaked bodies. Tullus continued to move among the ranks, alternating between sharp admonishments and rare words of encouragement.

'Dig deep, you lot!' he shouted. 'Show me there's still some Roman pride buried under all that filth!'

As the halfway point approached, Marcus raised his vine-stick, signalling the column to halt one more time. He turned to face the exhausted garrison soldiers.

'Now,' he said, raising his voice, 'you will prove that there are still legionary hearts beating within your chests.' He pointed towards the fort visible on the horizon. 'From here, we will break ranks and run to the fortress. The last ten men to arrive will spend the next two days on latrine duty. And don't think that excuses you from training.'

The men groaned again as they looked up at the distant gates of the fortress shimmering in the midday heat, but before anyone could question the order, he raised his arm.

'Break ranks, advance at speed... *move!*'

The men hesitated for a heartbeat, their muscles screaming in protest, but the threat of punishment spurred them into action. One by one, they broke into a run, their caligae pounding against the cracked earth as they raced toward the distant fort. Some surged ahead with renewed determination, while others lagged, their bodies barely able to maintain the pace.

Marcus and Tullus ran behind them observing the unfolding chaos with grim satisfaction. By the time they reached the gates, the first of the soldiers had already arrived, their chests heaving as they leaned against the walls. Others stumbled in minutes later, their faces pale and drenched in sweat. The final ten men dragged themselves through the gates, their expressions a mix of shame and exhaustion.

Marcus stepped forward, his vine-stick pressing each of their chests in turn.

'Latrine duty. Two days. Dismissed.'

The men groaned but knew better than to argue. As they trudged away, Marcus turned to Tullus.

'They're rough,' he admitted, his voice low. 'But I see heart. Tomorrow, we do it again and every day after that until we expose what they are really made of.'

'As you wish, Centurio,' said Tullus and walked away to join the men as they headed down the ancient steps of the nileometer to fill their flasks.

The soldiers took turns filling their flasks and basins, splashing water over their faces to wash away the grime of the march. Some drank directly from cupped hands, savouring the cool, slightly mineral tang of the water as it coursed down their parched throats.

Once refreshed, the soldiers were ordered back to their tents to begin the next phase of their recovery: restoring their appearance and equipment to the standards of the Roman military. The men paired off, taking turns cutting each other's hair with sharp shears and long, unkempt locks fell to the ground in heaps, followed by scraggly beards, leaving faces clean and jaws sharp. Tullus strolled among them, stopping occasionally to inspect their work.

'That looks much better,' he said to one. 'But keep your hand steady, you're not shearing a sheep.'

Leather armour and straps were stripped down next and re-coated with a thin layer of oil, the sheen bringing life back to cracked and dry surfaces. Swords were drawn from scabbards, their edges inspected with the wary eye of veterans who once knew the value of a sharp blade and once more, whetstones scraped against steel, sending up faint sparks as weapons were honed to deadly precision. Shields were reinforced where splinters and cracks had formed, while helmets were polished until they gleamed in the late afternoon sun.

Tullus walked the line continuously, his gaze sharp as he scrutinized the soldiers' efforts.

'That helmet looks like it's been dug up from Hannibal's time. Polish it again.' He moved on, jabbing a boot at a half-heartedly repaired shield. 'This won't stop an arrow, let alone a Nubian spear. Do it properly.'

By dusk, the men were assembled on the parade ground once more, forming ranks with weapons and shields ready. The sun cast long shadows over the fortress walls as Tullus stepped forward to conduct the inspection.

He moved methodically down the rows, pausing to check every detail: the gleam of a sword blade, the snug fit of a tunic, the alignment of shields. When he spotted something amiss, he barked his disapproval, forcing the offender to step out of line and fix the issue.

As he finished, Tullus stood before the ranks, his hands clasped behind his back. He gave a single, curt nod.

'Better,' he said gruffly, his voice carrying across the square. 'But not good enough. The standards of a Roman legionary are not 'better,' they are perfection. You will start again tomorrow and remember, it won't be me inspecting you tomorrow, it will be your Centurion, and he is not as accepting as me.'

The soldiers shifted uneasily, their gazes flicking toward Marcus, who stood at the edge of the parade square, his expression inscrutable.

'Dismissed,' Tullus barked.

The men broke ranks and trudged back towards the barrack block and tents, their faces a mixture of exhaustion and determination.

----

As the sun set, Marcus headed to the officers' quarters. The sick Tribune still lay in a cot, his pale, sweat-slicked face turned toward the ceiling of the small room.

Marcus entered and stood over him, watching as the man's laboured breathing finally evened out. A faint flicker of lucidity returned to his eyes, though his voice was barely above a whisper when he spoke.

'Centurion…' The Tribune rasped, his gaze meeting Marcus's. 'You've come to a place where shadows linger too long.'

'What happened here, Tribune?' asked Marcus. 'Why is the garrison in such a state?'

The Tribune exhaled heavily, his body shuddering under the strain.

'This fort… it was once the pride of the legion,' he began. 'The men were drawn from the best cohort. Disciplined. Loyal. But then… then the dreams started.' His voice faltered, and his eyes grew distant as if reliving the memories.

'Dreams?' asked Marcus.

The Tribune nodded weakly.

'Yes. All of us. They came every night, relentless. Horrors in the dark. Visions of the Egyptian gods… Anubis, Horus, Sobek. Feeding on our souls while we slept.' He paused, his voice trembling. 'They spoke to us, Centurion. They whispered… things

No man should hear.'

'And you believed them?'

The Tribune gave a weak chuckle, cut short by a coughing fit that left him clutching his chest.

'At first, no. I dismissed it as exhaustion or sickness. But the dreams... they didn't stop and eventually, even I began to believe.' He took a shaky breath, his hand gripping the edge of the cot. 'They've faded now but the men... they couldn't shake it. The fear infected them, poisoned their discipline. They refused to train, to guard, to fight. And then the supplies slowed, raiders struck, and... here we are.'

He tried to say more, but his strength gave out, and he sank back into his cot, his face pinched with pain. Marcus regarded him for a moment before turning back towards the door.

'Rest, Tribune,' he said, 'we need you back out there where you belong.'

The Tribune's eyes closed as Marcus left the dim room and stepped into cooler night air. Nearby, a soldier stood by one of the tents, his posture straighter than most. He carried himself like a man accustomed to discipline, though his armour bore the marks of wear, and his face was lined with fatigue. Marcus strode over, recognizing him as one of the Decurions.

'You there,' Marcus said. 'What is your name?'

The soldier turned sharply and saluted, his expression showing a glimmer of respect.

'Decurion Flavius, Centurio, at your service.'

Marcus studied him for a moment, then gestured for him to relax.

'Flavius, you seem more of a soldier than the others. What's going on here? Tell me the truth.'

'The dreams, Centurio... they broke the men. I've heard their tales, gods feeding on their souls, shadows whispering secrets. I haven't had the dreams myself, but it's hard to lead men when half of them think they're cursed.'

'And the other half?' Marcus asked.

'They're beaten down, my lord. Supplies haven't come regularly in months. Raiders hit the convoys hard, and what little gets through isn't enough. With no officers or Centurions... the men fell apart.' He grimaced, glancing toward the parade ground. 'Some tried to hold things together, but when morale fell, standards went with it. It's been chaos. Even my own contubernium were affected.'

'What about you, Decurion?' asked Marcus. 'Why didn't you step in?'

Flavius straightened.

'I tried, Centurio. But with no support, no punishment for deserters or cowards... it became impossible. I'm just one man.'

Marcus nodded slowly, his mind working through the problem. He clapped Flavius on the shoulder.

'You've done better than most would in your position, Decurio, but things are going to be different from now on, and I'll need men like you to help enforce it.'

Flavius's eyes flickered with something akin to hope, and he saluted again.

'Yes, Centurio. You can count on me.'

----

## Chapter Fifteen

### Alexandria

The small, dimly lit room smelled strongly of sweat and oil, the close walls reverberating with Falco's anger. He paced back and forth like a caged predator, his powerful frame taut with frustration. Sica leaned back against the wall, watching his companion's temper flare with a mix of amusement and exasperation.

'Throw the fights?' Falco shouted, his voice laced with fury. 'Three of them? Has he lost his mind, or does he think I'm a fool?'

Sica sighed, knowing the reaction was inevitable.

'Falco, listen. It's not about the fights themselves. It's about the story. Think of it as... setting the stage.'

Falco stopped pacing, fixing Sica with a glare.

'Setting the stage? For what? A reputation as a clumsy oaf?'

Sica stopped himself responding with something unflattering but thought better of it. This was not the time for banter.

'No,' he said instead, 'for a legend. Look at you. You're a mountain of muscle, a gladiator who looks like he was sculpted by the gods themselves. The moment you step into the arena, people will remember you. If you win now, they'll remember, yes, but they'll also expect it, and the odds will shrink at the bigger fights.'

Falco's scowl deepened.

'So, you want me to lose? To look weak?'

Sica pushed off the wall, stepping closer.

'No, not weak. Mortal. Flawed. The kind of underdog that makes people lean forward in their seats. And when the time comes, when the bigger tournaments arrive, you'll prove them all wrong. The odds will skyrocket, the wagers will pour in, and when you destroy whoever stands against you, you'll be hailed as a miracle. The fame, the fortune, it'll be yours again, just like the old days. But only if we play it right.'

Falco turned away and stared at the room's worn stone walls.

'You're asking me to risk my reputation. My pride.'

'I'm asking you to trust me,' Sica replied, his tone softening. 'You're not a gladiator, any more Falco, you are something more, something better. You are a member of the Occultum, and we have a mission to complete. This is just a means to an end and the sooner we can get it done, the quicker we can all get back to what we do best.'

The silence stretched, broken only by the faint sounds of the ludus outside. Finally, Falco turned back, his expression less thunderous but no less resolute.

'If this damages my name, Sica,' he said, ' I'll make you pay for it, I swear.'

The words were sharp, but the glint in Falco's eye betrayed the camaraderie behind the threat. Sica grinned, sensing the shift.

'Fair enough. But trust me, no one will be mocking your name when this is over.'

Falco sighed, his shoulders relaxing slightly.

'Fine. But I don't like it.'

'You don't have to like it,' Sica replied, clapping him on the shoulder. 'You just have to win when it matters.'

With the agreement reached, Sica left the room to deliver the news to Julius. The ludus master listened intently, his calculating mind already churning with possibilities. He leaned back in his chair, a slow smile spreading across his scarred face.

'Good,' he said, his tone full of anticipation. 'Then I'll make sure his opponents are perfect. Someone big. Someone fierce. The kind of fighter that makes an upset look impossible. And when the time comes, we'll all be swimming in silver.'

----

Across the city, Decimus and Cassius walked through the backstreets. The city's vibrant energy dimmed into shadows here, the air thick with the scent of refuse and lowlife. The buildings leaned tiredly against one another, their walls stained and crumbling, as though the weight of history bore down upon them.

As they turned down another narrow street, Decimus cast a glance at the scrap of information that had brought them here: the words of a one-armed man in a smoky, decrepit taberna. The man had ranted against the modern gods, his bitterness palpable as he clutched a crude cup of wine with his good hand. Yet, beneath the venomous words, there had been a thread of truth, a lead they couldn't afford to ignore.

'Silver crosses a priest's hand,' Decimus murmured to Cassius, repeating the man's cryptic advice, 'and the door to the hidden gods opens.'

Cassius snorted softly, his lips quirking in a faint smirk.

'If he wasn't halfway to drunk, maybe I'd trust that more.'

They rounded a corner and saw their destination: a nondescript building nestled between two dilapidated structures. Its façade was unremarkable, no carvings or statues to mark its purpose, no grand columns or painted reliefs to draw the eye. The only hint of life was the beggar slumped on the steps, his tattered robes barely covering his emaciated frame. His face was obscured beneath a hood, but his outstretched hand held a battered bowl, fingers trembling slightly.

'This is it?' Cassius said. 'Doesn't exactly scream hidden gods. To me.' Looks more like a place to get stabbed for your purse.'

'The best secrets usually hide in plain sight,' said Decimus. Stay sharp.'

As they approached, the beggar shifted, the faint clink of coins audible as his bowl wobbled. He didn't look up, but his presence seemed to anchor the space, as though he were more than just another desperate soul in the city's labyrinth. As they approached, he held out the bowl.

'A coin for the poor, my friends,' he said, 'and perhaps I'll show you the path to the truth.'

Cassius reached into his pouch and retrieved a small coin. The beggar's hand twitched expectantly as he tossed the coin into the bowl, the dull ring of metal against clay breaking the tense silence.

'Fortune favours the generous,' Decimus said, repeating the pass phrase the one-armed man had told them in the taberna.

The beggar made no reply but after a few seconds pause, turned slightly to bang three times on the door beside him, the sound echoing faintly in the stillness.

The heavy door creaked on its hinges as Decimus and Cassius stepped inside, their boots scuffing against smooth, worn stone. The air was cool, a stark contrast to the oppressive heat of the Alexandrian streets and carried a faint scent of beeswax and incense. As their eyes adjusted to the dim light, they froze in surprise.

Before them was a steep set of steps descending deep into the earth. Dozens of candles lined the walls, their flickering flames casting eerie shadows that danced across the jagged surface.

'Not what I expected,' Cassius muttered.

Step by step, they descended, the flicker of the candles guiding them into the depths. The air grew cooler, the faint echoes of their movements bouncing off unseen walls. The stairs spiralled downward for what felt like an eternity until, finally, they emerged into a vast chamber, carved out of solid rock.

Both men stopped in their tracks, momentarily overwhelmed. The room stretched farther than they'd anticipated, its vaulted ceiling held aloft by rows of intricately carved columns. Painted murals adorned the walls, each depicting scenes of Egypt's ancient gods: Ra, Anubis, Osiris, and Hathor stood resplendent in faded pigments, their once-vivid colours now dulled by time. Beneath each mural knelt men and women in various stages of prayer, their heads bowed, hands clasped, or arms outstretched.

Offerings lay scattered before the painted deities, simple bowls of grain, finely wrought jewellery, and small statues of gold and alabaster. The wealth ranged from modest tokens to treasures that gleamed even in the dim light, a testament to the devotion of their givers.

Two priests stood at the far end of the chamber, dressed in flowing linen robes that shimmered faintly as they moved. Their serene expressions were unreadable as they watched over the room, occasionally shifting to gather offerings that threatened to spill from the overflowing piles.

'This is...' Cassius trailed off, his eyes scanning the chamber, 'incredible.'

Decimus nodded slowly, his expression unreadable.

'This place is ancient,' he said. 'In its prime, it must have been magnificent.'

They walked further into the chamber, their footsteps muffled against the smooth stone floor. Decimus feigned interest in one of the murals, bowing his head as if in reverence, while his eyes darted around the room. The priests didn't move from their post, their backs pressed against a heavy, ornate door. It was an odd position, almost as if they were guarding it.

Cassius, meanwhile, lingered near an offering pile, muttering under his breath before re-joining Decimus.

'Grain, trinkets, even wine. These aren't secrets, they're scraps. If this is the hidden faith we've heard about, it's more like a back-alley forgeries den. This is a dead end, Decimus. A shrine for fools and relics. Let's go.'

Decimus hesitated for a heartbeat, then gave a short nod. 'You're right. Let's get out of here.'

They ascended the stairs in silence, the weight of the chamber pressing against their backs. By the time they emerged onto the streets, the heat and light of Alexandria felt almost welcome.

'Well, that was a waste of time,' said Cassius. 'That place was no better than the rest, a few prayers, some dusty murals, and enough offerings to keep a pair of priests fat for A month.'

Decimus didn't respond immediately, his mind racing.

Cassius glanced at him, his annoyance giving way to curiosity.

'What is it? You've been quiet since we left.'

Decimus exhaled slowly and stopped walking to turn to face his comrade.

'The priests by the door. Did you notice them?'

'Of course. What about them?'

'They weren't just standing there to look holy, Cassius, they were guarding something. And above the door...' Decimus paused, his voice lowering. 'I saw something carved into the stone. It was faded and barely visible, but it was there.'

'What was it,' asked Cassius.

'A Scarab,' said Decimus.

'So what?' asked Cassius. 'I know Lepidus claimed that those afflicted across Egypt dreamed about such things, but it could be a coincidence.'

'The scarab isn't just a symbol,' replied Decimus, 'it's one of the oldest icons in Egyptian belief and I don't think its position above that door was there by chance. It's a marker, Cassius, a sign that whatever lies beyond is tied to something more, something hidden. That door is a lead, my friend, and we can't afford to ignore it.'

----

## Chapter Sixteen

## Pselchis

For ten days, Marcus drove the legionaries hard, his relentless pace gradually transforming the dishevelled men into something resembling a disciplined unit. Though the beginning had been rough, with grumbles and glares aplenty, the discipline ingrained in the men from years of service began to resurface. Slowly but surely, the camp came alive with the sounds of training drills, clashing weapons, and barked orders echoing off the weathered wooden walls.

The animosity between the seasoned soldiers and the recruits faded as they found common ground in their shared struggles. The daily runs to the Nile became a unifying challenge rather than a dreaded punishment, with the men helping one another through the gruelling trek, and, by the tenth day, the entire group crossed the finish line together, their collective determination shining through in their exhausted but triumphant expressions.

Standing before them, Marcus allowed himself the briefest smile.

'One cup of wine for each of you,' he declared, earning a subdued but genuine cheer. 'And tonight, the camp cooks will add extra meat to the evening meal. You've earned it.'

----

That night, the mood in the camp shifted. Laughter and low conversation filled the air as the soldiers relaxed around their fires, enjoying the rare luxury of a hearty meal and the camaraderie of a shared victory. Marcus seized the opportunity to walk among them, his vitis tucked under one arm, exchanging quiet words and asking questions of their experiences before his arrival.

The men spoke candidly, their tales of sleepless nights haunted by dreams surprisingly similar. Each man described visions of shadowy figures, oppressive whispers, and strange, foreboding presences. But all agreed on one curious fact: the dreams had begun to fade as the daily drills, structure, and discipline returned to the camp.

Marcus listened carefully, his brow furrowed. The mystery still hung over the fort like an unbroken storm cloud, and though he was relieved the dreams had abated, he knew there were still unanswered questions. He nodded solemnly to each man, offering quiet encouragement before moving on. When the fires burned low, Marcus stood in the center of the camp and addressed the weary but contented soldiers.

'Tomorrow, there will be no run,' he announced, a ripple of surprise passing through the gathered men. 'Instead, I will lead a patrol up to the escarpment to survey the land to the south. One hundred of you will join me. The rest will remain here to repair the palisades and maintain the camp. The names will be posted at first light. Rest well.'

As the soldiers dispersed to their tents, Marcus turned to Tullus at his side.

'The garrison's making progress,' he said, 'But I feel we are isolated. I need to see the lay of the land in case of any conflict.'

Tullus nodded grimly.

'The men will be ready, Centurio. It's good to see some fire in their eyes.'

Marcus nodded and after a circuit of the fort to check the sentries were in place and alert, he retired to his own quarters, leaving strict instructions with the camp servants to wake him well before dawn.

----

Hours later, the clang of the alarm bell tore Marcus from

the depths of a dreamless sleep. As he automatically reached for his gladius, the door burst open, and Tullus stood silhouetted against the torchlight of the fort, his expression grim.

'Centurion,' he barked. 'You need to see this. *Now.*'

Marcus threw on a cloak and followed the Optio out into the night, fully expecting to see the garrison assembling to repel an attack. Instead, the scene in the parade square stopped him in his tracks. A chaotic circle of men had gathered, their faces a mixture of anger and confusion. At the center, two of the night guards pinned someone to the ground. Marcus stepped closer, his eyes narrowing as he recognized the struggling figure... *the Tribune.*

The young officer thrashed beneath the guards, his frothing mouth twisting into curses and snarls. His tunic was soaked in blood, the crimson staining his arms and hands. Nearby, a pugio glinted dully in the torchlight, abandoned in the dirt.

Marcus turned to Tullus.

'What in Hades happened here?'

Tullus gestured silently and led Marcus toward a nearby tent. Outside, a body lay sprawled in the dirt, its outline grotesque in the flickering light. Marcus stepped closer, his stomach tightening. The recruit's face was unrecognizable, a mess of blood and shattered bone, the ground beneath him dark with pooled blood. Members of the dead man's contubernium stood nearby, some of them nursing minor cuts and scratches.

'Tell me what happened here,' demanded Marcus.

'Most of us were asleep, Centurio,' said one of the men, 'but I heard someone come into the tent and thought it was one of the guards. But then I saw the Tribune, he was carrying the pugio.'

'Continue,' said Marcus.

'His eyes... they were wild, like he wasn't even seeing us. He went straight to Verus.' His voice cracked as he gestured to the body. 'He pounced on him and started stabbing, over and over.

We tried to pull him off, but it was already too late.'

Another soldier interjected, his face ashen.

'He was screaming, Centurio. Screaming that Verus was possessed, and he was coming for him. That he had to die.'

The words hung in the air, heavy with unease. Marcus's gaze shifted back to the bloodied Tribune, still thrashing and cursing as the guards struggled to hold him down. The Tribune's fever had broken but it seemed something far worse had taken its place.

'Restrain him and take him to his quarters,' he shouted. 'Tie him down if you must, but he is not to leave that room.'

The guards hesitated only for a moment before snapping to action, dragging the Tribune toward the timber building at the edge of the fort. The Centurion's voice boomed again, this time addressing the assembled men.

'This will not break us!' he said, 'and I will get to the bottom of it. But it does not excuse us from our duty. Tomorrow's patrol will go ahead as planned. Try to get some rest.'

The men shuffled uneasily before dispersing into the shadows of the camp. Marcus stood still, watching them go, knowing that his words had offered little comfort. The night would be long, and sleep would be scarce.

'Wrap the body and secure it somewhere until we have time to burn him,' he said, turning to Tullus. 'Once done, meet me outside the Tribune's quarters.'

'As you wish,' said Tullus and turned away.

----

The timber door creaked on its hinges as Marcus stepped into the Tribune's room. On the small cot, the Tribune writhed, his arms and legs bound tightly with leather straps. Two legionaries stood at the bedside, their faces etched with a mixture of duty and discomfort.

'You're dismissed,' Marcus said curtly, gesturing toward the door.

The guards saluted and filed out, leaving the Centurion alone with the tormented officer. Marcus moved closer, pulling a chair to the bedside. The Tribune was a wretched sight. His face, pale and gaunt, glistened with sweat that soaked the bedding beneath him. His glassy eyes stared at nothing, darting erratically as his lips moved, forming words that barely made sense.

'Demons… shadows... they're coming for us… must protect…'

Marcus stared, his expression grim as he studied the man. He had seen madness before, on the battlefield, in men broken by bloodshed, but this felt different. There was something unnatural about it, something he couldn't place.

His gaze fell to the small bedside table. A goblet of wine stood half-filled, beside an empty bowl smeared with traces of stew. He picked up the goblet, sniffing its contents carefully. The sour tang of cheap wine was familiar but unremarkable. For certainty, Marcus dipped a fingertip into the liquid and touched it to his tongue. The taste was ordinary, no bitterness, no metallic tang that might suggest poison.

Setting the goblet down, his attention turned to the empty bowl. He lifted it, inspecting it from every angle, but it too revealed nothing. It had contained the same stew served to the rest of the garrison: goat, lentils, seasoned broth. Whatever afflicted the Tribune hadn't come from his meal, or if it had, he alone had been affected.

Marcus rose and searched the room, his sharp eyes scanning every corner. He checked the floorboards, the small storage chest, even the folds of the bedding, but there was no sign of anything unusual. The room was ordinary.

The Tribune's thrashing grew weaker, his mumbled words trailing off into incoherent murmurs. Marcus watched him for a moment longer. Whatever was happening, the answers weren't here, and he left the restrained Tribune alone, closing the door behind him.

Outside, Tullus stood waiting, the faint light from the torches along the palisade casting his weathered face in sharp relief.

'Well?' Tullus asked.

'Nothing,' Marcus replied, shaking his head in frustration. 'The food, the wine, it's the same as everyone else. The room's bare. No poison, no strange markings, no talismans. Just him, raving like a lunatic.'

Tullus frowned, his dark eyes narrowing.

'It doesn't make sense. If it's not something he ate or drank, then what? The dreams have stopped for everyone else. The men are steady. But him... it's like he's possessed.'

Marcus let out a heavy sigh, his gaze drifting toward the palisade. The fort was eerily quiet now, the earlier commotion a distant memory.

'Possessed or not, it's a mystery we can't solve tonight. What matters is keeping the men calm. If they think the gods, or worse, spirits, are at play, discipline will unravel faster than we can stop it.'

For a moment, the two stood in silence, the weight of the situation settling heavily between them.

'Double the guards,' Marcus said finally. 'Along the palisade and in the watchtowers. It may not make any difference but at least the men can see we have done something.'

'It'll be done,' said Tullus. 'And you?'

'I'll check the perimeter,' said Marcus, his voice betraying the exhaustion he refused to acknowledge. 'But you need rest, Tullus. You've been at my side every step today. Get some sleep while you can.'

The Optio hesitated, his lips pressing into a thin line.

Then, with a slow nod, he stepped back.

'You'll wake me if there's anything?'

Marcus smirked faintly, the closest thing to humour he could muster.

'I'll save the best trouble for you.'

Tullus snorted softly and turned toward the barracks, his measured strides disappearing into the shadows. Marcus remained where he was, his gaze sweeping over the quiet fort. Somewhere in the darkness lay answers, but for now, like the sleep he desperately craved, they eluded him.

----

## Chapter Seventeen

## Alexandria

The days at the governor's palace in Alexandria had settled into a routine of political tedium and mounting frustration. Seneca, as a Tribune of Rome and a representative of Senator Lepidus, had been granted a seat at the governor's side during audiences with emissaries from the nomes. These meetings, meant to address the grain quotas crucial to Rome, had devolved into a litany of excuses and fearful tales.

Every delegation from the fertile stretches of the Nile brought the same message: shortfalls in quotas, dwindling productivity, and a populace paralyzed by dread. The emissaries painted grim pictures of villages beset by whispers of evil spirits, hauntings, and strange omens in the night. Farmers abandoned their fields, priests performed endless rituals to appease unseen gods, and panic rippled through the countryside.

Through it all, Seneca maintained his composure, though his mind often wandered to Lady Callista. Since their first dinner together, they had shared several more private moments in the palace gardens and halls, their conversations growing increasingly intimate. Her sharp wit and entrancing presence captivated him in a way he hadn't anticipated, and he found himself looking forward to their encounters with a mixture of anticipation and dread.

But his distraction did not go unnoticed.

One afternoon, as the sun hung high over the city, a servant summoned Seneca to the audience chamber. He entered to find Governor Postumus seated on a raised dais, his stern expression a stark contrast to the opulent surroundings.

'Tribune,' Postumus began, 'I believe we need to speak plainly.'

Seneca stepped forward and inclined his head respectfully.

'Of course, Governor. What concerns you?'

Postumus leaned back in his chair, steepling his fingers.

'You are here at the behest of Senator Lepidus, a man whose reputation is apparently impeccable and whose influence certainly stretches far. He has sent you here to support me, to address the mounting chaos in my province, and to ensure that Rome's lifeline remains intact.'

Seneca nodded, sensing the weight of what was coming.

'And yet,' Postumus continued, 'you have allowed yourself to be distracted.'

'Distracted, excellency?'

'Do not play coy with me,' Postumus snapped. 'You have been seen, Seneca. You and Lady Callista and whilst I am fully aware that we are all adults and free to do whatever we please in life, there are limits and I must remind you that this is not a social visit. You are a Tribune, and though you may come highly recommended, your station is still far beneath hers. Lady Callista is of royal lineage, her family one of the most esteemed in Egypt. A misstep with her could bring consequences far greater than you realize.'

Seneca felt the sting of the rebuke but kept his expression neutral.

'You are right, Governor. I have allowed myself to stray from the task at hand. It will not happen again.'

Postumus studied him for a long moment before nodding.

'Good. See that it doesn't. Egypt is in a precarious position, and we cannot afford further distractions. Focus on your mission, Tribune. That is why you are here.'

Dismissed, Seneca left the chamber feeling the weight of Postumus's words pressing heavily on him. He knew the governor was right, he had allowed himself to be drawn into something that could jeopardize not only his position but also the mission itself.

Shaking off the haze of distraction, Seneca resolved to

refocus. Leaving the palace, he made his way through the bustling streets of Alexandria, weaving past merchants and beggars, scholars and soldiers, until he reached the nondescript building that served as a meeting place for his men.

----

The dimly lit room above the quiet backstreets had become their haven of secrecy and the four men gathered around a battered wooden table, its surface marked with the scars of countless uses. Seneca poured four cups of wine and sat down, ready for any updates from each of his men.

'Before we start,' said Sica, 'can I ask what happened to Talorcan? I thought he would be here by now.'

'Talorcan stayed in Britannia,' replied Seneca. 'It wasn't an easy decision, but we had to think strategically and leaving a man there allows us to maintain a foothold. He will keep an eye on things, gather intelligence, and ensure that if and when we return, we're not going in blind.'

Sica tilted his head slightly, his dark eyes narrowing.

'So, he's not with the Occultum anymore?'

'Temporarily reassigned,' Seneca clarified. 'He's back with Vespasian's legion for now, embedded with the auxiliaries. It keeps him close to the local situation while giving him the resources to remain effective. When we return, he'll rejoin us.'

Sica's lips twitched into the faintest of smirks.

'He'll like that. Less talking, more hunting.'

Seneca allowed himself a small smile.

'It suits him. And knowing Talorcan, he's already tracking every whisper worth hearing. So, tell us about Falco.

'Falco is progressing well,' began Sica. 'The ludus master has entered him into a tournament in a few weeks' time. It's an excellent opportunity and should give us options.'

Cassius raised an eyebrow, leaning back in his chair.

'Remind me, Sica,' he said, 'why is this tournament so

critical to the mission? I see little point in Falco returning to the arenas so where does this path lead?'

'Possibly nowhere,' said Sica, 'but it is certainly worth exploring. The fact is that the hierarchy of every city in the empire loves a successful gladiator, but Alexandria is on another level altogether. Here, the rich and powerful thrive on status and connections. They sponsor fighters, they brag about knowing them, and many of the women take them as lovers. It's a path that leads straight to the highest circles of influence and if Falco wins, and I believe he will, he'll be celebrated, sought after and invitations will pour in. That puts him, and by extension us, at the very heart of Alexandria's elite. If anyone amongst the rich and powerful is conspiring against Rome, that's where we'll hear whispers. It's the perfect cover.'

Decimus leaned forward and took a sip from his cup.

'I hope this plan of yours doesn't get us all killed, Sica. Gladiators draw attention, sure, but they also draw danger.'

Sica shrugged.

'Danger is part of the job, and besides, it's not just about Falco.' His tone shifted, becoming more serious. 'I've been asking around, in the backstreets and tabernas. There's fear everywhere, more than I've seen in a long time.'

'Fear of what?' asked Seneca.

'Of the malady,' Sica said grimly. 'It's spreading, affecting everyone, but there's something strange about it. From what I've gathered, it's hitting those with Roman blood the hardest. Egyptians are not immune as we know, but the pattern is there. Something's happening, and it's no coincidence that Rome's strength is being targeted.'

Seneca frowned, his mind racing. The pieces were beginning to fit together, though the picture they formed was still shrouded in shadow. He turned his attention to Decimus.

'Decimus,' he said. 'What about you? Any progress?'

Decimus leaned forward, his chair creaking under his weight.

'We've covered a lot of ground,' he began. 'Cassius and I have been to most of the city's temples, the bigger ones and the smaller shrines tucked into alleys. We've watched the rituals, attended festivals, and listened to the priests, at least, as much as they'll let outsiders listen.'

'And?'

'Not much to be honest. The people are nervous, and they don't want to talk about anything out of the ordinary. But there is one thing that keeps cropping up.'

'What's that?'

'The scarab,' said Decimus. 'Not as a subject of conversation, but in passing. A mention here, a symbol there. It's subtle, almost as an afterthought. Like it's something people respect, or fear, but don't want to draw attention to. Ordinarily, it wouldn't be worth mentioning, but...' He let the thought hang for a moment.

'But Lepidus mentioned it back in the Hornless Bull,' replied Seneca.

Decimus nodded.

'Exactly. It's a connection, faint though it might be. And then there's the underground temple Cassius and I found.'

'The one in the backstreet?' Sica asked, leaning forward.

'That's the one. We went inside and down a long set of steps. The place is ancient, far older than most of what's standing above ground. The walls were covered in paintings of the old gods. Offerings were piled high, and there were men praying at each shrine. Two priests were watching over it all, serene and quiet.'

'And?'

'There was a door at the back of the chamber,' Decimus said, his tone sharpening. 'It was closed, and the priests made sure to stand in front of it the entire time. As we were leaving, I saw a symbol painted above the lintel. Faded, almost invisible in the dim light, but unmistakable.'

Seneca leaned forward, his eyes narrowing.

'A scarab?'

Decimus nodded.

'A scarab. It could be nothing, or it could be everything. Either way, it's worth looking into. If the priests are guarding it, there's something behind that door they don't want anyone to see.'

The room fell silent for a moment, the weight of the revelation settling over them.

'We certainly can't ignore it,' said Seneca eventually, 'the scarab keeps showing up, and now we have a place tied to it, we need to explore the idea further.'

Decimus nodded.

'I agree. But we'll need to tread carefully. If the priests are guarding it, there's a good chance it's not just another dusty storeroom.'

The men exchanged uneasy glances, the flickering lamp casting shadows that seemed to echo the growing unease in the room. The scarab, once a faint and insignificant clue, now loomed large, its implications impossible to ignore.

'What about you, Seneca?' asked Decimus. 'Any news from the palace?'

'I have a better understanding of the spread of the issue,' said Seneca with a sigh. 'This affliction, whatever it is, has a firm grip across all the nomes. Reports come in from every delegation, the same patterns repeating themselves: panic over evil spirits, reverence for the old gods, and disruptions that are choking the grain supply.' He paused, his gaze shifting briefly to the flickering lamp in the center of the table as he recalled his own recent nightmares. 'But as to the cause, I have nothing. No leads, no clear answers.'

'What about the governor?' asked Cassius. 'Any insights there?'

'He's exasperated,' Seneca replied. 'The shortfalls are mounting, and the reports of unrest only grow worse. He's doing his best to keep order, but even he is at a loss as to what's truly happening. The same issues persist everywhere, and yet there's no central figure or group we can point to as the source.'

'What about Marcus?' asked Decimus. 'Do we have any word from him?'

Seneca shook his head.

'Nothing beyond his initial deployment orders. We know he's at the southern border, near Syene. That's where the reports of the affliction were most concentrated, so if there's anything to be uncovered there, Marcus will find it. But for now, we'll have to wait for news.'

The group exchanged uneasy glances. The unknowns of the situation weighed heavily on them all, the scope of the problem growing more daunting with every meeting.

'So, what's the plan now?' asked Decimus.

'We proceed with what we have,' said Seneca. 'Keep asking questions and hopefully Falco's contest will put us in the orbit of Alexandria's elite. If that path yields nothing, we'll send word to Lepidus. He needs to know the scope of the problem, even if we can't yet offer him a solution.'

'Agreed, said Decimus, 'but let's hope Falco's performance shakes something loose. We're overdue for a breakthrough.'

Seneca stood, the others following his lead.

'We'll meet again the day after the contest,' he said. 'If anything changes, no matter how small, I want to know about it immediately,' and with that, the group dispersed, their minds heavy with the weight of the mission ahead.

----

## Chapter Eighteen

## Britannia

Veteranus stared at the scene before him, unable to reconcile the man before him with the man who had put him through so much fear and pain in the previous few weeks. Mordred, the shadowy druid leader whose name was spoken in dread, and with so much blood on his hands, was laughing softly as he played with his three small grandchildren.

The children were small and innocent, their shrill laughter filling the warm space as they clutched wooden figurines of warriors and animals, weaving battles with childish glee. Mordred was down on his knees, guiding their game with a patient smile that seemed impossibly genuine but as soon as he noticed Veteranus standing at the doorway, he rose with deliberate grace, brushing dust from his simple woollen tunic. The firelight reflected off his long black hair, bound loosely at his neck, and for a moment, he seemed like any other grandfather indulging his young kin.

Mordred stepped to a low table near the fire. He took up a clay jug and filled two earthen mugs with wine, his gaze briefly flicking to Veteranus before crossing the room, holding the mugs with a casual confidence. He extended one towards Veteranus as he approached.

'Drink,' he said, his tone conversational but with the undeniable weight of command.

Veteranus hesitated. He had not been drugged for several days now, an unexpected reprieve after weeks of torment, but the memory of the sickly-sweet tinctures that had clouded his mind still lingered.

'I've had enough of your poisons,' he said.

'It's just wine,' replied Mordred, taking a long sip from his own mug before holding Veteranus's out again. 'Or do you think me so craven I'd strike you down with a cup in my own home in front of my grandchildren?'

Veteranus hesitated for a moment longer, then reached out, his fingers closing around the mug.

Mordred lowered himself onto the bench opposite Veteranus, close enough to speak softly but still outside striking range. His gaze lingered on the mug in Veteranus's hands as though waiting to see if the Roman would drink.

Reluctantly, Veteranus lifted the mug to his lips and took a cautious sip. The wine was simple but clean, its earthy tang unfamiliar but not unpleasant. He set the mug down on the bench beside him, determined not to let this unexpected civility lower his guard.

'You don't look like a man enjoying his freedom,' Mordred remarked, taking a sip from his own mug.

'Freedom,' Veteranus echoed. 'Is that what you call this?'

Mordred shrugged, unbothered by the veiled anger in Veteranus's voice.

'You're free to speak. Free to sit at my table. Free to drink my wine. More than I've given others in your position.'

'Others like me? Romans, you mean. How many have you tortured in this place? How many have you...'

'Enough.' Mordred's voice was calm but carried an unmistakable edge. He leaned forward slightly, resting his elbows on his knees. 'This isn't about what I've done. It's about what you'll come to understand, in time.'

Veteranus snorted, his anger flaring despite his exhaustion.

'Understand? You've spent weeks breaking my body, drugging my mind, and now you want me to sit here and pretend you're some wise old man with lessons to teach?'

Mordred's expression didn't change, though his eyes seemed to darken.

'You think you know me, Roman,' he said softly. 'You see the druid, the war leader, the butcher. But you don't see this.' He gestured toward the room, where his wife now helped one of their daughters lay plates on the long table, and the grandchildren giggled as they chased each other around a pillar.

'This is who I am,' Mordred continued. 'A husband, a father, a grandfather. This land is more than a battlefield to us. It's home. And while you may not understand it now, you will. Before your time here is done, you'll see what it is you and your empire seek to destroy.'

For a long moment, the only sound was the crackle of the hearth fire and the faint chatter of the grandchildren as they played nearby.

'How are you feeling, Roman?' Mordred asked at last, his tone almost conversational.

Veteranus stiffened slightly, wary of the shift in tone.

'As well as can be expected, given the circumstances.'

Mordred's smile was faint but insistent, the kind that seemed to coax truth from even the most reluctant of tongues.

'And the dreams?' he pressed. 'The headaches? Have they stopped?'

Veteranus hesitated, his fingers tightening around the mug of wine. The memories of those first days in captivity, dark, twisted visions that felt all too real, still haunted him, though they no longer had the same grip.

'The dreams are still there,' he admitted. 'But they're... easier to bear now. The headaches, though, they have stopped.' He paused, narrowing his eyes slightly. 'And I'm under no illusion why, Mordred. That vial of white liquid your servants bring me every morning... that is the reason.'

'Perhaps,' replied Mordred with a small shrug, as though the matter was of no great consequence. 'I take it myself, you know. Daily. And I find it very beneficial.'

Veteranus stared at him, the admission catching him off guard. He had imagined the liquid as some form of control, a tool to weaken him, not something Mordred would willingly subject himself to.

'Is it derived from the poppy?' he asked.

Mordred's smile widened, a hint of mischief in the curve of his lips.

'No,' he replied simply, shaking his head. 'It comes from a place far away, beyond the lands you Romans know.'

The cryptic answer only deepened Veteranus's frustration.

'What is all this?' he demanded, setting his mug down with a dull thud. 'What do you want from me, Mordred?'

Mordred studied him for a moment, the silence stretching just long enough to unsettle. Then he chuckled softly, taking another slow sip of his wine.

'In time, all will be clear,' he said, 'but not tonight. Tonight, we will share food.'

Before Veteranus could press further, Mordred stood and gestured toward the table.

'Come,' he said, "a man cannot think clearly on an empty stomach.'

Veteranus hesitated, his body taut with distrust, but the smell of the food and the unyielding authority in Mordred's voice left him little choice. Slowly, he rose, his gaze never leaving the druid as they moved toward the long table, his every sense alert, knowing full well that this was no ordinary man.

----

The meal unfolded in a way that Veteranus had not anticipated. Plates of roasted meats, spiced roots, and crusty bread were passed with little ceremony, the hum of quiet conversation punctuated by the occasional laugh or clatter of a cup. Mordred sat at the head of the table, a commanding yet oddly relaxed presence, while Veteranus remained more guarded, his movements cautious.

Raven joined them shortly after the food was served, slipping into a seat beside Mordred with the easy familiarity of a trusted lieutenant. For a time, the conversation steered clear of anything significant. Mordred asked about Veteranus's years in the legions, a polite curiosity in his tone, while Raven offered the occasional jest, his dark humour aimed more at Mordred than their guest. Veteranus responded in clipped sentences at first, but the wine and the disarming normalcy of the scene slowly loosened his tongue.

It wasn't exactly friendly, but the tension that had defined their earlier interactions began to ease. The soft warmth of the fire, the rhythmic clinking of plates and cups, and the simple, grounding presence of food all worked against Veteranus's defences.

But unease still simmered beneath the surface. Mordred and Raven exchanged glances from time to time, silent signals that Veteranus couldn't decode. They weren't pressing him for anything, not information, not confessions, but the air of unspoken understanding between them gnawed at his nerves.

Finally, he couldn't take it anymore. He set his cup down heavily, the sound drawing both men's attention.

'What are you playing at?' he asked, his gaze shifting between Mordred and Raven. 'You go from drugging and beating me to inviting me to your table. What do you want from me?'

Mordred leaned back in his chair and took a deliberate sip of wine, letting the silence stretch before answering.

'All will be revealed in time,' he said with maddening serenity.

'You've said that before,' said Veteranus. 'You're dragging this out. Why?'

Mordred's smile returned, faint and knowing.

'Because timing is everything, Veteranus. You'll

understand soon enough. But for now, eat. Rest. There is much yet to come.'

Veteranus glanced at Raven, searching for some hint of an answer in the traitor's expression, but Raven only smirked and reached for another slice of bread.

The night dragged on. The servants cleared the dishes, and the fire burned lower in the hearth, casting long, flickering shadows across the room. Mordred and Raven spoke idly of local matters, tribal disputes, the movement of herds, even the weather, as though Veteranus weren't sitting there, stewing in his unanswered questions.

Eventually, Mordred rose, signalling the end of the evening. He clapped Veteranus lightly on the shoulder as he passed.

'Goodnight, Roman. Sleep well.'

Raven stood and gestured for Veteranus to follow. The two men stepped out into the cool night air, the longhouse behind them glowing faintly with the remnants of the firelight.

As they approached the hut that had served as Veteranus's prison, something immediately struck him as odd. He stopped and turned to Raven, suspicion tightening his chest.

'Where are the guards?'

Raven shrugged.

'There aren't any. You're no longer a prisoner.'

Veteranus stared at him, his mind racing.

'I'm not a prisoner?' he repeated, scepticism thick in his voice.

'You heard me,' Raven said. 'You can go if you want. No one will stop you.' He paused, tilting his head slightly. 'But if you did, you'd miss one of the greatest moments in history.'

Veteranus's stomach twisted. He hated how effortlessly Raven toyed with him, how easily he planted seeds of doubt and curiosity.

'What are you talking about?' he demanded, but Raven only turned and began walking away, his figure soon swallowed by the night.

Left alone, Veteranus hesitated at the door. The absence of the guards was a revelation, but it didn't feel like freedom. Not yet.

He stepped into the hut, its familiar confines both a comfort and a torment. The small cot in the corner awaited him, but sleep would not come easily. He sat on the edge, staring into the dark for what felt like an eternity, his mind whirling. What did they want? Why this sudden shift? And what had Raven meant about a moment in history?

He lay down eventually, but his thoughts refused to quiet. He replayed the events of the evening, the cryptic words, the missing guards, the strange calm of the meal. None of it made sense, and as the hours crawled by, he stared at the ceiling, his mind a battlefield of doubt and determination. Whatever game they were playing, he would uncover it. But not tonight. Tonight, he just needed to sleep.

----

## Chapter Nineteen

## Alexandria

The cell was dim, the flickering torchlight from the corridor outside casting long, shifting shadows across the rough stone walls. The distant roar of the crowd rumbled through the arena like the growl of a hungry beast, each surge of noise a reminder of the bloodlust waiting above.

Falco sat on the bench, his broad shoulders hunched, his elbows resting on his knees. His gladius leaned against the wall beside him, its blade clean and untouched, as though waiting for a master to claim it.

Across from him, Sica leaned against the opposite wall, his arms crossed, his small, wiry frame blending into the shadows. He watched Falco in silence, his dark eyes studying his companion with an intensity that bordered on discomfort. Falco had been unusually quiet since they were led into the cell, and the silence wasn't sitting well with Sica.

'You've never been this still before a fight,' Sica said finally. 'Usually, you'd be pacing by now… or bragging.'

Falco didn't respond immediately. He reached down, picking at a splinter on the edge of the bench. When he finally spoke, his voice was low and distant, like a man speaking to himself.

'Maybe I don't have anything to brag about anymore.'

Sica straightened, his brows drawing together in a rare display of emotion.

'What are you talking about? You've fought a hundred men in a hundred places. You've got nothing to prove.'

Falco let out a short, bitter laugh.

'That was before,' he muttered. 'Before the last three fights. Before I lost.'

'You let them win,' said Sica. 'You had to. You were following orders.'

Falco finally looked up, his dark eyes meeting Sica's. They were filled with something Sica had never seen in his companion before, hesitation.

'Tell that to the crowd,' he said. 'You didn't hear them, Sica. The way they jeered, the way they laughed. They think I'm a joke now. The great Falco, beaten by some nobody with a wooden shield and a cheap trick.' He shook his head, his hands balling into fists. 'I've fought my whole life to be the best, to make them cheer my name. And now... now they think I'm finished.'

Sica pushed off the wall, stepping closer to Falco.

'The crowd's cheers don't mean a damn thing,' he said firmly. 'You're not here to impress them. You're here for a purpose. Don't forget that.'

Falco looked away.

'It's not about the cheers,' he said after a moment. 'It's about who I am. I'm supposed to be the fighter they fear. The one they can't beat. But if I can't even beat some local champion in this... this nothing arena, then maybe they're right. Maybe I don't have it anymore.'

Sica crouched down in front of him, his sharp gaze unwavering. 'Listen to me,' he said. 'You've faced worse odds than this. You've fought in the grand arenas of Rome, against men who could've torn you apart. You're still standing, Falco. You're still breathing. That's not luck, that's because you're a fighter. A damned good one.'

Falco met his eyes again, and for a moment, there was a flicker of the old fire, the spark of confidence that had carried him through so many battles. But it was fleeting, swallowed quickly by doubt.

'But what if I'm not anymore?'

Sica exhaled slowly, his face softening just enough to show

he cared.

'Then you prove it to yourself,' he said. 'Not to the crowd, not to me, and not to anyone else. Just to yourself.'

The words hung in the air. Falco didn't reply, his gaze drifting to the gladius by his side. Above them, the roar of the crowd grew louder, the sound of a name being chanted in drunken unison echoing down the stone corridor. Falco's opponent, no doubt, basking in the adoration of the masses. Sica stood, brushing dust from his hands.

'They're calling for him now,' he said. 'But when this is over, they'll be calling for you again. You'll see.'

Falco didn't respond, his focus remaining on the blade at his side.

Sica paused at the cell door, glancing back at his companion.

'Don't overthink it, Falco. Just do what you've always done,' and with that, he stepped out, leaving Falco alone with his thoughts.

Falco sat there for a long moment, the noise of the crowd washing over him like a distant tide. His fingers brushed the hilt of the gladius, the wood familiar and steadying. He wasn't sure if Sica was right, but there was only one way to find out.

----

Combatants came and went, walking past the iron bars, drenched in sweat, blood, and sand. Most were alive, these games weren't for killing, after all, but some were as good as dead in spirit.

A young man staggered by, his face pale and his hands trembling, clutching a purse of silver as though it were both prize and punishment. Another strode proudly, his chest heaving but his head high, victorious. There were murmurs that one fighter had won the rudis, the wooden sword that granted liberty, his skill so undeniable that even the crowd had demanded his release.

None of it interested Falco. For him, this fight wasn't about wealth or liberty, it was about respect. Regaining what he had lost, or, perhaps, proving to himself that it wasn't gone at all.

The muffled noise outside reached a crescendo as another match ended. A competitor stumbled past the bars, blood dripping from a cut above his eye, but his grin was as wide as the horizon. Behind him, a defeated fighter dragged himself back down the corridor, shaking his head in bitter disbelief. Falco closed his eyes, trying to block it all out until the noise faded suddenly, replaced by an anticipatory murmur, like the crowd was collectively holding its breath.

The cell door creaked open, and a messenger stepped inside.

'It's time,' he said simply.

Falco stood slowly, his body heavy with the weight of expectation. He reached for his sword and shield, their familiar weight a strange comfort.

'Who's my opponent?' he asked, almost disinterested.

The messenger hesitated, then shook his head.

'You'll see when you get there.'

Falco nodded once, adjusting the strap on his shield, and, without another word, stepped past the messenger and into the corridor, heading toward the arena.

The heavy gates groaned as they began to open, the sound reverberating through the stone passage. Falco paused, just before stepping into the blinding sunlight of the arena. The moment felt familiar, yet alien.

He had done this so many times before, back in Rome and beyond, stepping out to the deafening roar of the crowd, their adoration tangible in the air. But he knew this would be different. He wasn't the invincible gladiator anymore. The last three fights had poisoned the crowd's faith in him.

As he stepped into the light, the full force of the sun hit

him, the heat immediate and oppressive. The arena stretched out before him, a vast oval of sand encircled by towering stands, packed with a capacity crowd. The reception was as cold as he had feared. Calls of derision came first, cutting through the hum of the crowd like daggers.

'Falco the Faker!' one voice jeered, followed by another: 'Go back to Rome, you fraud!' A few threw insults laced with mockery, their words echoing across the sands.

Falco kept his head high, his face impassive, but the sting of the crowd's disdain settled like a weight on his chest. He marched to the centre of the arena, the sand shifting beneath his boots, and turned to face the elevated box where the sponsors sat.

The governor of Alexandria sat in the centre. Beside him were members of the Egyptian royal family, their regal bearing unmistakable even amid the pageantry of the day.

Falco stared up at them, scanning their ranks. The pomp and wealth displayed there were a sharp contrast to the boiling tension below. And then, just a few rows behind the governor, he saw Seneca. The two men's eyes locked for the briefest of moments. Falco felt his heart jolt, though his expression betrayed nothing. Seneca's face remained calm, unreadable, as though he were merely another spectator drawn to the spectacle. No nod of recognition, no flicker of acknowledgment passed between them. They both knew why. It was all part of the plan.

Falco tore his gaze away, forcing his attention back to the crowd. The unease in the arena had settled into a restless murmuring, the crowd shifting in their seats, waiting for something to happen.

From the edge of the arena, an announcer stepped forward, his voice carrying easily over the throng. He was a wiry man, draped in vibrant robes, and his presence alone drew the crowd's attention.

'Citizens of Alexandria!' the announcer called, spreading

his arms wide. 'Today, you witness a rare spectacle! You know him well, Falco, the Iron Gladiator of Rome, known for years as Falco the undefeated! But today, he faces a test unlike any other!'

The crowd stirred, whispers rippling through the stands.

'For the first time in many months,' the announcer continued, his voice rising, 'we welcome back the undefeated champion of Egypt! A man whose strength and skill are the stuff of legend! The lion who has never been tamed!'

A roar of approval erupted from the crowd, the stands trembling with the force of their excitement. Falco's blood chilled.

The announcer paused, letting the tension mount before he bellowed the name:

'Behold! The mighty, the unstoppable... *Darius!*'

The crowd's roar became deafening, a wall of sound that reverberated through the arena. Falco turned his head toward the gate as it began to creak open again, his pulse quickening despite himself.

He had heard the name before, in the Ludus. Darius, the Champion of Egypt. Seldom seen, never defeated. The crowd's reaction told him everything he needed to know: this man wasn't just a fighter; he was a legend.

Falco adjusted his grip on his gladius, the familiar weight suddenly feeling heavier and, as the shadow of his opponent loomed in the gateway, his doubts gnawed at him. This wasn't just about regaining respect. This was about survival.

----

The roar of the crowd was deafening as Darius emerged fully into the arena. The Egyptian champion was a towering figure, his muscular frame accentuated by the golden light of the sun. He wore a breastplate adorned with intricate engravings, the gleam of polished bronze catching every flicker of movement. His weapon, a curved khopesh blade, looked wickedly sharp, the kind of blade that didn't just cut but tore. The crowd adored him.

The two men saluted the officials staring down from the royal box before turning and saluting each other, and, seconds later, a horn blast echoed through the arena signalling the start of the contest.

Falco barely had time to steady himself before Darius surged forward, his attack immediate and ferocious, his strikes precise and unrelenting. Falco raised his shield just in time to deflect the first blow, the force of the impact reverberating through his arm.

Darius pressed the attack, his movements fluid and aggressive. Every swing of the khopesh came with the intent to dominate, to overwhelm and Falco backpedalled, parrying desperately as he tried to regain control. But Darius gave him no room to breathe, his relentless assault forcing Falco closer and closer to the edge of the arena.

The crowd cheered wildly, their voices a thunderous wave of approval for their champion.

'Fight back, Falco!' someone yelled from the stands, but the words felt distant, buried beneath the onslaught. Darius swung again, the khopesh carving a brutal arc toward Falco's head. Falco ducked low, his gladius coming up instinctively to counter, but Darius pivoted with startling speed, delivering a powerful kick to Falco's chest. The force sent him sprawling into the sand, the air driven from his lungs and the crowd erupted, roaring their approval.

Darius stepped back, raising his arms to the crowd, soaking in their adoration. He bellowed something in his native tongue, his voice carrying across the arena, and the crowd responded with frenzied cheers. He turned to them fully, his back to Falco, basking in the glory of the moment.

Falco gritted his teeth, coughing as he forced himself onto one knee. His vision swam, but he could feel the grit of the sand beneath his fingers, grounding him. Get up, he told himself. Get up, or it's over.

Darius turned back, his grin fading as he saw Falco rise once more, and with a growl, launched himself forward again, resuming the attack.

The fight dragged on, each clash of steel punctuated by the roar of the crowd. Falco struggled to keep pace, his arms growing heavy, his movements sluggish. Darius cut him again and again, small, shallow wounds that bled but didn't cripple. The Egyptian champion was toying with him, showing the crowd his dominance.

Another swing, another cut. Blood trickled from Falco's arm. Another lunge, another strike. His shield arm burned with the effort of absorbing blow after blow. Falco's footing slipped, and he went down hard, the sand scraping against his already battered skin. He rolled onto his back just as Darius loomed over him, his khopesh raised high, its blade gleaming in the sunlight. The crowd surged to their feet, chanting for the kill.

*'Death! Death! Death!'*

Darius paused, his chest heaving, his gaze fixed on the fallen Roman. For a moment, the din of the crowd faded as his dark eyes locked with Falco's. And then, inexplicably, he lowered his weapon.

The crowd groaned in disappointment, but Darius ignored them. There was something in Falco's eyes, something defiant, unbroken. He took a step back, giving the Roman room to rise.

Falco stared up at him, his breaths coming in ragged gasps. He could see the decision in Darius's face, the faint glimmer of respect that hadn't been there before. Slowly, Falco pushed himself to his feet, his legs trembling beneath him.

He met Darius's gaze, his own eyes hard with resolve. He should have been dead. Darius could have ended him, and the crowd would have cheered.

But he wasn't dead, and the two men stood facing each

other, the tension between them palpable. Darius gave the faintest of nods, acknowledging something unspoken.

Falco nodded back and without a word, they moved back into position, their weapons at the ready. The fight wasn't over, not yet.

Falco steadied himself, the gladius feeling heavier in his hand with every passing second. His chest heaved as he drew in ragged breaths, his muscles screaming with fatigue. Across the sands, Darius mirrored his stance, his khopesh raised but his movements slower now, the early dominance replaced with a wary respect for his opponent. The crowd, sensing the shift, grew quieter, the air heavy with anticipation.

This time, when Darius attacked, Falco met him with renewed purpose. The narrow escape from death had ignited something deep within him, a fire he thought had long since gone out. His strikes, though still slower than at his peak, carried precision and intent and for the first time in the fight, Darius was forced to step back, his confidence shaken as the Roman pressed forward.

But Darius wasn't just a brute; he was a master of the arena. He adjusted quickly, sidestepping one of Falco's lunges and countering with a sweeping blow that clipped the edge of Falco's shield. The Roman stumbled, the crowd roaring as the advantage shifted once again.

Back and forth they went, the sand beneath their feet churned to a chaotic mess. Each strike and parry drew gasps from the spectators, who now watched in stunned silence, their earlier derision forgotten. The fight had transformed into something extraordinary, a clash of equals, two warriors pushing themselves beyond their limits.

Falco ducked under a high swing, his gladius flashing upward to score a shallow cut on Darius's side. The Egyptian grunted in pain but retaliated instantly, slamming the rim of his shield into Falco's shoulder. Falco staggered, barely staying upright as Darius pressed the attack, his khopesh slicing through the air in brutal arcs.

The two men came together in the centre of the arena, their weapons clashing in a relentless rhythm. Their breaths were ragged, their movements slower but no less deadly. Each strike was met with a block, each feint countered, until it seemed neither had the strength to finish the other.

The crowd erupted into chants, their allegiance shifting with every exchange.

'Fal-co! Fal-co!' some cried, their earlier mockery replaced with awe.

'Da-ri-us! Da-ri-us!' others roared, their champion still standing firm.

Falco's arms felt like lead, his vision blurring at the edges. He knew Darius was just as drained, the Egyptian's swings had lost their earlier power, his footwork no longer as crisp.

They circled each other now, weapons raised but barely moving, their gazes locked.

Darius struck first, a desperate swing that Falco deflected at the last second. The counter was instinctive, a sharp thrust aimed at Darius's shoulder, but the Egyptian twisted away, catching Falco's blade on his shield.

For a moment, neither moved, their weapons held in a tense deadlock. Then Falco faltered. The stumble was small but decisive. Darius saw the opening and lunged, his khopesh raised high for the final blow.

The crowd surged to their feet, their voices a deafening roar of anticipation.

But Falco wasn't finished.

With the last reserves of his strength, he dropped low, spinning on his heel to evade Darius's strike. The move was fluid, almost instinctive and before Darius could recover, Falco drove his shoulder into his opponent's back, sending him sprawling into the sand. As Darius spun around onto his back, Falco's gladius came down, the blade stopping just short of his opponent's throat.

The Egyptian froze, his chest heaving as he stared up at Falco, the cold edge of the blade resting on his skin. The crowd erupted in a single, thunderous roar, the arena shaking with the force of their reaction. The fight had been nothing short of magnificent.

Falco knelt over his fallen opponent, his breath coming in ragged gasps, his body trembling from exhaustion. His gaze never left Darius's, a silent understanding passing between them.

The crowd roared, their chants of 'Fal-co! Fal-co!' rising to a fever pitch, echoing through the arena like the crashing of waves. For a moment, he was caught in the din, the sheer magnitude of the noise around him overwhelming his senses. He looked up, his gaze sweeping across the packed stands. Thousands of faces stared back at him, their expressions twisted in bloodlust, their chants growing louder and more unified.

'Kill… Kill… Kill!'

The words struck him like a physical blow, repeated over and over, a relentless drumbeat demanding death. He looked back down at Darius, the man who had pushed him to his very limits. The Egyptian lay still, his chest rising and falling in heavy breaths, his dark eyes meeting Falco's. There was no fear in them, only acceptance.

Falco's grip tightened on the hilt of his gladius as he stared into the crowd, his pulse pounding in his ears. The faces blurred together, their chants merging into a single, primal scream. And then something shifted.

In that moment, Falco saw himself in Darius's place, a man at the mercy of a crowd, his life reduced to a spectacle. He saw the countless fighters who had fallen before him, their blood staining the sands for nothing more than fleeting applause. He saw himself, a gladiator whose name had been both praised and jeered, caught in a cycle of violence that would never end.

The noise of the crowd faded in his mind, replaced by a single, resounding thought:

'*This isn't who I am anymore.*'

With deliberate slowness, Falco lowered his blade and stepped back from Darius. The crowd faltered, their chants wavering in confusion.

He looked again at his opponent, then back up at the audience, his voice cutting through the sudden lull.

'*No,*' he shouted, the single word ringing around the arena.

The crowd fell silent, the tension in the air almost palpable. Falco took a step forward, turning to face the sponsors' box where the governor of Alexandria and the royal family watched intently. His voice grew louder, his words gaining strength with each breath.

'No more,' he shouted, his tone filled with conviction. 'I will not stain my blade with the blood of an ally.' He pointed the gladius toward Darius, his voice rising above the crowd. 'This man is the true champion of Egypt. He fought with honour, and he let me live when I was defeated. I will not dishonour him or myself by taking his life for your entertainment!'

The crowd murmured again, confusion rippling through the stands. Falco raised his sword high, his voice now booming, carried on the wind like a war cry.

'This gladius, this symbol of Roman strength, was never meant to spill the blood of Rome's allies. It was meant to spill the blood of her enemies! If you seek death for sport, find it elsewhere.' The crowd was silent now, their rapt attention fixed on him. 'Let it be known,' he continued, 'Falco has fought his last battle in the arena. Never again will I step onto these sands to spill blood needlessly, and from this day forward, will only fight for the glory of Rome, not as a pawn for your amusement.'

He held the gladius aloft one final time, the blade catching the sunlight in a dazzling flash. Then, with a sharp movement, he cast it away, the weapon landing in the sand with a muffled thud.

For a moment, the crowd remained stunned, the weight of his words hanging heavy over the arena. Then, slowly at first, they began to cheer and as the noise grew, they rose to their feet, sending his name upwards to the watching gods.

'Fal-co! Fal-co! Fal-co!'

Falco turned without another word and walked slowly toward the gates. The cheers followed him, the sound washing over him like a tide. For the first time in years, he felt free, not from chains or debts, but from the life he had once lived, and as he walked out of the arena, leaving the gladius and the sands behind, he knew that everything had changed. The roar of the crowd was still deafening, but in his heart, there was only silence, a clarity that told him this was the beginning of something new.

Falco was no longer a gladiator.

He was something more.

----

The noise of the crowd still thundered above, their chants echoing through the stone corridors beneath the arena. Falco walked slowly, his body heavy with exhaustion but his mind sharp and alive. Men lined the sides of the corridor, fighters, trainers, slaves, all clapping and slapping his back as he passed.

'Incredible,' one man muttered, his voice thick with awe.

'Never seen anything like it,' said another.

Falco offered no response, his face stoic as he kept moving. He didn't need their words. Their admiration wasn't what mattered anymore.

When he reached the familiar confines of his cell, two slaves were waiting for him with bowls of water and clean cloths. They set to work immediately, washing the sweat, blood, and sand from his battered frame. The water was cool, a stark contrast to the heat of the arena, and Falco let his body relax for the first time in hours.

Once they were finished, the slaves bowed and left him alone. Falco sat back on the wooden bench, staring at the far wall. He closed his eyes and exhaled slowly, his mind racing. He had done it. He had walked away from the arena for the last time, from the life he had known before joining the Occultum, the life he had thought he missed. And not as a broken man, nor as a defeated one, but on his own terms. He was still lost in thought when he heard the soft creak of the door. He opened his eyes to see Sica standing there, but something was different.

Sica's expression was unreadable, his sharp eyes fixed on Falco with an intensity Falco wasn't accustomed to.

'Well?' Falco asked, his voice rough but laced with humour. 'Are you happy now?'

Sica stepped forward, holding a small scroll in his hand.

'I have never seen anything like it,' he said, 'and don't know what to say. So perhaps this might say it for me.'

Falco frowned, taking the scroll.

'What is it?' he asked, unrolling it carefully.

'An invitation,' Sica said, a faint smile tugging at the corner of his mouth. 'To a dinner tomorrow night… with the royal family of Egypt.'

Falco looked up sharply, his brow furrowing.

'You're joking.'

'Do I look like I'm joking?' Sica replied. 'You did it Falco, this is exactly what we wanted.'

Falco's eyes flicked back to the scroll, scanning the elegant script. It was real. The words were unmistakable: a formal invitation, addressed to him by name, to dine with the most powerful family in Egypt. He leaned back, letting the parchment rest on his lap.

'So, they didn't hate my speech, then.'

Sica chuckled, shaking his head.

'Hate it? Falco, they're calling you a hero. You turned the entire crowd on its head. I've seen you fight a hundred times, watched you kill men from one end of the empire to the other, but today? Today was something else altogether.'

'What do you mean?' asked Falco.

'You had the skill to win against the best gladiator Egypt had to offer, but more than that, you had the humanity to walk away. To leave him alive and the humility to admit what most men in your position never could, that this arena, all of it, is just blood and dust.'

Falco's gaze remained fixed on his friend, his lips twitching into the faintest of smiles.

'Don't get all sentimental on me, Sica,' he said, 'you're making me feel weird.'

Sica smirked.

'Someone's got to keep you grounded, Falco. Wouldn't want you getting a big head after all this.'

They sat in silence for a moment, the weight of the day settling over them both.

Finally, Falco rolled the scroll up and set it aside. He leaned forward, resting his elbows on his knees, and looked at Sica with an intensity that made the Syrian pause.

'I exorcised many ghosts today, Sica,' he said, 'you know that, don't you?'

Sica nodded.

'I know. And after today, so will everyone else.'

Falco let out a long breath, his gaze drifting to the flickering torchlight on the far wall.

'A dinner with royalty,' he said, his voice breaking the silence. 'Guess I'll need to be on my best behaviour.'

'Don't worry,' said Sica, 'I hear they serve good wine. Might even make this whole mess worth it. Come, your time here is done.'

Both men left the cell and headed for the ludus doors. As they went, Falco glanced down at his friend with and a smile tugged at his mouth.

'I was magnificent in there, though wasn't I.'

'Shut up, Falco,' said Sica with a sigh. 'We still have work to do.'

----

## Chapter Twenty

## Pselchis

The day after the killing of the recruit, Marcus stood near the fort gates, his sharp eyes scanning the horizon as his men gathered behind him in disciplined silence. The events of the previous day hung heavy in the air, the tension palpable among the ranks. The murder had left a sour taste in every man's mouth and Marcus knew it would take more than time to restore morale, it would take action and leadership.

'Form up,' he ordered, and the patrol moved into position. Each man wore his Lorica Squamata, the glinting scales of the leather armour catching the morning sun. Their helmets hung from straps on their shoulders, and their shields rested comfortably against their backs. Extra waterskins bounced heavily at their sides with each step, their importance outweighing the additional weight.

Marcus nodded in approval.

'We'll head for the escarpment,' he said, addressing his Optio. 'The sentries in the watchtowers reported seeing lights there a few nights ago. It could be nothing, it could be trouble. Either way, we'll find out.'

Beyond them, in the distance, the escarpment rose like a jagged scar in the otherwise flat landscape, its edges darkened by patches of sparse vegetation. The patrol set out across the sunbaked ground, their sandals crunching against the hard-packed dirt. The morning air was still tolerable, a stark contrast to the heat that would come later. Marcus led the column with measured strides, setting a steady pace that allowed them to cover ground quickly without exhausting themselves.

'You handled yesterday well,' said Tullus after a moment, his voice low enough not to carry to the men behind them.

'I did what I could,' said Marcus. 'But the men need more than words. They need focus, direction. That's why we're out here.'

Tullus glanced over his shoulder at the column of legionaries trudging behind them.

'They trust you, Centurio. You've earned their respect.'

They marched on in silence for a while, the landscape stretching out before them in endless shades of ochre and brown. The ground was cracked and parched, the occasional thorny shrub breaking the monotony and small clouds of dust kicked up with each step, clinging to any exposed skin.

Despite the heat, Marcus insisted they wear their armour. The fishscale lorica offered protection without stifling movement, and he would rather have his men sweat now than bleed later.

As the sun climbed higher, he adjusted his pace slightly, mindful of the strain on his men. He glanced back periodically, his keen eye ensuring that the column maintained its discipline. Eventually, they stopped for a water break ordering the men that they were to take two swallows only. Once rested, they continued on, the distant escarpment growing larger with every step. Marcus's mind raced as he considered their course. Today's patrol was about more than just investigating movement in the distance, it was about reminding his men of their purpose, about rebuilding their confidence in the face of uncertainty. But more than this, he had to remember that behind it all was the mission given to the Occultum by Lepidus, and so far, he had found out nothing.

By midday, they had reached the base of the escarpment. The rugged cliffs loomed above them, their jagged edges casting thin slivers of shade over the parched landscape. The sun blazed overhead, and Marcus raised a hand to shield his eyes as he scanned the faint path winding its way up the steep slope. The path was narrow, barely wide enough for one man at a time. It twisted and turned, often vanishing around sharp outcrops before reappearing higher up. Marcus gestured for the men to fall into single file, their shields secured to their backs as they began the climb.

The first stretch was manageable, the uneven terrain forcing them to concentrate but not yet pushing their limits. The cool stone offered a brief reprieve from the relentless heat as they navigated the shaded crevices along the path, but the final ascent was brutal. The path narrowed further, and the incline steepened to the point where they had to scramble, their hands and feet clawing at the rocky surface. Dust clung to their sweat-soaked bodies, their breaths coming in short, sharp gasps as they pulled themselves upward.

Marcus reached the top first, hauling himself over the edge with a grunt. He stood for a moment, hands on his knees, before straightening and turning to help the next man up.

One by one, the patrol emerged, collapsing onto the rocky plateau to catch their breath. The men sprawled out, gulping from their waterskins and wiping the sweat from their faces. Marcus turned to Tullus.

'Keep them here for now,' he said. 'Let them rest.'

Tullus nodded as Marcus turned, and walked up the last slope to the plateau, finding an unobstructed view of the arid plains to the south. Marcus stopped just short of the edge, his gaze sweeping across the landscape. The air shimmered with heat, the horizon a distorted mirage of ochre and gold. Moments later he was joined by Tullus and both men stared in silence, their breaths slowing as the endless expanse stretched before them.

'There,' Tullus said suddenly, pointing into the distance.

Marcus followed his line of sight, squinting against the glare. At first, he saw nothing, just the rippling waves of heat. Then, gradually, a faint line of movement came into focus, a caravan snaking its way across the desert, its long column trailing like an ant line over the sands.

'It's a big caravan,' Tullus said, shading his eyes. 'Looks like camels, donkeys... carts too.'

As they watched, the rest of the patrol joined them, the men standing silently behind them. The caravan had grown more distinct now, the shapes of animals and wagons becoming clearer with every passing moment.

'That's not a normal caravan,' one of the men muttered, 'it's too big.'

Marcus frowned, his sharp gaze fixed on the distant line. It was enormous, far larger than the typical trade caravans that often passed through the region.

The men murmured among themselves as they took in the sight, the sheer scale of the caravan unsettling in its abnormality.

'What do you think it's carrying?' asked Tullus.

'I don't know,' said Marcus. 'But we're going to find out.' He turned to his men. 'Sort yourselves out, we're going down there.'

Ten minutes later, Marcus led his men carefully down the far side of the escarpment, their caligae skidding slightly on the loose gravel. The descent wasn't as steep as the climb, but the distant caravan remained their focus, a long, winding thread of movement across the barren expanse.

By the time they reached the desert floor, the sun was unforgiving, its heat pressing down on them like a heavy hand. The men adjusted their shields and water skins, their faces streaked with sweat and dust. Marcus wiped his brow, his gaze locked on the caravan, calculating the best point to intercept.

'Centurio,' called Tullus, 'look.'

Marcus turned, following the Optio's outstretched arm. At first, it was difficult to make out against the heat haze, but as the moments passed, his stomach tightened.

From the far side of the caravan, a line of mounted men was emerging, some on horses, some on camels. The riders were spread out at first, their mounts pacing easily alongside the wagons, but soon their movements changed. More and more appeared, forming into a single, ominous mass.

'Who are they,' asked Marcus, 'some sort of armed escort?'

'It could be,' said Tullus, 'but why would a trade caravan have so many.'

'How many do you think there are?' asked Marcus.

Tullus squinted.

'At least a hundred,' he said, but however many there are, they are coming this way.'

Marcus's looked nervously around at his men. There was no indication of any danger yet, but he did not want to take any chances, and, against a hundred mounted warriors in open terrain, they were at a clear disadvantage. He looked back at the oncoming riders. The horsemen were forming into a wedge and heading towards them, the cloud of dust they kicked up spreading wide across the horizon. He turned to his men, raising his voice.

'To the base of the escarpment! Move quickly but stay together!'

The order was obeyed without question, the column turning sharply and heading back toward the safety of the rocks.

'Drink the rest of your first waterskins,' he ordered, his voice cutting through the tense silence. The men obeyed quickly, uncorking their waterskins and draining what little remained. Tullus moved among them, his presence a steadying force as he checked their shields and ensured their weapons were ready.

'We don't have much time,' said Marcus, 'so listen carefully. 'We do not know their intentions but for now, we will assume the worst. Yes, they have horses, and in the open that gives them the advantage, but here, among the rocks, they'll have to dismount. That evens the odds and if that happens, you are more than a match for them. So, prepare your weapons, ready your shields, and stay together.' He turned to face the oncoming riders, their wedge formation now clearly visible as they approached. The lead horses were sleek and powerful, their riders draped in black thawbs, their faces mostly obscured save for dark, piercing eyes.

Marcus watched them approach with a calm intensity, his eyes taking in every detail, the strung bows across saddles, the glint of steel, the grim efficiency in the riders' movements. These were no merchants; they were fighters, well-organised and prepared for bloodshed.

The riders pulled up a few hundred paces away, a cloud of dust settling around them as their mounts pawed the ground. A tense silence fell over the rocky terrain, broken only by the occasional snort or shuffle from the animals. One man urged his horse forward, riding ahead of the group. He halted a short distance from the Romans, lowering the cloth that covered his face.

Marcus adjusted his grip on his shield and stepped forward, his movements deliberate but unthreatening. The weight of command rested on his shoulders as he stopped a few paces from the mounted man.

'What are you doing here?' the rider demanded 'The fort in Pselchis is the limit of Roman control. You've broken the unwritten agreement by coming beyond the escarpment. Turn back.'

Marcus's expression remained impassive, his tone firm as he replied.

'Rome controls all of Egypt. That includes this land. The fact that we rarely travel this far south doesn't make it any less true.'

The rider's eyes narrowed, his anger simmering beneath the surface.

'You speak as though you own the ground beneath your feet,' he spat. 'But this is not your land. The escarpment is an agreed boundary meant to keep the peace. You've crossed it.'

Marcus stood tall, refusing to yield even an inch.

'Boundaries shift. Rome's reach is long, and its presence here is not a matter of debate.'

The rider's knuckles tightened on the reins, his fury evident.

'Turn back,' he demanded again, his voice rising. 'Return to your fort and leave this land in peace, or you will suffer the consequences.'

Marcus said nothing for a moment, his sharp gaze drifting beyond the rider to the caravan in the distance. Now that they were closer, he could see its scale more clearly, dozens of camels, wagons loaded to their breaking point, and people moving purposefully alongside. This was no ordinary trade caravan. He turned back to the rider.

'We will leave,' he said, 'but first tell me, what is that caravan carrying and where is it headed?'

The man's expression darkened, his lips curling into a snarl.

'That is none of your concern, Roman. Turn back now.'

'Not answering questions only raises more,' Marcus replied.

'And giving you answers will only give Rome more excuses to interfere. This is your last chance. Leave, now.'

Marcus held his ground, his gaze unwavering as he stared at the mounted man. The silence stretched between them, the tension growing thicker with every passing moment. Finally, the rider jerked the reins and, wheeling his horse around, rode back to his men, his posture stiff with rage.

The Romans held their formation, their shields braced and weapons ready, but their unease was clear. The horsemen huddled together, their leader issuing sharp commands in a language Marcus didn't understand. Then, without warning, the riders spread out forming a wide line, every archer among them pulling a bow from their saddles.

Marcus's stomach tightened and he turned sharply to his men, his voice ringing out.

'Testudo! *Now!*'

The Roman soldiers snapped into action, their training taking over. They formed two tight squares, the front ranks kneeling and raising their shields forward while the men behind them held theirs overhead, locking the formation into an impenetrable shell. Marcus stared in horror as the desert wind carried the faint creak of bending wood towards him and he took his place at the edge of the first formation.

'Brace!' he roared as he ducked beneath the shields, and seconds later, the first volley crashed into the Roman position, some splintering on impact, others lodging deep into the thick shields. The men grunted under the force of the assault, but the testudos held, their interlocked shields forming an unyielding barrier.

'Hold steady!' barked Marcus, peering out from his position.

The second wave of arrows rained down like a black storm, hammering against the shields with a relentless drumbeat. The men adjusted instinctively, shifting their positions, closing any gaps, their discipline the only thing keeping them alive. The attack was unrelenting, the thud of arrows against wood, the hiss of incoming shafts, the occasional grunt of pain when a missile found a weakness.

Marcus crouched low, his shield locked into place with the others. The testudo was their salvation, a disciplined wooden shell that turned them from men into a fortress and though the arrows continued to fall, the line did not break.

Another volley rained down, the sound of arrows striking shields mingling with the grunts of exertion from the soldiers.

Most were deflected harmlessly, bouncing off the layered wood and metal, but two found their mark. One man cried out as an arrow pierced his thigh, another as it buried itself in his arm.

The wounded men were pulled into the centre of the formation, their comrades shielding them with grim efficiency as the rest of the patrol tightened ranks, their shields overlapping even more closely to close the gaps.

'Centurio,' called one of the men, 'we can't just sit here, let us take the fight to them!'

Marcus didn't respond immediately, his sharp gaze fixed on the enemy through a gap in the shield wall. The riders remained at a distance, their black-clad figures blurred by the heat haze. Another volley of arrows flew toward them, the shafts striking with a ferocity that tested even the most steadfast nerves.

'No!' Marcus shouted. 'If we leave the rocks, they'll pick us off before we reach them. Hold your ground.'

His words carried the weight of experience, and although the arrows kept coming, gradually, the pace of the volleys began to slow until finally, the riders wheeled their mounts around and rode back toward the distant caravan. Only when they were well out of range did Marcus give the command to stand down.

'Shields up!' he called. 'Report casualties.'

The men emerged from the testudo, the tight formation breaking apart as they stood and surveyed the damage. Shields were riddled with arrows, some bent and splintered from the force of the impacts. The wounded men were tended to quickly, their injuries painful but not life-threatening.

Marcus stood at the edge of the rocks, his gaze fixed on the retreating riders as they rejoined the caravan. The line of camels and carts had paused during the attack, but now it began to move again, heading northeast toward the horizon. Tullus stepped up beside him, staring at the caravan.

'What are your orders, Centurio. Do we follow them?'

'No,' replied Marcus. 'We head back to the fort. Get the men formed up.'

The patrol moved quickly, the wounded supported by their comrades as they began the climb back up the escarpment. Marcus lingered for a moment, his gaze lingering on the distant caravan, his thoughts consumed by the question that hung over them all: What could be so important that it warranted such a brutal response? Whatever the answer, he was determined to uncover it. But for now, they would regroup and look after their wounded.

----

## Chapter Twenty-One

### Alexandria

Two days after the fight, Falco and Sica approached the entrance of the royal palace, their steps faltering as the sheer scale of the opulence before them came into focus. The stairway leading to the palace doors was flanked by two rows of Egyptian soldiers, each standing perfectly still, their ceremonial robes bright with gold and turquoise accents. Their spears, tipped with polished bronze, gleamed in the fading sunlight. The soldiers' faces were stern, their gaze fixed ahead, but their presence alone was intimidating.

Falco adjusted the gold-trimmed toga draped over his powerful frame, its folds feeling unnatural on his shoulders. The garment had been supplied by the Roman governor himself, and while it fit well enough, he couldn't help but feel out of place in such finery. Beside him, Sica walked with his usual quiet intensity, though his sharp eyes darted about, taking in every detail of their surroundings.

'This is... something,' Falco muttered under his breath.

'It is,' Sica replied dryly, 'and then some.'

As they climbed the stairs, their eyes were drawn to the four men standing near the massive, ornate doors at the top. Each held a thick iron chain, and at the end of each chain was a leopard, sleek and powerful, their coats shimmering like liquid gold in the evening light.

One of the leopards growled as Falco passed, its amber eyes fixed solidly upon him. Its handler tightened his grip, the muscles in his arms straining as the big cat pulled against the chain. Falco slowed for a moment, his gaze meeting the animal's, his body instinctively tensing.

'Easy, now,' Falco murmured. 'There's a good cat.'

The handler gave a sharp tug on the chain.

'Move along, Roman. She doesn't take kindly to strangers.'

Falco snarled back at the cat before walking through the great doors, leaving the leopards and their watchful handlers behind.

----

Inside, the palace was even more astonishing. Every surface seemed to gleam. Gold, polished marble and intricate mosaics stretched in every direction, catching the light of countless oil lamps and torches.

Servants in fine linen robes moved through the space, guiding guests toward a wide marble staircase. Falco and Sica followed the flow of people, their boots clicking softly against the polished floor. At the top of the stairs, they entered an ornate antechamber, its walls lined with intricately carved columns and shelves filled with priceless ornaments. The room was filled with guests, many lounging on low couches or standing in small groups, engaged in polite conversation. More servants moved gracefully among them, offering trays of delicate cups filled with honey-sweetened wine.

Falco and Sica hesitated for a moment, both feeling distinctly out of place in such opulence.

'This is insane,' Falco whispered, before making their way through the crowd, weaving between clusters of finely dressed men and women. Falco could feel eyes on him, admiring, curious, envious. A few men stopped him to offer hearty congratulations on his recent victory, their voices filled with genuine awe.

'Magnificent fight, my friend!' one said, clapping him on the shoulder. 'The way you bested Darius... it will be spoken of for years!'

'You made us proud,' said another. 'Rome could use more men like you.'

Falco nodded politely, offering his thanks, though his discomfort was clear.

The women, however, were bolder. A few sidled up to him as he passed, their eyes lingering on his broad shoulders and powerful frame.

'You're even more impressive in person,' one woman said, her voice low and sultry.

Another, clearly married but unbothered by the presence of her husband nearby, smiled coyly.

'Such strength,' she murmured, her fingers grazing his arm. 'It's no wonder you're the talk of Alexandria.'

Falco forced a smile, brushing off the attention as tactfully as he could.

Sica, walking just behind him, smirked but said nothing, his amusement clear in the glint of his eyes. Toward the far end of the room, Seneca stood near the governor of Alexandria, the two deep in conversation. Seneca's posture was relaxed, but his sharp features were as focused as ever, his expression unreadable.

Falco nudged Sica subtly, nodding toward Seneca.

'There he is.'

Sica's gaze flicked to their comrade, then back to Falco.

'Avoid him. We can't risk drawing any unwanted attention.'

Falco nodded in agreement, the two of them shifting their path to avoid crossing directly into Seneca's line of sight.

They continued to weave through the crowd, their unease growing with every passing moment. The luxury of the palace was stifling, its beauty almost oppressive to men who had spent their lives in the dirt and blood of the battlefield.

Finally, another set of ornate doors at the far end of the room swung open, the sound of horns cutting through the chatter.

'The banquet is served,' a servant announced, and the crowd began to move, a steady stream of finely dressed guests heading toward the grand dining hall. Falco and Sica exchanged a glance before joining the procession, stepping further into a world of power, politics, and danger.

As they walked through the doors, they were met sight that made even the most opulent corners of the palace pale in comparison. The room was a masterpiece of craftsmanship, a testament to the wealth and splendour of Egypt. The walls were adorned with intricate mosaic frescoes in vibrant hues, each depicting the gods of ancient Egypt. Ra, Anubis, Hathor, and others gazed down serenely, their forms rendered in precise detail, the colours so vivid it seemed the gods themselves were watching.

Massive pillars rose to the ceiling, their surfaces completely covered in gold that gleamed like molten sunlight. Between them, delicate silk draperies swayed gently, stirred by the soft breeze flowing in through hidden vents.

In the centre of the room stood two long marble tables, each a marvel in its own right. The tabletops shimmered under the glow of countless oil lamps, their surfaces adorned with an array of crystal ornaments that refracted the light into dazzling patterns. Solid silver plates, their rims inlaid with gold filigree, caught the eye, while magnificent statuettes of gods, both Egyptian and Roman, were arranged artfully along the length of each table.

Around the walls, gilded cages hung at intervals, their delicate frames home to songbirds whose gentle trills filled the air with a melodic undercurrent. It was a subtle but enchanting addition, turning the room into a living symphony of sight and sound.

Falco's eyes widened as he took it all in, his breath catching.

'By the Gods…' he muttered, barely audible.

Beside him, Sica stood equally stunned, his usually sharp expression softened by wonder.

Falco's attention was drawn to the far end of the room,

where a single, unchained leopard strolled leisurely between the tables. Its sleek coat shimmered under the warm glow of the lamps, its movements fluid and languid. Guests gave the animal a respectful berth, though their eyes followed it warily. Its handler remained close, the unattached chain hanging loosely from his hands.

'I don't even know where to look,' Falco murmured, still trying to process the grandeur around him.

'Then don't,' Sica replied dryly. 'You'll just get lost in it all.'

The guests gathered around the tables, each standing behind their designated chair. The hum of conversation filled the room, the awe-struck murmurs of even the wealthiest Romans betraying their astonishment. Falco and Sica exchanged a glance, silently acknowledging that they were far removed from their usual world of dirt and blood.

A sudden fanfare cut through the room, and all conversation ceased as the guests turned their attention to the grand entrance at the far end of the dining room. Moments later, the royal family of Egypt appeared, stepping through the doorway with serene grace.

The man who once would have been called a pharaoh led the way, his figure tall and regal, his robes a cascade of white linen embroidered with gold. A broad collar of lapis lazuli and turquoise adorned his neck, and a ceremonial staff rested lightly in his hand. Beside him walked the queen, her beauty striking, her gown flowing like liquid gold as she offered warm smiles to the gathered guests.

Behind them, the younger members of the royal family followed, their presence equally commanding. Their faces bore the same serene composure, their smiles generous but measured as they acknowledged the guests on either side.

The royal procession moved slowly down the centre aisle,

their pace unhurried, their every step a display of elegance and authority.

Falco straightened unconsciously, his gaze fixed on the scene before him. For all the battles he had fought, for all the commanders and senators he had stood before, he had never encountered anything like this. He leaned closer to Sica, his voice low enough not to carry.

'So, the man in front. Is he the pharaoh?'

Sica smirked faintly, shaking his head.

'Not quite. They call him the pharaoh, and to the people of Egypt, he's royalty. But in reality, he's little more than a figurehead. A puppet, if we're being honest.'

Falco raised an eyebrow, glancing up towards the top table.

'A puppet?'

'Egypt's been a province of Rome since Cleopatra's time,' Sica explained. 'When she and Antony lost to Octavian at Actium, it was the end of Egypt's independence. Rome rules now, but they let the royal family keep their titles, their palaces, and all the trappings of power. It keeps the people happy, or at least quiet.'

Falco nodded slowly, his gaze distant as he considered Sica's words.

'So, they're royal in name only.'

'Exactly,' Sica replied. 'Rome has the power. The governors, the legions, they're the ones really in charge. But this?' He gestured vaguely around them, indicating the opulent surroundings. 'This is theatre. A show to keep the populace placated. Let them worship their gods, honour their traditions, and they won't look too closely at the fact that it's Rome pulling the strings.'

Falco frowned slightly, his thoughts turning inward. The spectacle, the wealth, the ceremony, it was all a gilded façade. And yet, it worked.

'Clever,' he muttered.

Sica gave a slight shrug.

'Clever, yes. But it only lasts as long as the people believe in it. Strip away the gold, and all you're left with is sand.'

Moments later, the royal family took their seats and almost immediately, a line of servants entered through side doors, their movements precise and perfectly choreographed. Each bore a large silver platter, laden with a dizzying array of delicacies and the air was soon filled with the mouth-watering aromas of roasted meats, fragrant herbs, and spices both familiar and foreign.

The servants moved quickly, placing dishes before each guest with quiet efficiency. Plates of Egyptian specialities, stuffed pigeon, spiced lamb, honeyed dates, were laid alongside Roman fare such as dormice in honey and fragrant garum sauces and crystal goblets of wine, their rims adorned with tiny, vibrant flowers, were filled without pause.

Falco surveyed the food with unabashed hunger, his eyes lighting up as the platters were set down. He wasted no time, catching the arm of a servant before they could retreat.

'Wait,' he said firmly, gesturing to the lamb. 'More.'

The servant hesitated, a flicker of surprise crossing their face, but complied, adding another heaping portion to Falco's plate.

'More,' Falco said again, his tone unapologetic.

By now, a few of the guests nearby had noticed. Some exchanged amused glances, while others smiled openly, entertained by Falco's blunt enthusiasm.

Sica leaned in, his voice a low hiss.

'You're making a scene.'

Falco ignored him, finally releasing the servant when his plate resembled a small mountain and picked up a piece of roast lamb with his hands, tearing into it without a shred of shame.

'I haven't eaten properly in weeks,' Falco muttered

between bites. 'I deserve this.'

Sica rolled his eyes, leaning back in his chair with a resigned sigh.

As Falco devoured his meal, the woman seated to his left turned to him with a bright smile. She was striking, her dark hair styled in intricate curls, her gown a rich emerald green that shimmered under the light.

'I don't think we've been introduced,' she said, her voice warm and confident. 'I'm Julia Marcellina, daughter of Senator Marcellus.'

Falco paused, swallowing a mouthful of meat before responding.

'Falco,' he said simply, extending his hand.

She took it lightly, her grip firm but graceful.

'I know who you are,' she said, her smile widening. 'You were the star of the games the other day.'

Falco chuckled, setting down his goblet.

'I was,' he said. 'But it was just one of many, many victories.'

They fell into easy conversation, Julia's wit and charm making the meal even more enjoyable. She laughed at his dry humour, and while Falco was no stranger to the attention of women, there was something refreshing about her directness.

Course after course followed, the feast seemingly endless and by the time the last platter was cleared, even Falco was sated, leaning back in his chair with a satisfied groan.

'I think they've outdone themselves,' Julia remarked, patting her stomach lightly.

Falco nodded, wiping his hands on the provided linen cloth.

'I think I could sleep for a week.'

Before long, the master of ceremonies stepped forward, his vibrant robes shimmering as he clapped his hands for attention.

The murmurs in the room ceased as all eyes turned to him.

'Honoured guests,' he began, his voice resonating through the space. 'It is my great pleasure to present the evening's entertainment. A celebration of the union of Roman and Egyptian culture, performed by the finest artists in Alexandria.'

The room erupted into applause as the first act took the stage, an ensemble of dancers, their movements hypnotic as they wove through their intricate formations. Fire-eaters took the stage next, their flames spiralling into the air with breathtaking precision while acrobats performed feats of agility that made them fly through the air like birds, accompanied by the hauntingly beautiful melodies of the aulos and lyre.

Each act surpassed the last, the audience captivated and even Sica, who rarely showed interest in such displays, found himself leaning forward, his sharp eyes following every movement.

Finally, the last performer stepped onto the stage, and the room fell into an almost reverent silence. A dancer, her figure draped in diaphanous veils that shimmered with every step, moved with a grace that was almost otherworldly. Her movements were fluid, her body telling a story that needed no words. The room was entranced, the light catching on the jewels that adorned her wrists and ankles, each turn and spin eliciting gasps of admiration.

Falco found himself leaning forward, his attention fully captured. It wasn't just the dancer's beauty or skill; it was the way she commanded the space, holding the entire room in the palm of her hand.

When she finished, the applause was thunderous, the sound reverberating through the gilded walls. The dancer bowed deeply, then disappeared as gracefully as she had come.

The master of ceremonies stepped forward once more.

'Honoured guests,' he said, spreading his arms wide, 'the night is still young! Please, join us in the antechamber to drink, mingle, and enjoy the company of your fellow esteemed visitors.'

As the guests rose, the room buzzed with conversation, the energy from the performance still crackling in the air.

'Quite the show,' said Sica.

Falco smirked.

'Let's hope the drinks are just as impressive.'

----

The antechamber was alive with energy, the hum of voices and laughter reverberating off the gilded walls. Guests moved about in clusters, goblets of wine in hand as they exchanged pleasantries and engaged in subtle games of influence and wit.

Falco, however, was the undisputed centre of attention. Men approached him with firm handshakes and hearty congratulations, their admiration evident in their smiles and words.

'That was a fight for the ages,' one man said, his tone reverent.

'You've given us something to talk about for weeks,' added another.

Sica, standing off to the side, watched with an amused smirk as Falco basked in the glow of newfound celebrity.

'You're quite the star, Falco,' he remarked eventually, taking a sip of his wine.

Falco turned, his grin broad and full of mischief.

'It's about time they recognised greatness,' he quipped, earning chuckles from the surrounding group.

But it was the women who seemed most captivated. They gathered around him in small groups, their eyes sparkling with admiration as he recounted his exploits from years past. Tales of his victories in the arena, his daring escapes, and his legendary strength flowed from his lips with an exaggerated flourish.

'And then,' Falco said, his voice dropping conspiratorially as he leaned closer to his audience, 'with nothing but a broken spear and sheer will, I took down the biggest beast you've ever seen. The crowd roared so loud, you'd have thought Jupiter himself had descended to watch.'

Gasps and laughter and admiration erupted from the group, and several women clutched their wine goblets as if to steady themselves. One of them, a striking brunette with a bold smile, slipped a folded piece of parchment into his hand.

'Should you wish for some…company during your stay,' she murmured, her voice low and inviting, 'this will guide you to my home. Just…be discreet.' She glanced over to where her husband was deep in conversation with another man, obviously under the influence of far too much wine.

Falco raised an eyebrow, his grin widening as he pocketed the note.

'I'll keep that in mind,' he said, his voice just as low.

Before long, he had a small collection of similar notes, each discreetly passed to him by women who lingered a little too long or smiled a little too brightly. Falco lapped it up, his charm on full display as he bantered and flirted outrageously, revelling in the attention.

But as the evening wore on, the heat of the room and the relentless buzz of conversation began to weigh on him. Slipping away from the crowd, he wandered toward a set of open doors leading to an ornate balcony.

The night air was cool and refreshing, the gentle breeze carrying the scent of jasmine from the gardens below. Falco leaned against the marble railing, his gaze drifting upward to the clear, star-filled sky and, for a moment, he allowed himself to relax, his thoughts quieting as he traced the constellations above.

'Beautiful, isn't it?' said a soft voice, as gentle as a melody carried on the wind.

Falco turned his head, and his breath caught. It was her… the dancer.

She stood close, her face illuminated by the pale glow of the moon. Her dark eyes, framed by thick lashes, glinted like polished obsidian as she gazed up at the stars. She was dressed simply now, her veil and jewels replaced by a flowing white gown that only accentuated her natural grace.

'Uh... yes,' Falco managed, his usual confidence faltering.

The dancer smiled, her expression warm and inviting.

'I'm Zarah,' she said, turning her gaze to him. 'And you are the man who turned the entire city on its head.'

Falco stared at her, uncharacteristically tongue-tied. For the first time in his life, the words he so easily summoned around women escaped him entirely.

'I, ' He cleared his throat, rubbing the back of his neck awkwardly. 'I'm Falco.'

'I know,' Zarah said with a soft laugh.

She leaned against the railing beside him, her attention once again on the stars. The silence stretched between them, not uncomfortable but charged with an unfamiliar energy. Falco glanced at her, his usual bravado completely at odds with the disarmed man standing beside her now. For the first time since as long as he could remember, he was totally out of his depth.

'Do you believe in the gods, Falco?' she asked softly, her voice carrying the same mysterious allure that had captivated the audience earlier.

Falco hesitated, his usual confidence wavering.

'I... suppose I do. Rome has its own gods, of course.'

Zarah smiled faintly, her eyes never leaving the stars.

'But do you feel them? Their magic? Their amazement?'

Falco swallowed, the gladius of his sharp tongue sheathed for once.

'I, uh, don't think I've ever thought about it like that.'

Her smile widened, and she turned to him fully, her face illuminated by the pale moonlight.

'You Romans,' she said, her tone equal parts teasing and fond. 'You're so practical. Everything must have a reason, a logic. But here in Egypt, we see the gods not just as ideas, but as forces that breathe life into the world.'

Falco nodded, his lips pressed together as he fought to keep from saying something foolish. He was completely out of his depth, yet utterly enchanted.

Zarah's eyes glinted as she misread his eager nodding for true understanding. Her voice grew quieter, more intimate.

'There are ways to experience their wonder, you know. To feel their presence, not from afar, but here.' She touched her chest lightly, just above her heart.

Falco leaned in slightly, caught in the spell of her words. 'How?'

She stepped closer, so close that he could catch the faint scent of jasmine clinging to her hair.

'I could show you,' she whispered, her voice barely audible over the gentle breeze. 'But not here. Not like this.'

His breath caught as she slipped even closer, her dark eyes holding his.

'Tomorrow night,' she continued, her voice dropping to a conspiratorial whisper. 'We'll meet somewhere more discreet. And I'll give you an experience you will never forget.'

Falco nodded quickly, his heart pounding.

'Yes. Yes, of course.'

Zarah smiled, her lips curving in a way that made his pulse race even more. She reached into a hidden fold of her gown and withdrew a small piece of parchment, pressing it lightly into his hand.

'The details are here,' she said softly. 'I will be waiting.'

Before Falco could reply, she turned away, disappearing back into the crowd with a grace that seemed almost otherworldly.

Falco stood there for a long moment, staring at the spot

where she had vanished, the faint scent of jasmine lingering in the air. His fingers curled around the parchment, its weight somehow heavier than it should have been.

'Well?' came Sica's voice from behind him.

Falco spun, startled out of his trance.

Sica arched an eyebrow, his expression a mix of curiosity and exasperation.

'Where have you been? I've been looking for you.'

Falco opened his mouth, then closed it again, shaking his head.

'Nowhere,' he muttered, tucking the parchment into his toga.

Sica's sharp gaze lingered on him, but he let it go.

'The party's winding down. We should leave before you end up with more trouble than you can handle.'

Falco nodded absently, still reeling from his encounter with Zarah and together, they slipped out of the palace, leaving the opulent splendour behind as they made their way back to their lodgings near the docks.

----

The transition was jarring. Their quarters, while serviceable, were a far cry from the grandeur of the palace. Inside, Cassius and Decimus were already reclining, sharing a pitcher of wine and trading stories about their younger days. They looked up as Falco and Sica entered.

'Ah, the hero returns!' said Cassius.

'How was the palace?' Decimus added. 'Was it what you thought it was?'

Falco dropped into a chair, his legs stretched out in front of him, his gold-trimmed toga now creased as it dragged on the floor.

'Like nothing you have ever seen,' he said. 'If the gods lived down here instead of the heavens, that is where they would live.'

'Actually,' said sica, 'the palace was all smiles and luxury, but beneath it, there's tension. You can feel it. Egypt might still glitter like gold, but it's held together by strings. The pharaoh might smile, but he won't act without Rome's approval. He can't afford to.'

'Did you learn anything useful?' asked Cassius.

'Not yet,' said Falco, 'but I have made a lot of contacts.' With a flourish, he reached into the folds of his toga and withdrew several pieces of folded parchment, spreading them out on the table.

'What's this?' Decimus asked, leaning closer.

'Leads,' Falco said, a broad grin spreading across his face.

Cassius picked up one of the notes, scanning the elegant script. His eyebrows shot up as he read.

'This isn't a lead, it's an invitation. To someone's bed.'

Falco laughed, shrugging.

'So? A bed can be just as good a place for information as a council chamber. Sometimes better.'

Decimus picked up another note, his expression equal parts amusement and disbelief. 'A senator's wife?' he asked, glancing at Falco.

'She was very persistent,' Falco said with mock innocence.

Cassius rolled his eyes.

'You collected these like trophies, didn't you?'

Falco shrugged, unbothered by the jab.

'Call them opportunities,' he said. 'You never know who's willing to talk after a glass of wine and a few compliments.'

Cassius shook his head in exasperation

'You're unbelievable, Falco. Absolutely unbelievable.'

Falco leaned back in his chair, a satisfied smirk on his face.

'I'm resourceful, Cassius. There's a difference.'

As the others laughed and shook their heads, Falco's

fingers brushed the inside pocket of his toga, where one piece of parchment remained hidden, the note from Zarah. The others didn't need to know about that one and though he smiled along with their humorous jabs, his mind was elsewhere, replaying her words and the promise of what awaited him the next night.

----

## Chapter Twenty-Two

### Alexandria

The oil lamp flickered weakly on Seneca's desk, casting long shadows across the scrolls and parchment strewn in chaotic disarray. He rubbed his temples, his eyes burning from hours of reading and rereading reports that offered little more than frustration.

Quotas unmet, productivity faltering. Always the same vague excuses, sickness, accidents, or, more troublingly, whispers of supernatural intervention. The word itself appeared over and over, scribbled in different hands: omens, curses, spirits.

Seneca exhaled sharply, tossing a quill onto the desk. Superstitious nonsense, he thought, though the repetition nagged at him like a persistent thorn. He had scoured every line for a thread to follow, some connection that could explain why certain estates were failing their quotas. But there was no pattern, no common denominator. Nothing but stories of shadows in the night, strange sounds, and workers fleeing in terror.

He leaned back in his chair, staring at the low ceiling, his mind churning with possibilities before a knock at the door startled him from his thoughts.

'Enter,' he called, his voice sharper than intended.

The door creaked open, and a young slave stepped inside, his head bowed. In his hands was a small, folded note.

'This came for you, dominus,' the slave said softly, placing the note on the desk before retreating as quietly as he had come.

Seneca sat up, his brow furrowing as he reached for the note. He paused, lifting it to his nose. The faint, unmistakable scent of perfume lingered on the parchment, light but deliberate. His pulse quickened.

He unfolded the note, his fingers unusually hesitant. The

lamp's weak flame illuminated the words, written in a delicate hand.

'Come straight away. A guide waits at the rear door of the palace.'

The message was short, almost cryptic, but its intent was clear. He glanced at the door, half-expecting the slave to return, but the corridor outside was silent.

Seneca stood, turning the note over in his hands as though it might yield some hidden meaning. There was no signature, no further explanation. But he knew who it was from.
He had thought of little else since their last meeting. The memory of her lingered like the scent on the note, her voice and laughter slipping into his thoughts at the most inconvenient moments.

But he had been told in no uncertain terms to keep his distance, to avoid complications. It was sound advice, pragmatic, logical. And yet...

He found himself gripping the note tighter, his gaze drifting to the cloak draped over the back of his chair. He knew he should ignore it and focus on the task at hand. But the pull was stronger than reason, an irresistible gravity that left him pacing the room. Ten minutes passed. Then he stopped, his decision made.

Snatching his cloak, Seneca threw it over his shoulders and tucked the note into his belt. He extinguished the lamp, plunging the room into darkness, and made his way down silent corridors towards the rear of the building. Once there, he hesitated for a fraction of a second, the governor's warning surfacing one last time in his mind, and then, sweeping all doubts aside, he walked through, closing the door behind him. He was committed.

----

Outside the guide stood in the shadow of the palace's rear gate, the hood of his thawb pulled low over his face. When Seneca stepped into view, the man straightened and took a step forward.

'Dominus,' he murmured, bowing his head slightly before gesturing for Seneca to follow.

The two walked in silence, the only sound the faint crunch of their sandals against the packed earth. The path wound through the outskirts of the city, past quiet alleys and shuttered homes, until the air began to carry the briny tang of the sea. The guide led Seneca down a narrow trail to a small dock, its timbers weathered and creaking faintly in the night breeze. A small boat waited there, its hull dark against the lapping waves.

The guide climbed in first, turning to gesture for Seneca to follow. Seneca stopped short, his instincts bristling. His eyes swept the scene, the empty dock, the gently rocking boat, the faint outline of the men at the oars. The guide said nothing, only watched him with quiet expectancy.

'Where are we going?' Seneca asked, his voice edged with caution.

The guide didn't answer, instead nodding toward the boat.

Seneca knew he should turn back, but something about the night, the whisper of the sea, the glint of moonlight on the water, the faint scent of perfume still lingering in his mind, kept him rooted. With a sharp exhale, he stepped into the boat, his hand gripping the edge as it swayed beneath him.

The guide gave a soft command, and the two men at the oars began to row, the faint creak of the oars the only sound breaking the silence. Seneca sat stiffly, his eyes fixed on the horizon, but his unease began to grow as the shoreline faded into the distance.

Seneca's nerves prickled as the land disappeared behind them, the open sea stretching out in every direction. But then, through the gloom, he saw it, a tiny island, rising like a jewel from the water. Its outline was faint at first, but as they drew closer, it became clear that it was no ordinary island.

Thousands of candles and lanterns lit the rocky slopes,

their golden light dancing across the water like stars fallen to earth. The effect was mesmerizing, and for a moment, Seneca's tension eased, replaced by quiet awe.

The boat glided to the island's dock, a small but intricately carved structure that seemed impossibly delicate against the rugged rock. The guide disembarked first, turning to gesture for Seneca to follow once more.

He hesitated, his sandals perched on the edge of the boat, but the enchanting glow of the island pulled at him like a tide. With a nod, he stepped onto the dock, the wood firm beneath his feet.

The guide pointed towards narrow path lined with candles, their flickering flames illuminating the stone steps that wound upward.

At the top of the path stood a small arbour, its roof supported by delicate wooden beams entwined with vines, open on one side to face the sea.

Seneca walked around to the open side, the breeze brushing against his face. He stopped, his breath catching in his chest as he took in the sight before him.

Callista lay reclining on a sumptuous bed draped in fine silks, the fabric shimmering faintly in the candlelight. The bed itself was low and wide, piled with pillows of vibrant colours, deep purples, rich golds, and soft greens. Around her, freshly cut flowers spilled from ornate vases, their petals scattered across the bed and floor in a display of indulgent beauty.

She was dressed in a gown of sheer, semi-transparent silk that clung to her form, revealing just enough to tease without exposing too much. The fabric seemed to ripple like water as she shifted slightly, reclining with effortless grace. Her dark hair fell loosely over her shoulders, its soft waves catching the light as if kissed by the glow of the lanterns.

In her hand, Callista held a crystal goblet, and she swirled the golden wine gently, the faintest smile gracing her lips as her eyes locked onto his.

'Seneca,' she said. 'You got my note.' Her smile widened, fully aware of the effect she was having. There was confidence in her gaze, a knowing look that seemed to pierce through his composed exterior and unearth something deeper. She tilted her head slightly, the gesture inviting and utterly disarming.

'Come,' she said simply, her voice laced with promise.

For a moment, Seneca stood frozen, caught in the spell of her presence. The combination of her beauty, the setting, and the intoxicating scent of the oils left him uncharacteristically unsure of himself. He approached slowly, his sandals brushing against the scattered petals on the ground, his eyes never leaving hers.

As he neared, Callista sat up, propping herself against the pillows with effortless elegance. She reached for a nearby carafe, the crystal catching the candlelight in dazzling bursts, and poured a measure of the golden wine into a second goblet. She held it out to him, her fingers brushing his as he took it.

'To moments worth remembering,' she said softly, her voice carrying an almost hypnotic quality.

Seneca raised his glass, his fingers tightening slightly around the cool crystal. He knew, even as the first sip of the sweet wine touched his lips, that this moment would stay with him for the rest of his life. Finally, she broke the silence, her voice as smooth as the silk that adorned her.

'Well,' she said, tilting her head slightly, a playful smile curling at her lips. 'What do you think of my special place? I spend a lot of time here alone. You are my first…visitor.'

Seneca took a moment to respond, his eyes flicking briefly to the shimmering sea beyond the arbour before returning to her. He set the goblet down carefully on a low table beside the bed.

'It's… extraordinary,' he said honestly, his voice quieter than usual. He gestured to the sea, the glowing lanterns and carefully nurtured cascading vines grown in pots of soil brought from the banks of the Nile. 'I've never seen anything like it.'

Her smile widened slightly, and she leaned back into the pillows with a languid grace.

'Good,' she murmured. 'I've gone to great lengths to make it so.'

'It's more than just beautiful,' Seneca added, 'It feels... untouchable. As though it's outside of the world.'

Callista's eyes sparkled at his words. She raised her goblet to her lips, taking another sip before speaking.

'That's precisely what it is,' she said. 'A sanctuary, free from the noise and expectations of the world. Here, there is no Rome, no Egypt, no governors, no rules.' She looked at him over the rim of her glass, her expression unreadable. 'Only what we choose to bring with us.'

Her words hung in the air, delicate yet laden with meaning. Seneca's brow furrowed slightly, his mind turning over the weight of them.

'And what is it you choose to bring here?' he asked quietly.

Callista set her goblet aside, and leaned forward slightly, her dark hair falling over one shoulder.

'Moments,' she said simply. 'Moments worth living, worth remembering.'

For a moment, the weight of her words pressed on Seneca's chest. He was a man of duty, always calculating, always bound to the expectations of Rome. But here, under the glow of the lanterns and with her eyes holding his, he felt untethered, drawn into a world far removed from the one he knew.

'And now,' she said softly, her voice drawing him back, 'I've chosen to bring you.'

Seneca opened his mouth, but no words came. For once, his sharp mind found itself adrift, unmoored by the intensity of her presence.

Callista's smile deepened, fully aware of the effect she was having. She reached out, her fingers brushing lightly against his wrist, the touch sending a ripple through him.

Despite the voice in the back of his mind, the cautious, calculating voice that always guided him, he let himself fall into her embrace.

Callista drew him closer, her breath warm against his cheek, her scent intoxicating as jasmine and honey mingled with the salty air of the sea. The vines around the arbour swayed gently in the night breeze, the flicker of the candles throwing shifting patterns of light across their entwined figures.

Time lost all meaning. The worries of the world, the demands of duty, the tension of his mission, the weight of Rome itself, dissolved as they gave themselves wholly to each other. Their passion was unrestrained, a raw expression that swept them both away, leaving nothing but the heat of their bodies and the rhythm of their breaths.

When it was over, they lay together on the bed, the soft silk sheets tangled beneath them. Callista's fingers traced idle patterns on Seneca's chest, her head resting lightly on his shoulder. For the first time in years, he felt truly at peace.

Sleep claimed him quickly, exhaustion and contentment washing over him like a tide. Callista's arms held him close as his breathing slowed, and soon the only sounds were the faint lapping of the waves against the rocky shore and the rustling of the vines.

----

The hours passed in silence, the night stretching on as the stars wheeled overhead. But just before dawn, the tranquillity shattered.

Seneca bolted upright, his body drenched in sweat, his chest heaving. His eyes were wide, wild with terror, as his screams tore through the stillness of the early morning.

The sound echoed over the dark expanse of the sea,

startling the birds in their nests along the rocky cliffs. The peaceful glow of the candles now felt sharp and jarring, their flickering light casting strange, dancing shadows that seemed to close in around him.

Callista jumped beside him.

'Seneca,' she said gasped, 'what is it? What's wrong?'

But Seneca didn't respond. His hands clutched at the silk sheets as he stared out toward the horizon, his face pale and stricken, as though he had seen something no mortal man was meant to see.

----

## Chapter Twenty-Three

## Pselchis.

Marcus stood at the top of the watchtower, his silhouette outlined against the deepening hues of the late afternoon sky. His hands rested on the rough wooden rail, his sharp eyes scanning the horizon. The air was still, save for the faint murmur of voices and the occasional clatter of boots from below.

Moments later, the sound of footsteps on the ladder broke his reverie and he glanced over his shoulder to see the Optio, climbing into view.

'You sent for me, Centurio?' said Tullus, stepping onto the platform.

Marcus nodded and gestured for Tullus to join him at the rail. They stood side by side, staring out over the rocky expanse that stretched beyond the fort. The silence between them lingered for a moment before Marcus spoke.

'The men are improving,' he said. 'Their drills are sharper, and their discipline is holding. That's your doing.'

Tullus blinked, glancing at his commander. Praise was rare from Marcus, and his tone carried an unusual weight.

'Thank you, Centurio,' he said cautiously, sensing something beneath the surface.

Marcus turned to him briefly.

'You've done well, Tullus. The men trust you. They follow you. That's important.'

Tullus frowned, his brow furrowing.

'I appreciate that, Centurio. But... what's this about?'

'The unit is growing stronger and under your guidance, it will fare well. But I... I have to go.'

'Go?' Tullus repeated, incredulous. 'Go where?'

'Out there,' he said simply, nodding over the palisade. 'There's something I must do.'

Tullus frowned, his confusion deepening.

'My lord, if this is about the caravan, we can send a detachment.'

Marcus shook his head.

'No. This is something I must do myself.'

'Then I'll go with you,' Tullus offered without hesitation.

Marcus allowed himself the faintest smile before placing a firm hand on Tullus's shoulder.

'No. You're needed here. The men need you. I trust you to keep them together, to keep them strong. If I don't return, send a message to the fort at Syene and tell them everything that has happened here. They'll send a replacement in due course.'

'But why? What aren't you telling me?'

Marcus stepped past him, the ladder creaking underfoot as he began his descent. He paused halfway, glancing back at Tullus.

'Don't worry about me,' he said, 'I'm used to this sort of thing. Oh, and I will need a horse.'

And with that, he disappeared below, leaving Tullus standing alone on the watchtower. He turned his gaze back to the direction Marcus had pointed, his mind racing with questions. *What in Hades is going on?*

----

The following morning, Marcus sat atop one of the few garrison horses, his figure almost unrecognisable in his newly acquired black thawb. Behind him, strapped tightly to the saddle, was his sarcina, packed with essential supplies.

At the gates of the fort, Tullus stood silently, watching Marcus ride out without a word. His expression was a mixture of confusion and unease. This wasn't like Marcus, the disciplined and pragmatic leader he knew, and yet, there he was, disappearing into the wilderness alone, his purpose as enigmatic as the man himself.

'What's going on?' came a voice from beside him.

Tullus glanced over to see the Decurion standing at his side, his brow furrowed in puzzlement as he followed Tullus's gaze toward Marcus.

'I don't know,' Tullus admitted, shaking his head slightly. 'But something is seriously wrong. Assemble the men, Decurio, we have things to do.

----

The desert stretched endlessly ahead, a sea of gold rippling beneath the morning sun. Marcus rode steadily westward, his horse's hooves crunching softly against the baked earth. The air was cool now, the fleeting reprieve of dawn, but the growing heat on his back was a reminder of the scorching day to come.

The horizon shimmered like a mirage, broken only by the faint traces of the caravan's path. Sparse vegetation dotted the landscape, gnarled shrubs and patches of coarse grass, but it offered little shade or comfort. Marcus paid it no mind. His thoughts were locked on the task ahead, as unyielding as the cracked ground beneath him.

He could still picture the caravan clearly: the long column of camels, wagons, and armed riders, their numbers far exceeding any typical trade caravan. It wasn't just the sheer scale that set it apart, it was the precision of its movements, the heavily armed guards who had ridden out in such force to repel his patrol. Whatever they were transporting, it wasn't common goods, a hundred mounted archers didn't accompany bundles of cloth or jars of spices. No, this was something far more valuable, or dangerous. The thought gnawed at him like a persistent itch he couldn't scratch.

He pressed onward through the day, the sun climbing higher until it burned relentlessly overhead, pausing only to ensure the faint tracks hadn't disappeared beneath the wind, and by late afternoon, his quarry finally came into view.

At first, it was nothing more than a smudge on the horizon, but as he drew closer, the shapes became clearer, dark silhouettes of camels and wagons, camped at the base of a rocky hill.

Marcus slowed his horse, guiding it off the trail and into the shadow of an ancient ruin, its stones worn smooth by centuries of wind. It offered little protection, but enough to conceal his horse from prying eyes. He dismounted, patting the animal's neck as he tethered it securely in the shade.

'Easy, girl,' he murmured. The horse snorted softly in reply and as the last light of day gave way to the cool embrace of night, Marcus leaned against the crumbling stone, watching as the stars emerged overhead.

Eventually, the last of the light disappeared completely, and he set out towards the encampment, his specialist training coming back to him as naturally as breathing. The nearer he got, the more his senses sharpened. He scanned for sentries, his eyes catching the faint glint of weapons as the guards patrolled in well-rehearsed patterns. Their movements were precise, overlapping just enough to leave no room for gaps.

Marcus pressed himself lower to the ground, his black thawb blending seamlessly into the darkness. He crawled along a shallow fold in the earth, the firelight dancing above him as he inched closer. The faint hum of voices drifted toward him, mingling with the occasional clatter of metal and the snort of camels until finally, he reached the edge of the camp, his chest pressed firmly against the sand as he lay motionless beneath the last wagon.

He slowed his breathing, his heart pounding in his ears as he watched young boys hauling water from barrels to the hobbled camels. Further away, the cart masters gathered around a central fire sharing food and conversation.

Marcus waited, his eyes fixed on the patrols. He studied the intervals between their movements, calculating the timing of each pass and when the next pair of guards moved on, he slid out from beneath the wagon.

He crept forward slowly, until finally, he reached a wagon near the centre of the camp. Larger than the others, it was sturdier, with intricate detailing along its wooden frame. This, he knew, was no ordinary cart. Whatever they were guarding would be here.

Marcus pressed his back against one of the wheels, his breath shallow as he scanned the area. The tail flap of the canvas covering was secured with tight knots, the rope pulled taut. He frowned, his fingers brushing against the bindings. Undoing them would take too long.

His hand moved to the hilt of his blade, his mind racing. Every second he lingered increased the risk, but he hadn't come this far to leave empty-handed. He drew the blade silently, the steel gleaming faintly in the firelight, and as his knife sawed through the heavy canvas, his heart hammered unsure what he would find inside.

----

## Chapter Twenty-Four

### Alexandria

Seneca sat hunched on the edge of the bed, his chest heaving as beads of sweat rolled down his temples and neck. His trembling hands gripped the edge of the mattress, his knuckles white, as though he feared the ground might vanish beneath him. The world around him was slowly sharpening, shadows returning to their rightful places, the oppressive weight of his dream lifting inch by inch.

Behind him knelt Callista, her arms draped gently around his shoulders. Her face was etched with worry, and she whispered soothing words, the melody of her voice like a balm to his frayed nerves.

'It's over, Seneca,' she murmured, pressing her cheek lightly against his damp shoulder. 'You're here. You're safe.'

He gasped for breath, his pulse thundering in his ears as the last vestiges of the nightmare clawed at him, refusing to let go. His eyes darted to the open sea, the gentle rhythm of the waves grounding him in the present.

Gradually, his breathing slowed, and the tightness in his chest began to ease. The haze of terror that had gripped him melted away, replaced by the faint hum of exhaustion. His hands relaxed, and he swallowed hard, his throat dry and raw.

Callista's arms slipped away as she rose gracefully, her bare feet silent on the cool tiled floor. She reached for a loose, gauzy gown hanging from a nearby chair, slipping it over her shoulders before walking to a gilded table by the wall. A carafe of water and two delicate glasses rested atop it, their surface catching the pale morning light.

Pouring slowly, she returned to the bed and offered him a glass, her concerned gaze fixed on his. Taking the glass, he raised it to his lips, the cool water a welcome relief as he drank deeply.

'It was just a dream,' he said finally.

'A dream that left you as pale as death,' she replied quietly. 'I have never seen anyone thrash and cry out as you did.'

Seneca said nothing, his gaze fixed on the horizon. The nightmare had been unlike anything he had ever experienced, vivid, terrifying, and powerful enough to drag him into its depths. It had felt real, far too real. He exhaled slowly, his shoulders sagging slightly.

'Thank you,' he murmured, glancing at her with a faint flicker of gratitude in his tired eyes.

Callista nodded, her expression softening as she placed a hand lightly on his knee.

'The sun is rising,' she said. 'Whatever haunted you in the dark cannot follow you into the light.' She rose gracefully and walked away from the bed to call softly for her slave.

'Prepare the boat,' she instructed. 'We are leaving.'

----

The journey back to Alexandria passed in near silence, broken only by the creak of the boat and the occasional lapping of water against the hull. Seneca stared out at the horizon, the weight of the night pressing heavily on him. He replayed every moment in his mind, the warmth of her touch, the passion they had shared, and the terror that had gripped him in the dark hours.

When the boat reached the dock, the city was beginning to stir. Callista stepped onto the planks first, her gown catching the early light, and Seneca followed close behind.

They stood there for a moment, side by side, the quiet hum of Alexandria rising around them. Seneca struggled to find the words to express what he felt. He took a breath to speak, but Callista turned to him, placing a finger gently against his lips.

'Don't talk,' she said softly, her voice carrying a warmth that both soothed and stung. 'Remember the parts that were wonderful. When you do, remember who we are and what we shared. Life should be filled with such moments.'

Her words lingered in the air like the last notes of a song. Then, she withdrew her hand and turned away, as though the night they had shared had been a fleeting dream.

'Wait,' Seneca said, his voice tight with emotion. 'When will I see you again?'

Callista paused, half-turning to glance back at him. Her dark eyes held his, but her gaze was distant, as if she were already far away.

'You won't,' she said simply, her tone final but not unkind. 'Our roads head in different directions.'

Before he could say anything more, she turned and walked toward a narrow side street, her two guards falling into step behind her. Seneca stood rooted to the spot, watching as she disappeared into the maze of Alexandria.

For a long moment, he remained there, trying to process her departure. The most beautiful, caring, and sensual woman he had ever met had walked out of his life as effortlessly as a breeze slipping through an open window. His mind raced, replaying her words and her touch, but he knew there was nothing more to be said or done. She was gone.

Finally, he exhaled deeply, the sound trembling slightly as he turned away from the dock. He walked slowly into the city, his steps aimless, his thoughts a whirlwind. The cries of vendors and the clatter of carts echoed in the streets, but they barely registered. He didn't know where he was going, but one thing was clear: whatever path lay ahead, it would not be the same without her.

----

Across the city, Decimus and Cassius moved through the shadows of the Alexandria's underbelly, their cloaks pulled tight as they wound their way through the maze of alleys.

For days, they had pursued more information about the

underground temple they had visited weeks earlier, chasing down rumours and piecing together fragments of information about what lay behind the closed door. It had been a frustrating endeavour, one marked by resistance and unease. Bribery, cajoling, and threats had pried open some mouths, but the answers they received were vague, evasive, and often tinged with fear.

'It's as if the temple doesn't exist,' Cassius had muttered earlier in the day. 'Except that it clearly does, and everyone's too afraid to admit it.'

Decimus had noticed the same pattern. Every mention of the temple was met with one of two reactions: stony denial or thinly veiled panic. A few men had bolted outright, their faces pale, as if even speaking of the place might bring them harm. It was unnerving. In the end, they had decided to return to the source. If no one would tell them what the temple was or why it was so feared, they would have to find out for themselves.

Now, they stood once more in the narrow street where the unassuming door waited. It looked no different than it had the first time, plain, weathered, and entirely forgettable, as though designed to be overlooked. Again, the same beggar sat on the step, his hand outstretched expectantly. Cassius glanced at Decimus.

'Still think this is a good idea?'

'I don't know,' he said, 'but we've come too far to turn back now.'

Cassius sighed, his hand reaching into his cloak to retrieve a silver coin.

'Remind me why we do this to ourselves?'

'Because no one else will,' replied Decimus, and as the coin rattled into the bowl, pushed the door open, revealing the narrow staircase that descended into shadows.

'You know,' said Cassius quietly, his voice barely above a whisper, 'the last time we came here, I thought we were just being paranoid. Now I'm starting to think we weren't paranoid enough.'

The staircase wound downward, the air growing cooler with each step. Finally, they reached the bottom, stopping before the door leading into the temple chamber they had visited weeks before.

Decimus and Cassius stepped cautiously into the vast room, their footsteps muffled by the sand-dusted stone floor. The walls were adorned with the same intricate carvings of gods and symbols, Ra, Anubis, Isis, all rendered with exquisite detail that seemed almost alive in the flickering light of the oil lamps. Cassius leaned closer to Decimus, his voice a low murmur.

'Feels the same as last time. Like we shouldn't be here.'

Decimus didn't respond immediately. His sharp eyes swept the room, taking in every detail, every shadow. Finally, his gaze landed on the far end of the chamber, where two priests were again flanking the heavy stone door beneath a faded emblem of a scarab.

'Ready?' he asked.

Cassius exhaled sharply.

'No. But let's get it over with.'

They crossed the chamber slowly, threading their way through the worshippers. Eyes turned toward them, brief, wary glances, but no one spoke or moved to stop them.

Decimus and Cassius stopped a few paces from the priests, who turned their heads slightly to acknowledge their presence.

'Who seeks the Scarab?' asked one of the priests?

Decimus hesitated, his mind calculating how to approach this delicate situation.

'We seek knowledge,' he said carefully. 'We've come to understand what lies beyond.'

'This is not a place for outsiders,' said the priest. 'You should leave.'

'We've come far,' Decimus pressed. 'All we seek is

enlightenment.'

'You speak as though you have a right to what lies beyond,' came the reply. 'You do not.'

Cassius tensed beside Decimus, his hand twitching near the hilt of his sword. Decimus raised a hand subtly, signalling for him to stay calm.

'We mean no disrespect,' said Decimus, his tone soothing. He reached into his cloak, pulling out a small golden scarab, its surface gleaming in the lamplight. 'We only wish to understand. Perhaps this will demonstrate our sincerity.'

The priests' eyes flicked to the offering, their expressions briefly betraying surprise.

The first priest leaned toward the second, exchanging hurried whispers before turning back to face them.

'Those that seek enlightenment often suffer the consequences,' he said. 'Are willing to see the truth, and if necessary, pay the price?'

Both men nodded silently, and the priest stepped aside, gesturing toward the stone door.

'Then go,' he said simply, and may your gods look down upon you.'

Decimus inclined his head slightly, slipping the scarab into the priest's hand and as he and Cassius moved past, they pulled the door shut behind them, the sound echoing ominously through the narrow corridor that stretched ahead. Decimus and Cassius exchanged a brief glance before continuing forward, their footsteps the only sound breaking the oppressive silence.

The corridor sloped downward, the flickering glow of oil lamps casting strange, dancing shadows on the rough stone walls until finally, they reached another door. Both took a deep breath and, after pulling the doors towards them, walked through into another chamber.

----

It was similar in size to the one above, but the atmosphere was suffocatingly different. The air was thick, oppressive, and at the centre of the room lay a massive stone scarab, its surface polished to a dull sheen that caught the light of the oil lamps arranged around its base.

But it wasn't the scarab that made Decimus and Cassius stop in their tracks, it was the figures lining the walls.

A complete circle of upright coffins surrounded the chamber, each one slightly tilted forward as if watching the scarab. And inside each coffin… was a man.

The figures were restrained by thick bands of leather across their chests, arms, and legs, and their heads were secured in place by blood red strips of cloth, each adorned with a golden scarab.

The sight froze the two men where they stood, their stomachs tightening with unease.

Cassius was the first to find his voice, though it came out as little more than a whisper.

'*What in Hades…?*'

Decimus didn't respond, his sharp eyes scanning the room as he tried to process what he was seeing. Eventually he stepped cautiously closer to one of the coffins. The man inside stirred slightly, his lips parting as if to speak, but no sound emerged.

'They're alive,' he murmured quietly, his voice barely audible over the pounding of his own heart.

One of the men in the nearest coffin stirred, his eyes fluttering open. Cassius froze as the man's unseeing gaze locked on nothing in particular, his pupils clouded like stormy glass. And then came the scream, raw, primal, and filled with unrelenting terror, a sound that clawed at the walls and burrowed deep into their minds.

Before either of them could move, more eyes snapped open. One by one, the bodies in the coffins began to writhe, their limbs jerking spasmodically. The screams multiplied, overlapping until the chamber vibrated with the sheer force of their collective anguish. Cassius staggered back, his hands flying to his ears.

'We need to get out of here!' he shouted over the cacophony.

The two men turned and bolted for the stone door, stopping abruptly when they realised it was closed. Decimus heart sunk, knowing that they had deliberately left it open. Both men placed their hands on the door to push it open, but the stone refused to budge.
Cassius pounded his fists against it, shouting at the top of his lungs.

'Open the door! Let us out!' But his voice was lost in the confined space, overwhelmed by the relentless screaming behind them.

Gradually, the noise began to fade, and Cassius stopped, his breath coming in short gasps as he exchanged a glance with Decimus. They turned slowly to face the room once more.

The men in the coffins had gone still, their screams replaced by a deep, oppressive silence. The stillness was almost worse than the noise, and Cassius felt a chill crawl up his spine. His eyes wandered upward for the first time, drawn by a flicker of movement.

High above them, balconies had been carved into the stone walls, where black-clad priests stood in eerie silence, their faces hidden beneath dark hoods. They watched the scene below without moving, their presence as heavy as the air in the chamber.

'What is this?' shouted Cassius, his voice shaking with fury and fear. 'Open the door! Now!'

The priests remained motionless, their gazes fixed on him like statues of judgment. For a long, suffocating moment, nothing happened. Then, as one, the figures turned in perfect unison and disappeared through unseen doors behind them, their flowing robes vanishing into the shadows.

'Cassius,' said Decimus quietly. 'Look.' He pointed toward the center of the room where tendrils of mist were seeping out from beneath the massive stone Scarab, like ghostly fingers, spreading slowly across the floor. The mist shimmered faintly, and with it came a scent, sweet and floral, tinged with something rich and intoxicating.

Cassius's stomach churned as the smell reached his nose. It was beautiful, almost hypnotic, yet there was an undercurrent of something wrong, something that made his instincts scream.

'Don't breathe it in,' he warned, backing toward the door again.

But Decimus remained still, his eyes fixed on the mist as it crept up his body.

'It's… warm,' he murmured, almost to himself.

'Decimus, don't, '

Cassius's words caught in his throat as his companion swayed slightly, his expression shifting from fear to something more serene.

'*Decimus!*' he shouted, but as he watched, his companion's eyes rolled back, and his body crumpled to the floor in a lifeless heap.

Cassius staggered back, panic clawing at his chest. He turned to the door again, pounding on it with every ounce of strength he had left but as his voice became weaker, he finally succumbed and his body slid down the stone floor, disappearing beneath the ever-rising mist.

----

## Chapter Twenty-Five

## Britannia

The chill evening wind of Britannia swirled through the narrow paths of the village like a restless spirit. Veteranus walked these paths alone, unhurried. There were no guards at his door anymore, no spears at his back, and yet he knew better than to believe he was unobserved.

Every so often, on the edge of his vision, a shadow shifted, a figure melting into the forest line or a fleeting glimpse of movement behind a wattle-and-daub hut. The village might have seemed calm to a stranger, but to a man of his experience, it was a stage of quiet vigilance, its players hidden but ever-present. Subtle as the watchers were, their presence was unmistakable to him. He had spent a lifetime reading the unspoken, and subterfuge was as natural to him as the air he breathed.

He came to a stop at a communal fire, the flickering flames casting a warm orange glow on the rough faces of the villagers who passed by. A teenage boy crouched low by the fire, methodically turning slender wooden arrow shafts in the heat. Veteranus watched for a moment, then stepped closer.

'May I?' he asked, gesturing to the empty log beside the boy.

The boy hesitated, his eyes narrowing as he regarded the older man. Finally, with a slight nod, he shifted just enough to make space, though he said nothing.

Veteranus sat, resting his elbows on his knees and holding his hands out briefly to the fire for warmth. The silence stretched, broken only by the crackle of the flames and the occasional snap of a twig underfoot in the distance.

Noticing the bundle of unfinished shafts beside the boy, he leaned forward, picked one up, and held it in his hands. It was crude but serviceable, the sort of weapon a hunter might rely on to fill his belly, not one destined for the battlefield. Still, there was promise in it, and the boy's diligence was clear in the careful scraping of bark and the smoothness of the grain.

Veteranus turned the shaft over in his hands, inspecting it, then picked up a flat stone and began scraping at a knotted imperfection near the tip. The boy glanced at him, wary, but said nothing.

Minutes passed, the two of them working in silence. Veteranus did not force conversation, he knew better. Instead, he let his actions speak, matching the boy's pace and precision as best he could, though his hands were more accustomed to wielding swords than shaping arrows.

Eventually, the boy grunted softly, breaking the silence as he held up one of his completed shafts for inspection. His expression seemed to challenge the older man: What do you know of this craft?

Veteranus met the challenge with a faint smile, lifting his own shaft and mimicking the boy's motion. It was a poor imitation, the boy's was smoother and straighter, but the gesture earned him a grudging nod.

The ice began to thaw, and though words were still sparse, the boy occasionally glanced at him now, his sharp eyes softened by curiosity rather than suspicion.

At one point, the shaft Veteranus was working on snapped in his hands, the brittle wood splintering with a loud crack. The boy's eyes widened, and then, to Veteranus's surprise, he laughed, a short, sharp sound that broke the tension like a blade through fabric.

Veteranus chuckled too, shaking his head at his own deliberate clumsiness. He tossed the broken shaft into the fire, and as it burst into flames, he reached for another.

The boy's laughter still lingered faintly in the air, mingling with the crackle of the flames as the two continued their work. Veteranus glanced at the boy, noting how his movements had become a touch looser, less guarded, as if the task before them had melted some of the tension. It was an unspoken rhythm, the kind that spoke to the simplicity of shared labour but suddenly, the boy looked up, his dark eyes narrowing as he peered into the shadows beyond the firelight.

Veteranus also looked up and recognised Raven walking towards the fire, carrying something slung over his shoulder. The boy muttered something under his breath and began gathering his things with hurried precision. He tucked the unfinished arrow shafts into a leather satchel, slung it over his shoulder, and vanished into the night without so much as a backward glance. As he left, Raven sat on a log opposite Veteranus.

'Shame,' said Veteranus, gesturing toward the boy's now-vacant spot. 'I was just starting to enjoy his company.'

Raven gave a low grunt of acknowledgment and tossed a skinned and gutted rabbit, its flesh still fresh and faintly glistening.

'Compliments of the hunt,' Raven said, also throwing over a wineskin before producing his own rabbit from a pouch at his side. He produced a pair of stripped saplings and skewered the carcass, before angling it over the fire from one of the rocks that ringed the flames.

Veteranus accepted the second sapling and followed suit, leaning forward to turn the meat slowly over the fire.

'It's been years since I've roasted a rabbit over an open fire,' he remarked.

'Then you've missed out,' said Raven, adjusting his own rabbit.

The mood was easy, the conversation relaxed as they settled into the quiet camaraderie of the fire. They spoke of hunting, and their respective times in the forests of Gaul, the glow of the flames casting flickering shadows on their faces.

'Do you favour the bow, then?' Veteranus asked after a while, watching Raven rotate his rabbit with care.

'For certain kinds of game,' Raven replied. 'It's clean. Silent. A good hunter can take down his prey before it even knows he's there. But for the woods here?' He gestured with a tilt of his chin toward the surrounding darkness. 'A spear gives you better odds if what's hunting you decides to fight back.'

Veteranus shook his head.

'I'll take a bow any day. But a man can't argue with a full belly.'

By the time the meat was cooked, the smell of roasted rabbit hung heavy in the air, mingling with the earthy scent of the night. They ate in companionable silence, tearing into the tender flesh with calloused hands and tossing the bones to the dogs that prowled at the edges of the firelight. The animals scrambled over the scraps, growling and snapping, their yellow eyes glinting like fireflies.

Once the meal was done, Veteranus leaned back on the log, wiping his hands on his cloak before taking a deep swig of the sweetened wine. It was strong but pleasant, warming him from the inside.

Above them, the stars hung cold and distant, and the village settled into the stillness of sleep. After a long pause, it was Veteranus who broke the silence.

'So, Raven. I suppose you know that Seneca thinks you are dead.

'A necessary arrangement,' said Raven. 'I still have work to do and had to disappear without questions being asked.'

'So you are, and always have been a traitor?'

'I have always been loyal to my people, but for years, they did not need me. Now, my place is here so I have returned.'

'As I said,' replied Veteranus, 'a traitor,'

Raven stared at him, his face calm.

'Are names really that important?' he asked. 'Are you not called Veteranus, the Butcher of Iberia?' He said the title without emotion, neither condemning nor endorsing it.

Veteranus chuckled, though it was a bitter sound.

'The Butcher. Is that what they're calling me now? I suppose it's not inaccurate. My methods were... efficient.' He tilted his head, his tone darkening. 'But they didn't like what they saw in the mirror when it was over. So, they cast me out. Easier to blame me than admit what they'd unleashed.'

'And yet here you are,' replied Raven. 'Summoned from disgrace. By Lepidus, no less.'

Veteranus's eyes sharpened at the mention of the name.

'You know of Lepidus?'

'I have had some dealings,' replied Raven, 'the Occultum handler with a taste for pawns. Men like you and me. The kind he burns through and discards once we've outlived our use.'

'A fair judgement,' said Veteranus. 'Some of us spent years playing a role, slipping deeper into the cracks, doing what needed to be done.'

Raven tilted his head, his curiosity piqued.

'You're obviously speaking from experience. What role did you play? You don't strike me as a legionary.'

Veteranus smirked, but said nothing, just raising his flask in mock deference.

'Fair enough, said Raven. 'A man like you doesn't survive this long by sharing secrets freely.

'So,' said Veteranus eventually, 'I'll admit I'm curious. You clearly know of me, but I don't know why I'm here.

'Why do you think you are here? asked Raven.

Veteranus's fingers tightened around his flask, the words forming on his tongue slowly, cautiously, as though pulling them from the shadows of his memory might summon something he'd rather forget. He stared into the fire, its glow reflecting in his dark eyes, before speaking in a low, deliberate voice.

'Back in the cavern… when I was drugged,' he said, 'Mordred said something strange. He kept rambling about a shared purpose. Something to do with a mark, a tattoo, on my shoulder.'

Raven's expression shifted at that, though only slightly, a subtle curve of his lips, a flicker of something knowing in his eyes. He leaned back, his gaze fixed on Veteranus.

'I was wondering how long it would take for you to bring that up,' he said. 'Show me.'

For a moment, Veteranus hesitated, but with a grunt, he set the flask aside, reached up, and pulled the collar of his tunic down to expose his left shoulder.

The tattoo was unmistakable, its lines bold and dark against his weathered skin. It was a beetle, its wings stylized, its body encased in sharp, angular detail.

'What does it mean?' Veteranus demanded, replacing his clothing.

'It would be better to show you,' replied Raven, and rolling up the sleeve of his tunic, revealing the inner side of his forearm. There, etched into his skin, was the same tattoo. The beetle.

Veteranus's breath caught, his eyes snapping from the tattoo to Raven's face. For the first time that night, his composure faltered.

'You have the same mark,' he muttered. It must be a coincidence. It doesn't mean anything. It's just ink on skin.'

Raven rolled his sleeve back down, the tattoo disappearing beneath the coarse fabric.

'You're wrong,' he said calmly. 'That mark has been borne by people for generations. It isn't a coincidence.'

'Generations? And what is that supposed to mean? It binds us all together in some grand fateful purpose?'

'It's not about fate,' Raven replied, 'It's a symbol, one that's travelled far beyond any single family or place. It's been carried by people across the world, chosen or marked for a purpose. One that's always been the same: unification.'

'Unification,' Veteranus repeated, his voice thick with scepticism. 'Unification of what? This miserable patch of forest and its collection of mud huts?'

'Of people who have been wronged and seek their true place in history,' he replied.

Veteranus shook his head, exhaling sharply as he leaned back against the log.

'I think you've got the wrong man, Raven. I'm no unifier. And I'll tell you this. I didn't get this mark for anything noble. I got it as a drunk youth, stumbling around the backstreets of Rome, looking for trouble and finding plenty. Some back-alley tattooist with hands as unsteady as mine took a handful of coin and marked me with this beetle because I accepted a wager from a stranger. That's it. There's no meaning. No destiny. Just a foolish boy who didn't know better.'

Raven studied him carefully, his dark eyes unblinking, as if searching for something beneath Veteranus's words.

'And yet here you are,' he said finally.

'What's that supposed to mean?'

'The mark doesn't care where it came from,' said Raven. 'It's not bound by family lines or places of birth, it's given to those who are seen as worthy, in some way, people who have something in them, something useful, something unique. That man must have saw something in you, Veteranus, even as a boy. Sometimes, they are right, sometimes, they are wrong but, on this occasion, I do not believe it was a mistake.'

Veteranus shrugged dismissively, though there was a flicker of something in his eyes, something uneasy. '

'Whatever they saw,' he replied, 'it's long gone now. All that's left is a tired man who's fought too many battles for causes he stopped believing in a long time ago.' He turned his gaze back to the fire. 'And I'll tell you this. I'm not, and never will be, part of these people. This land, these Druids… they mean nothing to me.'

'Perhaps,' said Raven. 'But that beetle on your shoulder? It means something. It's also the only reason you're still alive.'

Veteranus's eyes snapped up to meet Raven's.

'What are you talking about?'

'When were brought before Mordred back at the Medway, he already knew you were an imposter and would've killed you without a second thought. But he didn't. Do you think that was mercy? No, it was the beetle. When he saw it, he stayed his hand. Whatever your reasons for carrying that mark, it has spared you… for now.'

Veteranus stared at him, the fire crackling softly between them. The weight of Raven's words pressed down upon him.

'And what happens when it stops being enough?'

Raven didn't answer immediately. Instead, he looked into the flames, his expression distant.

'That,' he said finally, 'will depend on what you do next.'

----

## Chapter Twenty-Six

## Pselchis

The night pressed in around Marcus like a living thing, heavy and suffocating, each sound amplified in the stillness. His blade worked quickly but carefully, slicing through the thick canvas that covered the wagon.

His eyes flicked from his work to the perimeter, scanning the darkness for any sign of movement. He knew the guards' routes, their predictable laps around the wagons, but knowing wasn't enough. His life depended on more than timing; it depended on instinct, the ability to sense the unseen.

The canvas gave way with a faint tear, and Marcus slipped his hand inside. His fingers met something coarse and dry…sacks. He made another incision and reached in, grabbing a handful of the contents. The faint moonlight revealed strands of something fibrous, but before he could examine it further, the crunch of boots on gravel reached his ears and his heart leapt. A guard was approaching.

Without hesitation, he shoved the handful of material beneath his tunic, letting it press coldly against his skin. Dropping to the ground, he slid under the wagon, his back scraping against the hard-packed earth as the guard passed by, his shadow flickering in the firelight.

When he was sure it was safe, he crawled out again and peered through the slit he had made in the canvas. Inside, he saw more sacks, identical to the first and a line of boxes stacked alongside.

Marcus glanced around again, checking the shadows again for any sign of movement. The next guard was still on his circuit, leaving Marcus a narrow window of opportunity.

Unable to resist, he reached through the slit again, cutting the cords on one of the boxes and lifting its lid. Inside, he found rows of small pouches, tightly bound and stacked in neat layers. The pouches were unmarked, and he had no idea what they contained, but the care with which they were stored suggested their importance.

He took one, slipping it into his belt. His hands itched to investigate further, to take more, but time was against him, and he couldn't risk lingering any longer. Carefully, he pulled the canvas back into place, securing it as best as he could with trembling fingers. Then, with one last glance around, he dropped to the ground and crawled back the way he had come, before stopping at the last wagon, his pulse pounding in his ears.

From his position, he could still see the faint glow of the campfires and the shadowy forms of guards patrolling the perimeter. He waited, as still as a stone, until the nearest guard's footsteps faded into the distance. Then, with painstaking slowness, he slid out from under the wagon and rose to a low crouch.

The rocks loomed ahead, a jagged line of cover between him and the open plains beyond. Marcus moved quickly, his feet silent on the soft ground He reached the rocks and slipped behind their cover, his body pressed against the cold stone and only when he was certain he was out of sight did he straighten up and begin his hurried retreat toward his horse.

The eastern sky was beginning to pale, the faint blush of dawn creeping over the horizon. Time was slipping away, and Marcus knew he had to move fast. Every passing moment brought the camp closer to waking, and with it, the chance of discovery.

He ran as quickly as the uneven terrain allowed but, in the gloom, he misjudged a step and pitched forward, the ground rushing up to meet him. He hit hard, his hands scraping against the rocky earth as pain shot up his leg. He bit down on his lip, stifling the cry that threatened to escape as he rolled onto his back.

His ankle throbbed with a sharp, stabbing pain, and when

he tried to move it, it felt as though fire was lancing up his leg.

'Damn it,' he hissed through gritted teeth, his face contorted in pain. He gripped his ankle for a moment, willing himself to push through it. The camp was too close, and dawn was coming fast. He couldn't afford to stop.

With a grimace, he forced himself to his feet, testing the weight on his injured ankle. The pain was excruciating, but he could manage it, barely. He shuffled forward, his gait uneven and laboured, each step sending jolts of agony through his leg.

The open ground stretched out before him, empty and exposed, and he was over halfway to the ruins where his horse was tethered before he heard the first calls of alarm, cutting through the stillness like a knife.

Behind him, the camp had erupted into chaos. Figures moved rapidly between the wagons, and Marcus could hear the unmistakable sound of men arming themselves, their voices barking orders as the first rays of dawn lit the horizon.

'They've found it,' Marcus whispered to himself, his stomach dropping like a stone.

He turned back toward the ruins and forced himself into a limping run, each stride a battle against exhaustion and pain. His breaths came in short, ragged bursts, his hands clawing at the air for balance. He risked a glance over his shoulder and his blood turned to ice. A column of riders was emerging from the camp, their dark forms silhouetted against the flickering firelight. They were moving fast, and their course was unmistakable, they were headed straight for him.

His heart pounded as he turned back toward the ruins, pushing himself harder despite the fiery pain in his ankle. The ruins loomed closer, their jagged outlines rising against the lightening sky. Marcus stumbled again but caught himself, his hands slamming into the rocky ground. He cursed under his breath, gritting his teeth as he hauled himself upright.

The sound of hooves grew louder, and he knew he was running out of time. He stumbled into the ruins, his chest heaving, gasping for breath. His horse whinnied nervously, its ears flicking back and forth as the scent of danger filled the air. Marcus ignored the pain and grabbed the reins, dragging himself into the saddle with a groan of effort.

He reached for the sarcina tied behind the saddle, cutting the ties to let it fall to the ground with a dull thud before digging his heels into the horse's flanks.

'Come on, girl,' he muttered, gripping the reins tightly, 'get me out of here.'

The animal surged forward with a snort and bolted out of the ruins. Marcus leaned low over its neck, urging it on as the first rays of dawn painted the horizon in pale golds and purples. Behind him, the thunder of hooves grew sharper, angrier.

The ground was merciless, pitted and uneven, but Marcus's horse flew over it, driven by the urgency of its rider. At first, he thought he might have a chance, the space between him and the riders seemed to hold steady, the wind whipping past his face as the horse powered onward, but as the terrain grew more unforgiving, the truth began to dawn on him. The horses behind him were stronger, more accustomed to the treacherous land, and, bit by bit, the distance between them shrank, and the shouts of the riders began to reach his ears.

'Faster!' Marcus hissed, digging his heels in harder. The horse responded with another burst of speed, its muscles straining beneath him. For a moment, it felt as though they were flying, the ground a blur beneath them… but it wasn't enough.

The riders were closing fast now, their dark shapes growing larger with every second. Marcus risked a glance over his shoulder and felt his stomach drop. They were nearly upon him, their faces indistinct but their intent unmistakable.

His mind raced, desperation clawing at his thoughts. He

couldn't outrun them, he knew that now. The realization settled over him like a cold weight, but with it came a grim determination. If this was the end, he would make it an end worth remembering.

Ahead, a low hill rose out of the landscape, its slopes littered with boulders and jagged rocks. It wasn't much, but it was something, a place to make a stand. He tightened his grip on the reins and turned his horse toward it, his jaw set, his breath coming in sharp bursts.

The horse scrambled up the incline, its hooves slipping on loose stones, but Marcus didn't relent.

'Just a little further,' he urged. Behind him, the riders' shouts grew louder, mingling with the rhythmic pounding of hooves. They were so close now that he could hear their bridles jingling, the snorts of their mounts, the scrape of weapons being drawn.

Marcus knew he could go no further and pulled his horse to a halt, sliding out of the saddle with practiced speed. His injured ankle buckled beneath him, and he staggered, catching himself against a nearby boulder. The pain was excruciating, but he pushed it aside, his focus narrowing to the moment at hand.

Drawing his blade, he limped deeper into the boulder-strewn hillside. The jagged rocks formed a loose maze, offering only the barest semblance of cover, but it was enough. He ducked behind one of the larger stones, his chest heaving, his lips pressed into a thin line of resolve. If they wanted him, they would have to pay for it.

He drew his gladius, the familiar weight a small comfort in the face of the inevitable, knowing this was where he would die. The realization didn't come with fear, only a cold, detached acceptance. He had made his choices, and this was where they had brought him.

The riders dismounted at the edge of the boulders,

spreading out to encircle him. Marcus caught glimpses of them through the gaps between the stones, figures cloaked in flowing thawbs, their curved swords gleaming faintly in the morning light. Their movements were efficient, disciplined, like wolves closing in for the kill.

He reached up and pulled his own thawb from his shoulders before tossing it to the ground. The loose fabric might have shielded him from the chill of the night, but now it was a hindrance, restricting the swift, precise movements his gladius demanded.

The first of the tribesmen came into view, stepping cautiously around the boulder. He was tall and lean, his thawb billowing slightly as he moved, his curved sword gripped in both hands. With a sharp, fluid motion, Marcus surged forward, his blade arcing upward in a deadly thrust. The tip of the gladius plunged into the man's chest, sliding between his ribs with brutal efficiency.

Marcus twisted the blade as he yanked it free, letting the body crumple to the ground. Blood dripped from the gladius, staining the rocky ground as Marcus stepped back, his eyes darting to the shadows beyond. He gripped the hilt tighter, his breaths shallow and quick.

The others would have heard nothing, just the faint scuff of feet and the body hitting the earth. But they would know he was here now, and they would come.

His heart raced, the pounding in his chest like the drumbeat of war. Marcus pressed his back against the cold, unyielding stone. He could hear the murmurs of the remaining tribesmen, their voices a low, menacing hum. The first assailant had fallen swiftly, but the element of surprise was fleeting. Now, the enemy moved with heightened caution, their curved swords glinting ominously as they navigated the labyrinth of boulders.

His muscles tensed as he caught sight of another warrior

approaching, his silhouette stark against the dawn's early light. With a swift, calculated movement, Marcus lunged, the gladius slicing through the air to again meet its mark. The warrior's eyes widened in shock before he too crumpled to the ground, lifeless, but there was no time to revel in the victory, another adversary was upon him and the clash of steel rang out as their blades met. Marcus parried the blow, using the momentum to drive his shoulder into the attacker's chest, sending him sprawling. More men appeared out of the gloom and despite his prowess, the sheer number of enemies began to take its toll. For every warrior he felled, two more seemed to take their place. He could feel his strength waning, the weight of exhaustion bearing down upon him.

 Forced back step by step, Marcus found himself cornered, the unforgiving rock face pressing against his back. The remaining warriors encircled him, their expressions a mix of respect and anticipation, recognizing a formidable foe brought to his final stand.

 Marcus's chest heaved as he prepared for the inevitable, a steely resolve settling over him. He would not go quietly; he would make them pay dearly for every inch. He readied himself to charge into the fray one last time, but before he could move, a thunderous roar echoed through the rocks, a sound that sent a jolt through both Marcus and his adversaries and from the ridge above, a battle cry rang out, unmistakably Roman.

 Marcus's eyes darted upward to see Tullus charging down the slope at the head of over a hundred legionaries. Gone was the precision of Rome's disciplined ranks, the strict formations that defined the legions. This was a tide of driven, battle-hardened men, their weapons gleaming in the early light, surging forward with one purpose, to save a comrade in desperate need.

 The enemy warriors panicked as the Roman legionaries charged into their midst with un-disciplined ferocity. The clash was swift and brutal, the tide turning in an instant with those tribesmen that survived, fleeing to their horses and racing back the way they had come.

Tullus reached Marcus's side, his expression a mix of relief and determination.

'Tullus,' said Marcus. 'How in the name of the gods are you here?'

'It took me a while to make a decision,' said the Optio, 'but yesterday, when you rode off alone, I knew you were heading into trouble. You didn't say it outright, but I could see it in your eyes. Whatever you were chasing, it wasn't going to end well.'

'So, you decided to follow me with half the garrison in tow?'

'More than half,' Tullus corrected. 'I couldn't let you go alone, so I mustered the men and marched through the night. We knew the caravan couldn't have gotten far.' He gestured to the battlefield around them. 'And here we are. You would have done the same for me.'

Marcus's gaze snapped back to Tullus, a retort on his lips, but it died in his throat. He couldn't deny it, and they both knew it.

'Next time,' Marcus said, 'send a messenger first. I'd like to know when a hundred legionaries are about to come charging in.'

Tullus chuckled, clapping Marcus on the shoulder with a heavy hand.

'And ruin the surprise? Where's the fun in that?'

Despite himself, Marcus let out a low laugh, shaking his head. He looked around at the men, the battered landscape, and finally back at Tullus.

'Well, you've saved my neck, so I suppose I owe you one.'
Tullus raised an eyebrow.
'You owe me more than one, Marcus. And don't think I'm

not keeping count.'

Marcus smirked, the weight of the moment easing slightly.

'Of course you are.'

The two men stood there for a moment longer, the faint glow of camaraderie pushing back against the exhaustion and bloodshed. Finally, Marcus sheathed his gladius, wincing as his ankle protested the movement.

'Let's get out of here,' he said.

Tullus nodded, turning to call out orders to the men.

'You heard him! Form up and move out! We're going back to the fort!'

----

## Chapter Twenty-Seven

### Alexandria

The streets of Alexandria were alive with the energy of the evening, the golden glow of the setting sun catching the vibrant colours of dyed fabrics and the gleaming mosaics of shopfronts.

Falco moved through the bustling crowds, his movements slightly stiffer than usual. The clean linen tunic he wore, belted neatly at the waist, clung awkwardly to his broad frame, its newness making it less forgiving with his every stride. Over it, he had draped a light cloak of fine material, nothing ostentatious, but it was freshly laundered and smelled faintly of lavender.

It was strange to see himself like this. He had spent most of his life in rougher attire, armour, or dust-streaked garments from long marches. Now, he felt like an impostor walking these polished streets, the fine sandals on his feet feeling too delicate for someone of his size and strength.

The sword at his side, though discreet under the draped edge of his cloak, was the one thing that felt natural. Everything else, the smooth tunic, the elegant lines of the cloak, the polished leather of his belt, felt alien. Falco tugged at the neckline of the tunic, where it clung too tightly around his neck. He had never known clothing to make him feel like a boy playing at being a man. But then, he thought wryly, he'd never known a woman to make him feel like this, either.

Her laughter still rang in his mind, soft and melodic, as if she had played a harp with her words. The way she moved, graceful, almost like water flowing, had left him unmoored. Falco had faced death countless times without blinking, but this was something entirely different. It wasn't fear that gripped him but something even less familiar: the overwhelming desire not to look like a fool.

'Get it together,' he muttered to himself, his deep voice barely audible over the hum of the marketplace. A merchant glanced his way, eyebrows raised, and Falco quickly looked away, his ears burning.

Ahead, the marketplace spilled out like a living tapestry. Hawkers and merchants called out from every corner, their voices a cacophony rising over the chatter of buyers. Stalls overflowed with bright silks, intricate jewellery, and exotic perfumes. Vendors thrust their wares at passersby, their hands extending with promises of beauty, wealth, or love.

'Bracelets of finest gold for your lady, Roman!'

'Oil of myrrh! A single drop will make her heart yours!'

'Amber from the east! Charms to bring eternal devotion!'

Falco slowed his pace, glancing over the offerings. He felt a pang of awkwardness deep in his chest. What was he supposed to bring her? His instinct was to bring nothing, he was a gladiator, not some Alexandrian poet, but a voice in the back of his head told him that this was different. She deserved something, something to show he wasn't completely hopeless.

He paused at a stall displaying delicate glass trinkets, running a massive hand over the smooth, shimmering edges of a necklace. It was fragile, like a spider's web spun into crystal. The merchant leaned forward eagerly, seeing an opportunity in Falco's hesitation.

'Perfect for a woman of beauty, no?' the merchant said, his grin as oily as the perfume he was selling. 'She'll remember you for this.'

Falco frowned and shook his head, pulling his hand back.

'No,' he muttered. 'It's not... it's not right.' He stepped away, ignoring the vendor's protest, and tried another stall, then another, but nothing seemed fitting.

As he pushed further into the marketplace, he found himself growing irritated. The merchants' endless chatter grated on his nerves, their wares, bracelets, silks, trinkets, seeming more and more like useless frills. Falco didn't want something shiny or grand. He wanted something real. Something simple.

Finally, at the edge of the market, he spotted a quieter stall. It was small and unassuming, lined with amphorae of wine neatly arranged in rows. An older man stood behind the display, his weathered face calm amidst the chaos. Falco approached, his eyes drawn to a small amphora near the front. Its dark clay was smooth, unadorned, but there was a quality to its simplicity that struck him.

'This one,' he said, his voice firm but awkward, pointing to the amphora.

The shopkeeper nodded knowingly, his hands steady as he picked it up.

'A fine choice,' he said, wrapping the amphora with care. 'It's sweet but balanced. Good for sharing.'

Falco handed over a few coins and took the amphora, its weight reassuring in his hands. He nodded his thanks to the shopkeeper and turned back toward the streets, tucking the wine under his arm. It wasn't much, but it felt right.

----

Falco adjusted his cloak as he approached the rendezvous, a quiet courtyard tucked away from the bustling streets. The soft glow of torches lit the scene, their light flickering against the marble columns of a small temple nearby. The faint murmur of fountains and the scent of jasmine hung in the air, lending the place an aura of refined elegance. It was a fitting backdrop for her, she who seemed to carry elegance effortlessly, like it had been crafted solely for her.

And there she was, standing alone in the center of the courtyard, her silhouette framed by the amber torchlight. She was everything Falco remembered and more. Her gown, a delicate shade of emerald, shimmered faintly as it caught the light, hugging her figure with just enough suggestion to leave the rest to the imagination. She stood poised, her hands clasped lightly in front of her, her dark hair cascading down her shoulders in loose waves. When her eyes found his, she smiled, the gesture soft and inviting, as though she had been waiting just for him.

Falco froze, the weight of the amphora suddenly feeling heavy in his hand. His heart thudded in his chest, and for a moment, he felt like a clumsy youth, unarmed and defenceless before the sheer power of her presence. Gathering himself, he took a deep breath and started toward her, his steps deliberate but betraying his nerves.

Halfway there, a sharp tug at his sleeve stopped him midstride. Falco frowned, his eyes darting to the source of the interruption. A man, a beggar by the look of him, stood hunched at his side. The man's clothes were threadbare, his face weathered and sunken, and his wide, searching eyes glimmered with desperation. Falco's brow furrowed in irritation.

'What is it?' he asked, as he glanced back at her. She was still watching, though her smile faltered, curiosity flickering in her expression. The beggar hesitated, his fingers still clutching the edge of Falco's sleeve.

'You are the gladiator, yes?' he rasped. 'You must come with me.'

Falco stiffened, his frustration mounting. He thrust a coin toward the beggar, eager to end the interruption.

'Here. Take this and leave me be.'

The beggar shook his head, his grip tightening.

'No, you don't understand,' he said, his tone growing more desperate. 'Your friends are at risk. They are in danger, and if you don't come now, they'll be dead within a few hours.'

Falco blinked, his irritation giving way to confusion. He glanced over his shoulder at her again. She was still watching, though now her smile had faded entirely, replaced by a look of uncertainty. His stomach churned with unease.

'What are you talking about?' he hissed.

The beggar leaned closer, his voice dropping to a whisper.

'I sit on the steps of a hidden temple in the back streets. I've seen your friends come and go, they are foreigners, like you. I followed them, hoping for coin and heard them speak of you when you won a big fight in the arena. But they've done something foolish. They went into the temple's inner chamber.'

Falco frowned deeply.

'What temple?'

'I will have to show you,' said the beggar, 'but not many come out alive. I know the ways of the temples and I know what goes on inside them.'

Falco stared at him, the weight of the man's words sinking in. He glanced back at her again. She was still standing there, but her face had lost its warmth entirely, her hands now clasped tightly in front of her.

'You're sure about this?' hissed Falco.

The beggar nodded vehemently.

'I swear it. I've sat on those steps for years. I know the secrets of that place, except what lies beyond the scarab door. But your friends… they went inside. If you do not go now, it could be too late.'

Falco's mind was torn. His loyalty to his comrades gnawed at him, but when his eyes met hers again, he felt a different pull, something deeper, more unfamiliar, that left him unsteady. He had never felt this way about anyone before, and the thought of walking away from her now, after all his preparation, left him with a hollow ache. Finally, his frustration boiled over.

'If you're lying,' Falco snarled, 'I swear I'll find you and you'll wish you'd never heard of me.'

The beggar met his glare without flinching.

'I'm not lying,' he said. 'I've risked much to find you.'

Falco let out a sharp breath and turned back toward her, determined to explain, to find some way to salvage this. But when his eyes reached the courtyard, the space where she had stood moments ago was empty, her absence as sharp as a dagger.

Falco stood there for a moment, the amphora heavy in his hand, the weight of disappointment pressing against his chest. He turned back to the beggar and nodded grimly.

'Lead the way.'

----

Half an hour later, they reached the temple, its facade hidden in the shadows of the narrow backstreets. The two men paused at the threshold, Falco's hand resting on the hilt of his hidden gladius as he turned to the beggar.

'What's your name?'

The beggar hesitated, his gaze darting to the ground for a moment before meeting Falco's.

'Erasmos,' he said finally.

'Well, Erasmos,' Falco said, 'if you want me to trust you, you're going to tell me everything. Start with my friends. What do you know about them?'

Erasmos shifted uncomfortably, glancing up at Falco before speaking.

'They've been here before, coming and going for weeks but only went inside once. Foreigners like you, and loud enough in their conversations that I learned their names. Cassius... Decimus... always looking over their shoulders, like they knew they were being watched.'

Falco's brow furrowed, but he remained silent, letting Erasmos continue.

'They've been asking questions. Dangerous ones. I don't know why or what they're looking for, but this time they went too far. They paid their way into the inner chamber.'

Falco's eyes narrowed.

'The inner chamber?'

Erasmos nodded.

'The temple is divided. In the first chamber, the people worship openly. They offer prayers, burn incense, make sacrifices to the gods.' He leaned in closer, his voice dropping to a conspiratorial whisper. 'But beyond that, past the scarab, there's another place. The inner chamber. Only the specially chosen or those with enough coin to bribe the priests are allowed to enter.'

'And what happens in there?' Falco demanded.

Erasmos hesitated, his voice trembling slightly.

'I don't know. No one outside the temple does. But I've seen the people who go in.' He glanced at the ground, shaking his head. 'Some come out... changed. Enlightened, they call it. Others come out broken, mad, raving, like their minds have been shattered. And some... some never come out at all.'

Falco's grip tightened on the hilt of his gladius, the weight of Erasmos's words sinking into his chest like a stone. His jaw clenched.

'Why are you telling me this?'

Erasmos looked up at him, his expression carefully neutral.

'Because I want coin,' he said bluntly.

Falco's eyes hardened.

'Coin? Is that what all this is about? I could hand over what you demand and end up stuck on the inside with my comrades. Do you think I'm going to fall for that?'

Erasmos raised his hands defensively, shaking his head.

'No, you don't understand. I want nothing now, nothing. But if you find your friends, and you make it out of there, I'll want payment then. Fair payment for risking my life to bring you here.'

Falco's eyes bore into Erasmos, searching for any hint of deceit. The beggar's face was calm, steady, but there was a flicker of desperation in his eyes, desperation not of a liar, but of a man who knew the danger they were both about to face.

'If you're telling the truth,' he said, 'and my friends come out of that place alive, I'll make you a rich man. But if this is a trick…' he leaned in closer, his tone as cold as steel, 'I'll cut out your heart with a blunt knife.'

Erasmos met his gaze without flinching.

'I'm not lying,' he said quietly. 'Your friends' lives hang by a thread. What happens next is up to you.'

----

Falco's mind was racing. If what the beggar said was true, Cassius and Decimus didn't have much time and every instinct told him to charge inside, blade drawn. But even a seasoned fighter like him knew better than to rush blindly into the unknown. He needed a plan. He needed help. His eyes snapped to the beggar.

'If what you're saying is true, then I can't do this alone. Someone has to bring reinforcements.'

The beggar blinked in confusion.

'Reinforcements?'

Falco nodded firmly.

'You're going to the governor's palace and ask for Seneca. Tell him I need him and bring him back here as quickly as you can. If he doesn't believe you, show him this.'

He reached down and twisted the heavy gold ring from his finger, holding it out to Erasmos. The gladiator's ring gleamed in the faint light, its weight and craftsmanship undeniable.

Erasmos stared at the ring, his expression flickering between awe and hesitation.

'This ring... It's worth a fortune. Why give it to me?'

'Because that ring proves who I am. Give it to Seneca and he'll come.'

The beggar shook his head, his expression uncertain.

'I'll never get past the gates, I'm a beggar.'

'You will,' Falco growled, stepping closer, his imposing

frame towering over the smaller man. 'You have to. Get to Seneca, tell him everything you've told me about Cassius and Decimus. Tell him what's happening here.'

Erasmos hesitated, before giving a reluctant nod and turning away to disappear into the maze of Alexandria's back alleys. As the beggar's figure faded from view, Falco's sense of resolve wavered.

'Damn it,' he muttered under his breath. He had trusted the beggar with one of his most valuable possessions, a ring that was worth more than the man would likely see in a lifetime. What if Erasmos was already on his way to sell it to the highest bidder? What if the promise of wealth had outweighed the urgency of saving lives?

Clenching his fists, Falco let out a soft curse and turned back toward the temple. There was no time to dwell on the possibility of betrayal. Either Erasmos would deliver the message, or he wouldn't. Either way, time was running out and he had to decide what to do next.

The door loomed before him and Falco stared at it for a long moment, his fingers flexing around the hilt of his gladius. With a deep breath, he stepped back into the shadows to wait. Whatever awaited him beyond that door, he would face it and if that meant he had to go in alone, then so be it.

----

## Chapter Twenty-Eight

## Pselchis

The sun was a blazing orb, sinking low over the horizon as Marcus and the column of weary legionaries approached the fort. The journey back had been gruelling, the desert's unforgiving heat bearing down on them during the day and the biting cold creeping in at night. Marcus sat astride his horse, his injured ankle bound tightly with a makeshift bandage.

As they passed through the creaking wooden gates, the column broke into subdued cheers. The men knew they had survived something harrowing, though the weight of exhaustion showed in their every step.

Among them were the wounded, men who limped, clutched hastily wrapped cuts, or leaned heavily on comrades for support. Blood had dried into dark streaks on their armour and tunics, and one man, pale and barely conscious, slumped forward on a makeshift litter carried by two of his comrades. His chest rose and fell shallowly, the wound at his side poorly bound and leaking crimson.

Marcus dismounted with effort, biting back a wince as his injured ankle bore his weight. A young medicus hurried toward him, his satchel of tools bouncing against his side as he scanned Marcus's leg.

'Your injury, Centurion, let me…' the medicus began, reaching for his bandaged ankle.

Marcus's hand shot out, gripping the man's arm firmly.

'No,' he said, gesturing to the soldiers around him. 'See to the men. That one first,' he pointed to the soldier on the litter, 'do what you can for him.'

'Yes, Centurio,' the medicus replied, hurrying toward the litter.

Around them, the rest of the column dispersed. Most of the men headed for the nileometer, dropping their gear with audible relief before bending to drink their fill from the buckets around the edge.

Marcus limped towards his quarters. A slave hurried to help him, steadying him as he removed his dusty tunic and easing him into a chair. Other slaves brought hot water and filled a wooden tub. Eventually he lowered himself in and let out a low groan as the heat seeped into his aching muscles, washing away the grime of the march. His ankle throbbed, but the water dulled the edge of the pain.

Once clean, Marcus emerged from the basin and dressed in a plain, unadorned tunic, tying a simple belt at his waist before sending a runner to fetch Tullus. The Optio was already issuing orders somewhere in the fort, ensuring that discipline returned after the chaos of the march, but Marcus needed to speak with him before night fell.

----

Several minutes later, the door creaked softly as Tullus stepped into the room. His armour was gone, also replaced by a simple tunic but his presence was as commanding as ever. Marcus stood by the table, gesturing toward the chair across from him.

'Sit,' he said.

Tullus raised an eyebrow but complied, dropping into the chair with a sigh. A slave entered quietly, balancing a platter of flatbread, dried figs, dates, and a small bowl of lentils. A jug of watered wine followed, its surface slick with condensation from the cool air of the storage cellar. The two men ate in silence at first, the silence punctuated by the occasional scrape of a knife against the wooden plates or the soft crunch of bread. Finally, Marcus broke the silence.

'You know you didn't have to come after me, Tullus.'

Tullus snorted, tearing a piece of bread in half.

'Don't start with that,' he said, shaking his head. 'I've heard enough *'thank yous'* for a lifetime. You'd have done the same for me.'

Marcus allowed himself a faint smile, nodding.

'Still, you saved my neck. I owe you.'

Over the next half hour or so, the food dwindled, the wine jug grew lighter, and Marcus's gaze turned distant, his thoughts shifting to the reason he had summoned Tullus.

After the servant had removed the platters, he pushed back his chair and walked to the wall where his cloak hung. From its folds, he retrieved the items he had taken from the caravan: a small handful of dried flowers and the pouch of fine white powder. Returning to the table, he placed them carefully in front of Tullus.

'This?' he said, gesturing at the items, 'is what we went through all that hell in the desert for. I need to find out what it is, and why it was worth protecting with an entire caravan of armed men.'

Tullus's frown deepened as he studied the items. He reached for the pouch, loosening the string carefully and peering inside. His expression shifted slightly, his lips pressing into a thin line.

'I think I know what this is,' he said after a moment, 'Henbane.'

Marcus leaned back, frowning.

'I've heard of Henbane,' he said. 'Isn't it a poisonous plant?'

'It is,' Tullus agreed. 'But not always.' He gestured toward the pouch. 'If it's prepared a certain way, it can be used as a drug… a powerful one. It's dangerous, unpredictable even, but some people use it for visions, for rituals, or…' he hesitated, his expression darkening, 'for control.'

'Control?'

Tullus nodded grimly.

'In the right hands, or should I say, the wrong ones, it can make people... pliable.' He paused, his gaze shifting to the dried flowers beside the pouch. 'What about that?'

Marcus shook his head.

'No idea. It was in one of the sacks. Why would they collect flowers?'

Tullus stared at the items on the table for a long moment before turning toward the door.

'Bakhet,' he called, 'come in here.'

A moment later, the servant reappeared, his eyes darting nervously between Tullus and Marcus.

'Yes, Dominus?' he said, bowing his head slightly.

Tullus gestured toward him.

'You're a local man, aren't you?'

The servant nodded quickly.

'Yes, Dominus. I was born not far from here.'

Tullus pointed to the dried flowers on the table.

'Do you recognize these?'

The servant stepped forward cautiously, his gaze lingering on the table. He reached out with tentative fingers, lifting the brittle flowers carefully. He held them close to his face, inhaling their faint, earthy scent. For a moment, he said nothing, his brow furrowing in thought. Then he nodded and placed the flowers back down on the table.

'Yes, Dominus. I know them. This is the blue orchid. It is a common plant across Egypt, but it grows in abundance further south, along the lands of the southern tribes near the Nile. It is very valuable.'

Tullus exchanged a glance with Marcus, then looked back at the servant.

'Why is it valued? What makes it important?'

'Because of its potency, Dominus. 'It is used by certain tribes in their rituals and ceremonies. They believe it opens the mind, lets them see beyond the veil of the living world.'

The room fell silent, the flickering lamplight casting long, restless shadows on the walls as Marcus and Tullus stared at the two substances on the table.

Marcus's brow was furrowed deeply, his thoughts racing. Both substances had hallucinogenic properties, that much was clear. Could this be the cause of the strange visions? The whispers of madness? The mere possibility gnawed at him, but he was certain of one thing: none of his men would have voluntarily taken such things. Yet, the connection was too strong to dismiss.

He turned sharply toward the servant, who had been lingering nervously near the doorway, as if hoping to slip away unnoticed.

'Which one is more potent?'

The servant hesitated, his fingers twisting the hem of his tunic.

'Both are strong, Dominus,' he replied carefully. 'On their own, when properly prepared, either can cause powerful visions and clarity. They can also cause madness.'

Marcus exchanged a glance with Tullus, whose silence had grown increasingly thoughtful. Then, as if struck by a sudden idea, Tullus leaned forward, his gaze fixed on the servant.

'What happens,' he said slowly, 'if you mix the two?'

The servant's eyes widened, his face paling visibly. He took an instinctive step back, his voice faltering as he replied,

'You... you should not do that, Dominus.'

'Why not?'

The servant swallowed hard, his gaze darting between the two men.

'It... it is possible, but it is forbidden. The process is complicated, only known to certain priests in the far south. Few know how to combine them safely, and even fewer would dare to try.'

'Why?' snapped Marcus.

The servant hesitated again, visibly trembling now, before finally lowering his voice to a near whisper.

'Because the resulting drug, Dominus, is said to provide a direct path to the gods themselves.'

The air in the room grew heavier as they digested the servant's words, the implications settling over them like a dark cloud.

'One more question,' said Marcus, his sharp eyes boring into the servant. 'Does this combined drug have a name?'

The servant's lips pressed into a thin line, and for a moment, Marcus thought he might refuse to answer. But then he bowed his head slightly, his voice trembling as he spoke.

'It does, Dominus. The people call it Scarab.'

----

## Chapter Twenty-Nine

## Pselchis

Marcus sat at the table, his mind still stunned at what he had just learned. His eyes remained fixed on the dried flowers and white powder on the table, the word Scarab echoing in his mind. That single word had changed everything and though clarity still eluded him, he knew without a doubt that he had stumbled onto something of immense importance, something Seneca needed to know.

He turned to Tullus, knowing that what he said next would not be reversable.

'I need to leave,' he said simply.

Tullus frowned.

'Leave? What are you talking about? You've only just got back.'

'There is something I need to do,' said Marcus. 'And this time there will be no coming back.'

Tullus leaned forward, his tone hardening.

'You can't just abandon your post, Marcus. You're a Centurion. You have responsibilities, your men, this fort. You're a soldier of Rome.'

Marcus exhaled deeply. He looked at Tullus and spoke carefully.

'I was a Centurion once, Tullus, but I'm not anymore. Not truly. I have… another path now. One I can't explain, but one I must follow.'

Tullus's eyes widened, astonished.

'You're telling me you're no longer serving?' he gasped. 'Then what in Hades are you doing here?'

Marcus shook his head.

'I can't say but I'm asking you to trust me. I need to leave as soon as I can, and I need your help to make that possible.'

Tullus sat back, his frown deepening.

'What do you want me to do?'

'I need time to get to Alexandria without half a legion chasing me down. Cover for me, just for a few days and after that, you can report me missing to the Legatus at Syene.'

Tullus stared at him, his mind clearly working through the implications.

'And what exactly do I tell him? That you just vanished into thin air?'

Marcus reached across the table, grabbing Tullus's wrist tightly.

'Tell him whatever you have to, but not before I'm long gone. This is bigger than protocol, Tullus. Bigger than my rank or my duty to this garrison. What I have to do… it's of the utmost importance to Rome. I wouldn't ask this of you if it weren't.'

Tullus's expression softened slightly, though his confusion remained. He studied Marcus's face, searching for some clue as to the truth of his words. Finally, after a long pause, he nodded slowly.

'Alright,' he said. 'I don't understand any of this, but I'll give you the time you need. Just a few days. After that, you're on your own.'

Relief washed over Marcus, and he released Tullus's wrist, his grip loosening into a gesture of gratitude.

'Thank you. I won't forget this, Tullus. But there is one more thing that needs resolution before I go, this situation with the Tribune.'

'I'll send a message to Syene after you have gone,' responded Tullus. 'I'll explain what happened. They'll decide what to do with him.'

'No,' said Marcus, shaking his head. 'You know what their decision will be. His actions, killing a fellow legionary, will not be excused, no matter the cause, no matter the circumstances.'

Tullus frowned, confusion etched across his face.

'Marcus, you saw him. The man wasn't himself. Whatever possessed him... it wasn't natural.'

'It doesn't matter,' Marcus replied. 'When the report reaches Syene, they won't care about causes. To them, he's a murderer. He'll be hanged, or worse, sent to the salt mines.' He paused, his voice softening. 'No man deserves that.'

'Then what are you suggesting?'

Marcus paused before responding.

'Apparently, the Tribune was a good man before this. Respected. Fair. He doesn't deserve to suffer for something he couldn't control. But...' his tone grew harder. 'We can't just let him walk free, either. The men wouldn't accept it. He murdered one of their comrades. Morale would break and discipline would crumble.'

Tullus stared at Marcus, the pieces slowly falling into place.

'What do you want me to do?'

'You're going to do nothing,' said Marcus, 'except bring him to the front gates at dawn and muster the garrison to man the walls. They need to see this.'

Tullus hesitated, clearly uneasy. But Marcus's tone left no room for argument. After a moment, he nodded reluctantly.

'As you wish, Centurio.'

----

The following morning, as the first glow of dawn appeared over the eastern mountains, Marcus stood outside the fort gates, the desert stretching out before him. He stood alone, his thoughts heavy as the weight of what was to come bore down on him.

Footsteps broke the silence, and he turned to see Tullus approaching with the Tribune. The man's hands were still bound, his face pale and gaunt from days of confinement. There was no fight left in him, only a quiet resignation in his hollow eyes.

Marcus nodded to Tullus, who hesitated briefly before stepping forward to untie the Tribune's hands. The man flexed his fingers weakly but made no move to resist.

'Come,' said Marcus quietly, gesturing for the Tribune to join him.

The air was still, the faint whispers of the desert wind the only sound as Marcus and the Tribune stood side by side, staring towards the east. The crimson glow of dawn painted the landscape, stark and unyielding, as if nature itself bore witness to what was about to unfold.

'Do you have family?' asked Marcus quietly, breaking the silence.

The Tribune nodded, a faint smile tugging at his lips despite the circumstances.

'A wife. Two boys. They're still young. I… I had dreams for them, you know? To grow strong, to join the legions, maybe even surpass me one day.' His voice faltered slightly, but he steadied himself. 'I wonder if they'll ever know what happened.'

Marcus exhaled deeply, his eyes fixed on the horizon.

'I'll make sure they know you served honourably. Whatever else has happened here, that truth won't change.'

The Tribune glanced at him, gratitude flickering in his tired eyes.

'Thank you, Centurion. It means something… to know they'll hear that.'

They stood in silence for a few moments, the distant call of a bird breaking the stillness.

'If I let you live,' said Marcus quietly, 'we both know what's waiting. A trial in Syene or Rome, disgrace, execution, or worse, condemnation to the salt mines. I know it's not right, but the law won't care about what possessed you. They'll only see the blood on your hands.'

The Tribune nodded, still staring out at the rising sun.

'I've made peace with it,' he said and turned to meet Marcus's eyes. 'Let's get it done.'

Marcus studied the man for a long moment, seeing no fear in his expression, only resolve. The Tribune dropped to his knees, the sand shifting beneath him as he turned to face the sunrise. His back straightened, his head high as he gazed at the blood-red sky, his lips moving silently in a final prayer.

Marcus stepped behind him, gripping the hilt of his gladius tightly.

'Think of them,' he said quietly, his voice almost a whisper. 'Your wife, your sons.'

The Tribune's shoulders rose and fell in a slow, steady breath.

'I am,' he replied softly. 'Tell them… I love them.'

For a moment, Marcus hesitated, the weight of the moment pressing down upon him. Then, with a swift, precise motion, he drove the gladius down through the back of his neck, severing the man's spine cleanly and ending his life in an instant.

The Tribune's body slumped forward, landing face down in the sand. Marcus stepped back, his gladius dripping red, his expression carved from stone.

Behind him, the fort's garrison watched from the walls in silence. To them, it was justice. To Marcus, it was far simpler. It was an act of mercy.

----

A few hours later, Marcus and Tullus rode in silence along the banks of the Nile, the rhythmic clopping of their horses' hooves the only conversation between them. The sounds of the river were a mix of gentle ripples and the faint shouts of boatmen preparing their vessels for the day's journeys.

A short time later, they reached the moorings, and Marcus dismounted carefully, before giving his horse a final pat and handing the reins to Tullus.

'That's the one you want,' said Tullus, pointing towards a Baris moored nearby. 'They are the fastest boats on the Nile. With a good current and fair winds, you should be in Alexandria within ten days.'

'Understood,' said Marcus. 'I don't know how to thank you for everything you've done, Tullus. I…'

Tullus raised a hand sharply, cutting him off.

'No more,' he said, 'I've already told you, you've said enough.'

Marcus paused, studying Tullus for a moment before nodding in acknowledgment and turning toward the waiting sailboat. But before he could take more than a few steps, Tullus's voice stopped him.

'I do have one question, though.'

Marcus turned back as the Optio stepped closer, glancing around to ensure no one else was near.

'When I was in Syene,' Tullus began, 'there was talk among some of the men who'd come fresh from Rome. Rumours about a secretive unit of exploratores who work behind enemy lines and answer to no authority. They called them the Occultum though knew little more.' He paused for a moment, staring deep into the Centurion's eyes, as if looking for a reaction. 'I don't suppose you have anything to do with them, do you?'

Marcus held Tullus's gaze, his expression unreadable. After a long moment of silence, he sighed before answering honestly.

'Even if I did, Tullus, what would you expect me to say?'

Tullus hesitated, then gave a slight shrug.

'You'd deny it.'

Marcus allowed the faintest trace of a smile to tug at the corner of his mouth.

'Then there's your answer.'

Tullus chuckled dryly, shaking his head as if he should have expected nothing less. Marcus stepped forward and clasped Tullus's arm firmly, a gesture of friendship and mutual respect.

'Take care of yourself, my friend,' he said, and before Tullus could respond, Marcus turned and boarded the Baris.

Tullus remained where he was, watching as the sails unfurled and the ship began its journey northward. He stood in silence for a long moment, his thoughts swirling as the vessel drifted farther and farther away, until it was little more than a speck on the wide, glimmering expanse of the Nile.

Finally, he mounted his horse and leading the other by the reins, turned back toward the fort. The questions Marcus left unanswered weighed heavily on his mind, but he knew better than to expect more. Whatever the Centurion was caught up in, it was far beyond his understanding, and perhaps, it was better that way.

----

## Chapter Thirty

## Britannia

The narrow trail twisted through the craggy hills and dense woodlands south of Isla Mona as the column of twenty druid warriors headed deeper into the lands of the Ordovices. Veteranus rode near the middle of the group, his eyes scanning their surroundings. The Celts flanking him were unlike any he had encountered before, taller, with broad shoulders and strong, defined features. Their hair was tied back from faces marked with subtle scars, signs of warriors who had lived their lives steeped in conflict.

Their silence was unnerving. Unlike the boisterous, defiant Celts Veteranus had encountered in battle, these men moved with quiet purpose. There was no idle chatter or laughter, only sharp eyes scanning the terrain as if every shadow concealed danger. Even the way they carried their weapons, axes, swords, and spears, suggested a deadly readiness that kept Veteranus on edge. Raven rode a short distance ahead, his lean frame blending effortlessly with the landscape. He spoke little, answering Veteranus's occasional questions with vague remarks.

Their journey south took them through harsh terrain, crossing jagged mountains and plunging into shadowed passes where the air grew cold and damp. Veteranus often caught glimpses of movement in the periphery of his vision, armed men watching from ridges or concealed within thickets. But none approached, their watchful eyes following the group in silence.

The second day ended with the party descending into a dense forest at the base of a towering mountain. The trees were ancient, their gnarled branches forming a canopy that cast the forest floor into perpetual twilight. Moss hung in heavy curtains from the limbs, muffling the sound of their passage.

Eventually, they made camp in a small clearing, a fire crackling to life as the shadows deepened. The warriors settled around the flames, eating and drinking in near silence as Veteranus lowered himself onto a log, the day's journey weighing heavily on his body. He rubbed his temples with calloused fingers, trying to ease the dull ache that had begun to throb behind his eyes.

Raven's eyes flicked across to him, recognising the symptoms. Without a word, he reached into the folds of his cloak and produced one of the vials that Veteranus had become accustomed to back in the village in Mona.

Veteranus stared at the vial for a moment, and with a small nod of acceptance, poured the liquid down his throat recognising the faintly bitter aftertaste. As the warmth began to spread through his chest and the pain in his head ebbed away, he stared into the fire, and his thoughts turned once more to the land he now found himself in. The evening stretched on, and as they finished their simple meal, he turned towards Raven.

'Can you tell me more about your people?' he asked.

'What do you want to know?'

Tell me about Mordred. What sort of a man is he?'

Raven leaned back against a fallen tree, the flickering firelight dancing across his face as he considered the question.

'Mordred was born into power,' he began. 'His father was the head druid at the time, a man feared and revered in equal measure and his mother was of royal blood. Mordred was the kind of man who was destined for greatness from the start. Even as a boy, he could manipulate men, bend them to his will and by the time he was grown, he was fearless in battle, clever in negotiation, and powerful in leadership. He united tribes that had warred for generations and commanded loyalty from everyone who followed him. Those who didn't...' Raven's dark eyes flicked toward Veteranus. 'Well, they tended to disappear.'

Veteranus's brow furrowed.

'And his enemies?'

'They respected him,' Raven said simply, 'but not enough to stop them from trying to destroy him. He has made more than his share of widows and orphans.'

There was a long pause before Veteranus asked quietly,

'And when you said he was going to change history, what did you mean by that?'

Raven's expression became guarded, his eyes narrowing slightly.

'You'll find out soon enough.'

Veteranus scowled but didn't push further. He had learned long ago that pushing too hard at a closed door often led to more trouble than it was worth. Instead, he shifted the conversation toward their pasts, probing gently at Raven's life before he had returned to the druids.

What began as cautious exchanges soon deepened into something more genuine. They spoke of battles fought and won, of blood spilled on foreign soils, and of the forests they had both come to see as home. Despite their differences, despite the opposing sides they had once stood on, they found common ground in the bonds of war and survival, until eventually, as the fires burned low, each man sought his sleeping blanket and fell into a fitful sleep.

----

The following morning, their journey continued with Veteranus none the wiser as to where they were going. By midday, a walled city appeared in the centre of a vast valley, its stout wooden palisades blending with the misty morning landscape. As they neared, the entire population of the town filed out of the gates, forming a loose semi-circle facing the oncoming column. Men, women, and children stood in solemn silence, their eyes fixed on the approaching party. The warriors slowed their pace and came to a halt, dismounting in unison. Raven swung down from his horse and turned to Veteranus.

'Come with me,' he said.

Veteranus followed as Raven strode forward, flanked by two of the druid warriors. They were met halfway by a group of village elders, their faces lined with age and weariness. The men carried themselves with a wary respect, clearly aware of the power the druid warriors represented.

After brief nods of greeting, one of the elders produced a clay jug, its surface stained from years of use. He poured mead into crude wooden cups, handing one to Raven and another to Veteranus. Satisfied, the elders gestured toward a long wooden bench set just outside the palisade.

'Sit,' one said gruffly.

Raven and Veteranus took their places, the bench creaking slightly under their weight. In front of them, the semi-circle of villagers shifted as a line of boys was brought out, herded forward by a man with a switch in his hand.

The boys ranged in age, size, and demeanour. Some looked eager, their eyes wide with hope or nervous excitement. Others seemed indifferent, their expressions blank as if resigned to their fate. They were paraded one by one in front of Raven, who inspected each one closely.

Veteranus leaned back slightly, watching the quiet procession. He wondered what Raven saw, what qualities he sought in these boys that set one apart from the others.

Moments later, Raven's brow lifted slightly, a flicker of interest breaking through his stoic mask as a tall boy took his place before him. His frame was wiry but strong, and he walked with a swagger that spoke of defiance, his gaze uninterested as though the entire affair bored him.

Raven rose to his feet, stepping closer. The boy tensed but held his ground, his disinterest giving way to a glimmer of defiance. Raven reached out, his fingers brushing the boy's jaw as he turned his head to inspect him more closely. When he opened the boy's mouth to check his teeth, the boy lashed out, shoving Raven's hand away with surprising speed.

The crack of the switch came instantly, the man behind the line of boys delivering a sharp lash across the boy's back. He stumbled forward, a hiss of pain escaping his lips, but he straightened almost immediately, his glare now fixed on Raven.

Raven said nothing and turned back toward the chieftain.

'Where did you find this one?'

The chieftain shrugged, leaning on his staff.

'A raid against a Deceangli settlement who had breached a treaty,' he said. 'His family fought hard, but in the end, he was all that was left worth taking.'

Raven's eyes flicked back to the boy, his lips pressing into a thin line as he resumed his inspection. He touched the boy's shoulders briefly, noting his frame, before returning to his seat.

The rest of the boys were paraded past, but Raven showed no further reaction. When the last boy was led away, the chieftain sat down opposite Raven, the firelight glinting faintly off his bronze armbands.

'I am interested in two,' Raven said finally. 'The one with the temper and the smaller one with the sharp eyes.'

The chieftain stroked his beard thoughtfully.

'Both are good stock. They'll cost you.'

Negotiations began, the two men haggling back and forth with the precision of seasoned traders. Eventually, silver coins changed hands, and the deal finally struck with a firm handshake.

As soon as the trade was complete, the villagers began to disperse, retreating within the safety of their palisade. There was no offer of food, no invitation to stay the night, only the clink of silver and the weight of mutual understanding.

Veteranus watched as the gates closed behind them

leaving him once again to wonder what kind of world he had stumbled into.

Ten minutes later, the riders sat astride their horses, the sound of restless hooves and the occasional snort of a mount breaking the quiet. Veteranus adjusted his reins and turned to Raven, who sat motionless atop his horse, his dark eyes fixed on the gates.

'What are we waiting for?' he asked.

Raven nodded toward the gate, his expression unchanged. 'Those.'

The gates creaked open slowly, revealing the two boys emerging together. They shared a single horse, the taller boy gripping the reins while the smaller one sat awkwardly behind him, clinging to his waist. The taller boy's face was set in a scowl, his defiance still flickering despite the lash mark across his back. His hair hung in wild, dirty tangles over his face, but his shoulders were squared, and his grip on the reins was firm. Behind him, the smaller boy hunched low, his head down and his arms wrapped tightly around the taller boy's waist. His slight frame seemed to sink further under the weight of the situation, his gaze fixed on the ground as if afraid to meet the eyes of the men waiting for him.

As they reached the riders, Raven turned his horse and began to head back toward the north without a word. The other warriors followed suit, their disciplined silence as unnerving as always.

Veteranus hesitated, his gaze flicking back to the two boys for a moment before urging his mount forward to catch up with Raven.

'Who are they?' he asked.

Raven's eyes remained on the trail ahead, as he answered.

'The taller boy, the one with spirit, is good stock. Strong, determined. With the right training, he'll make a fine druid warrior.'

245

Veteranus frowned.

'And the other?'

At this, Raven's expression shifted, a faint trace of something, perhaps intrigue, perhaps something darker, flickering across his face.

'He is weak, with no spirit. He is destined for something else altogether.'

Veteranus studied Raven for a moment, his brow furrowing.

'What do you mean by that?'

Raven glanced at him briefly, a faint, almost cryptic smile playing at the edges of his lips.

'Time will tell.'

The answer left more questions than it resolved, but Veteranus had learned by now that pressing Raven for answers was rarely fruitful. He let the silence stretch between them as they rode on, the two boys following behind under the watchful eyes of one of the druid warriors.

Though the forest around them was alive with the sounds of birds and rustling leaves, to Veteranus, the quiet among the riders carried an unspoken tension, as if the events of the morning had set something far larger into motion. Something he wasn't yet privy to, but knew he soon would be.

----

## Chapter Thirty-One

### Alexandria

The air outside the temple seemed thick and heavy, a palpable weight pressing down on Falco as he lingered in the shadowed doorway across the street. He adjusted his cloak for the hundredth time, cursing the stiff folds of the finery he still wore since leaving the abandoned meeting with the dancer. Here, every thread felt out of place, every polished line of his attire marking him as a man who did not belong here.

The hours seemed to stretch endlessly, his nerves tightening with each passing moment. Finally, his patience frayed to breaking, and he stepped forward, his hand reaching for the concealed gladius beneath his cloak, but before he could take another step, a voice broke the silence.

'Falco.'

He turned sharply, and relief washed over him as Seneca stepped into view alongside Sica. Behind them, Falco caught a glimpse of the beggar, lingering in the shadows like a wisp of smoke.

'Seneca,' he replied, his voice taut with urgency. 'You're here.'

'Thanks to our friend,' Seneca replied, nodding toward the beggar without looking at him. 'He said it was urgent. Start talking.'

Falco wasted no time and outlined everything. When he was finished, they fell silent, all three men processing what little information they had.

'What do we do?' Falco asked eventually.

'I don't see that we have any other option,' said Seneca. He glanced at Sica. 'Falco and I will go in first. You follow a few moments later, as if we've arrived separately.'

Sica grunted in acknowledgment, and, decision made, Seneca and Falco crossed the street and after a final pause, pushed the door open and stepped inside, following the steps down into the earth.

----

The interior of the temple was dimly lit, the flickering light of oil lamps and candles casting shifting shadows across the walls. Falco's eyes swept over the intricate images of Egyptian gods with imposing animal heads and unreadable expressions, doing his best to appear as inconspicuous as a man of his stature could manage.

The temple itself was quiet, with only a few dozen worshippers scattered throughout. They knelt or stood in silent reverence before the deities, their focus elsewhere, posing no immediate threat. Seneca, however, took note of each one, his sharp eyes flicking over their faces and postures. He had the practiced air of a man who was always assessing, always calculating, always ready for trouble.

When they reached the far end of the temple, they saw it, the door with the mark of a scarab carved above. A robed priest stood at either side, watching the newcomers with distrusting interest, their gazes flicking briefly over Seneca before lingering on Falco. It was no surprise, Falco's broad shoulders and imposing height drew attention wherever he went.

'Ready?' murmured Seneca.

Falco grunted softly, his hand brushing the edge of his cloak where his concealed gladius rested.

'Always.'

The two men strode forward in unison. As they approached, the priests straightened instinctively, their postures stiffening as if to assert authority. A flicker of unease passed through their eyes.

Seneca's gaze locked onto theirs.

'We're looking for two men,' he said, 'Romans. They

came here earlier today. We need to know if they passed through this door.'

The priests exchanged a brief glance before the taller of the two responded.

'We cannot say. Those who seek enlightenment here are promised complete anonymity. We honour their privacy.'

Seneca's eyes narrowed slightly.

'This isn't a matter of privacy. It's a matter of urgency. These men are in danger, and we need to find them immediately.'

The priest's expression remained neutral, his tone unyielding.

'We understand your concern, but the sanctity of the temple's traditions cannot be broken, even for urgent matters.'

A flicker of frustration crossed Seneca's face, and he drew in a slow breath, clearly working to maintain his composure.

'I'll ask you once more,' he said, his voice tightening. 'Did they enter?'

Before the priest could repeat his vague answer, Falco's large hand shot out and closed around his neck, and in one swift motion, hoisted the man off his feet to slam him against the wall.

The priest let out a strangled gasp, his feet kicking uselessly in the air as Falco's grip tightened.

'Open the door,' hissed Falco, 'or I'll break your neck and take the keys myself.'

The second priest froze for an instant, his eyes wide with panic, before his hand darted beneath his robe, reaching for a blade hidden at his side. But Seneca was faster and, in a single smooth motion, drew his pugio, the short dagger gleaming as he pressed it firmly against the second priest's throat.

'Don't,' he said softly, his full of menace.

The moments stretched unbearably, the second priest's chest heaving as he weighed his options. Finally, with a shout of desperation, he cried out.

'Let him go, we'll open the door!'

Falco's eyes burned with fury as he held the priest against the wall for another second, before releasing him. The man crumpled to the ground, clutching his throat and gasping for air, his face flushed and drenched in sweat.

Behind them, the worshippers in the temple had seen enough. One by one, they slipped out quietly, casting nervous glances over their shoulders. Within moments, the temple was nearly empty, the last few stragglers disappearing out the main entrance.

Seneca slowly withdrew the blade and stepped back. He nodded toward the scarab-marked door.

'You've delayed us long enough.'

The second priest, his hands trembling, withdrew a heavy brass key from within his robes. He hesitated for a moment, his gaze flicking nervously between Falco and Seneca, before he stepped toward the scarab-marked door. The key slid into the lock with a loud, metallic scrape, and with a sharp twist, the mechanism clunked heavily. The priest pushed the door slightly, and it swung open on well-oiled hinges, revealing a dim corridor beyond.

Falco gestured inside with a tilt of his head.

'After you. Both of you.'

The taller priest swallowed hard and stepped into the passageway, his companion following close behind. Falco and Seneca moved after them, the sound of their boots echoing in the confined space.

The air grew heavier as they descended the narrow corridor, the walls damp and unevenly cut, bearing the marks of tools that had shaped them centuries earlier. At the end of the passage, they came to the second door, this one a heavy slab of stone mounted on a steel pivot embedded into the floor. Its surface was worn smooth, save for faint markings etched near its edges.

Across the door lay a long steel bar, slotted into the walls to prevent it from being forced open from within.

'Open it,' said Falco.

One of the priest's pivoted the steel bar upward with visible strain, the weight of it making the task awkward and slow. Once the bar was clear, they pulled the door toward them, its hinges grinding faintly as it swung open.

Beyond the door, a faint light flickered, casting shifting shadows that danced across the uneven walls of the chamber beyond. Falco stepped closer, his piercing gaze fixed on the opening. He nodded sharply at the priests.

'Inside. Both of you.'

Reluctantly, the two priests stepped into the chamber. Falco followed close behind with Seneca a step behind him.

In the center of the room, the massive stone scarab loomed, its intricately carved body radiating an unsettling sense of presence. Around it, against the walls of the chamber, lay the perfect circle of coffins that Cassius and Decimus had already witnessed hours earlier. Inside each coffin, men lay restrained, their slack faces pale, their eyes half-closed as if trapped in a waking nightmare. Their bodies leaned forward, looking downwards as though anticipating something from the silent scarab.

Falco felt a chill crawl up his spine, a cold, unnatural fear. The room was oppressive, thick with an energy he couldn't name, and for a brief moment, he faltered, his hand tightening around the hilt of his gladius.

Seneca, too, was silent, his usual composure slipping as his sharp eyes darted from one coffin to the next. It was a scene out of a nightmare, something beyond anything he had encountered.

The sound of hurried footsteps behind them snapped Falco back to attention and he turned just in time to see the taller priest sprinting out through the door, slamming it shut behind him. Falco roared, charging the door and throwing his weight against it but the stone didn't budge, the bar on the other side already in place. He pounded against it with his fists, the dull echo reverberating through the chamber.

'Open it!' he shouted, turning on the remaining priest.

The shorter priest stood calmly near the scarab, his hands folded before him, his expression unnervingly placid.

'It is impossible,' he said, his voice eerily steady. 'There is only one way in and out of this chamber. The door is now barred, and my brother will not open it.'

Falco's face twisted with fury as he strode toward the man, his gladius half-drawn from its sheath.

'You will open it,' he growled, or I swear I will gut you like a fish.'

The priest didn't flinch.

'Even if I wanted to,' he said, 'I could not. We are all now bound to the will of this place.'

Falco's rage boiled over, his hand snapping forward to grab the priest by the throat, but Seneca's voice cut through the tension like a blade.

'Falco,' he said sharply, 'come here.'

Falco froze, his grip still tight on the priest, and turned to see Seneca standing a few paces away, his face pale and his eyes wide. He was staring at two of the coffins near the far side of the chamber.

Falco's eyes followed his gaze, and his breath caught in his throat. Inside the two coffins, restrained like the others, lay the unconscious forms of Cassius and Decimus.

----

The shock of finding their comrades quickly gave way to urgent action and the two men rushed to the coffins, their hands fumbling with the leather straps restraining their comrades. The bindings were thick and cruelly tight, biting into their skin, and it took several slashes of Seneca's pugio to cut them away.

As the last straps fell, the two men slumped forward like broken marionettes. Seneca caught Cassius as he fell, his heavy frame almost too much to manage while Falco lowered Decimus to the floor with more care.

'Decimus,' Falco growled, shaking him gently. 'Wake up.'

Decimus's head lolled to one side, his eyes barely open, their unfocused gaze moving sluggishly. His lips moved as though trying to form words, but all that came out was a slurred mumble, unintelligible and weak.

'They're drugged,' muttered Seneca, as he leaned over Cassius, trying to bring him around. He patted his comrade's cheek, then lightly slapped it, his tone rising. 'Cassius. Look at me. Come on!'

Cassius's eyelids fluttered, but his head lolled back, his body limp and unresponsive.

'They're breathing,' Seneca said with frustration, 'but we need to move fast before…'

A loud thud from the direction of the door interrupted him.

Falco had abandoned Decimus for a moment and was back at the stone barrier, throwing his shoulder into it with brute force. Each impact sent echoes through the chamber, but the door remained firmly shut. He turned, his face a mask of frustration and fury, and stormed back toward the priest now kneeling at the base of the scarab. The priest's arms were now stretched toward the stone effigy, his head tilted back, and his eyes closed as he recited prayers in a low, rhythmic tone. His calm was maddening.

Falco grabbed him by the collar and yanked him upward. 'How do we open that door,' he snarled.

The priest opened his eyes slowly, his expression serene.

'It is too late,' he whispered, his eyes drifting upward, 'look.'

Falco followed his gaze, his breath catching as he noticed the recessed balconies above the chamber. Silent figures stood in the shadows, black-clad sentinels, their faces hidden.

'Seneca!' he barked, 'look up!'

Seneca glanced upward, but as he watched, the priests above began to move, their black robes swirling as they filed out silently through their hidden exits.

'Can we get up there?' Seneca asked, his mind racing but before Falco could answer, the priest in his grip began to laugh, softly at first, then louder, until it turned into a hysterical, grating cackle. Tears streamed down his face as he gasped between bouts of laughter.

'It's too late,' he choked out. 'They're coming.'

Falco shoved him back toward the floor with disgust.

'Who's coming?' he demanded, but the priest only laughed harder, pointing weakly toward the scarab.

Wisps of pale mist began to creep from beneath the stone effigy, curling across the floor like grasping fingers and Falco stepped back instinctively, his eyes wide.

Seneca had already seen it, his sharp mind frozen for a brief moment as he watched the mist spread across the chamber. The mist thickened, the pale tendrils spreading out and rising as it engulfed the floor. Cassius and Decimus, still lying prone, were quickly being engulfed, the haze swirling around their faces, threatening to drown them in its eerie embrace.

'We need to move them,' shouted Seneca, *'now!'*

Falco grunted in response, hefting Cassius upright with one arm slung over his broad shoulders. Seneca did the same with Decimus, dragging him free of the mist and over to the door. The sound of the priest's manic laughter echoed behind them, a chilling counterpoint to the growing hiss of the mist as it spread like a living thing, climbing ever higher. Falco reached the door first, his free hand once again slamming against the unyielding stone. The sound reverberated through the chamber, each blow desperate and furious.

'*Someone open the damned door!*' he roared, his voice nearly cracking with the effort.

Seneca joined him, propping Decimus against the wall while he pounded on the door with the hilt of his pugio.

'*Sica!*' he shouted, his voice carrying over the priest's cackling. '*Sica, we're in here!*'

The mist climbed higher, licking at their necks.

Falco slammed his fist against the door again, panic creeping into his voice.

'*Sica! If you're out there, open the bloody door!*'

Just as the mist began to curl around their throats, a metallic sound echoed from corridor beyond and the door slowly opened, revealing Sica standing above the corpse of the priest who had escaped a few minutes earlier. He looked at them with a calm that only years of violence could bring, a bloody knife still held in his hand.

Falco didn't hesitate, dragging Cassius through the opening without a word. Seneca followed close behind, pulling Decimus with him as the oppressive mist swirled just inches behind them, its level lowering as it crept into the corridor.

Sica stepped aside, letting them through. Once past, he gripped the edge of the door, ready to slam it shut.

'Wait!' Falco gasped, and thrusting Cassius into Sica's arms, turned to return to the chamber.

'Falco!' Seneca shouted, 'what are you doing?' But Falco was already gone, disappearing back into the swirling mist.

For several agonizing seconds, Seneca and Sica stood frozen, their strained breathing the only sound breaking the silence. Then, as suddenly as he had vanished, Falco reappeared and draped over his broad shoulders was the limp body of the unconscious priest.

Sica's jaw dropped in disbelief.

'What are you doing?' he demanded. 'You should have left him there!'

'None of us have any idea what's going on here,' growled Falco, 'but this bastard does. He knows something and I'll be damned if I leave him to die in that hell without finding out what it is.'

Seneca and Sica exchanged a stunned glance. Falco's reasoning was sound, unexpectedly so. It was rare to see such calculated thinking from the usually brash and impulsive soldier. Seneca gave a curt nod.

'Fine. Let's move before something worse comes out of that place.'

Together, the group hurried back up the narrow corridor, Seneca and Sica supporting the groggy forms of Cassius and Decimus while Falco carried the priest's body like a sack of grain. They burst out into the street, the cool night air washing over them like a lifeline. The faint torchlight from the surrounding buildings cast long shadows, and the street was eerily empty, the temple's earlier visitors long gone.

Leaning against the far wall of the alley stood the beggar, his wiry frame shrouded in shadows. His presence was as quiet and unobtrusive as it had been earlier, yet his eyes gleamed with curiosity as they fixed on the strange procession emerging from the temple. He straightened slightly but said nothing, simply watching as the group sorted themselves out, catching their breath and finding their bearings.

Eventually, the men moved past him without a word, their focus on putting distance between themselves and the cursed temple. Falco took several paces before something pulled him to a halt. He froze mid-step, then slowly, he turned, his gaze falling on the beggar.

The beggar straightened further, his back no longer

touching the wall. Their eyes locked in a moment of silent recognition. There was no malice, no threat, just a quiet understanding that passed between them.

'Do you still have the ring?' asked Falco.

The beggar hesitated briefly before nodding. He reached into the folds of his tattered cloak and produced the ring, holding it up so it glinted faintly in the torchlight.

Falco stared at it for a moment, memories flashing through his mind like fragments of a half-forgotten dream.

'It was given to me by Emperor Gaius,' he said, his voice quieter now, almost reflective. 'It's now yours. Do with it what you will.'

The beggar's eyes widened slightly, but he said nothing, clutching the ring tightly in his calloused hand. Falco didn't wait for a response, and, with a curt nod, he turned away, his broad shoulders disappearing into the shadows as he followed Seneca and the others out of the alley.

The beggar remained where he was, staring at the ring in his hand. His fingers tightened around it, a flicker of something indescribable passing over his face. Then, with a glance toward the retreating figures, he slipped the ring back into his cloak and melted into the night.

----

## Chapter Thirty-Two

### Alexandria

The men of the Occultum gathered once more in the rented rooms near the docks. Cassius and Decimus sat slumped in chairs by the window, their faces pale and gaunt, their recovery slow despite the time that had passed. The ordeal in the temple had left its mark, though neither man spoke of it.

Falco paced the room like a caged animal, his footsteps a steady rhythm on the wooden floor. His tunic was rumpled, and his face was taut with frustration, the silence eating away at him. He stopped by the table long enough to pour himself another cup of wine, then resumed his restless movements, the drink barely touched as he muttered under his breath.

The others said nothing, their weariness matched by their shared unease. They had been holed up in the rented rooms for over a week, waiting, always waiting. Waiting for Seneca to return from the governor's palace. Waiting for a plan. Waiting for answers.

The sound of the door opening shattered the heavy quiet and Falco stopped mid-step, his head snapping toward the entrance as Seneca strode in.

Seneca closed the door behind him and crossing the room without a word, picked up the jug of wine and poured himself a cup, the liquid sloshing faintly as it filled the cup to the brim. The others watched him in uneasy silence, exchanging wary glances, but Seneca made no effort to fill the gap. Instead, he placed the cup down carefully, the faint clink of ceramic against wood the only sound.

'Well?' he said finally, his sharp eyes cutting through the room. 'What have you learned?'

'Nothing,' muttered Cassius 'The bastard refuses to talk.'

'Where is he now?'

'Locked in a room below a house down the alley,' said Cassius. 'Nobody will find him there.'

'We can't keep him much longer,' said Decimus. 'If he doesn't talk soon, we'll have to let him go.'

'Leave me alone with him for an hour,' said Sica. 'I'll make him talk.'

'You can't just kill a priest, Sica,' said Cassius.

'Not kill him,' said Sica, lowering his gaze to meet Cassius. 'Just cut him a little. You'd be amazed how much truth is hidden under the skin.'

'Enough,' Seneca snapped, cutting through the tension. 'This isn't a game, Sica. After what happened in that temple, we know something is going on, something dangerous. We need answers.'

'Do you think we don't know that?' said Cassius. 'The priest is useless, Seneca. He just sits there, muttering riddles and smiling like he knows something we don't.'

Seneca rubbed his temples, clearly restraining his frustration.

'There's possibly no direct link between what's happening in that temple and the chaos spreading across Egypt,' he said, 'but it's the only thread we have, and we're running out of time.' He reached into his robes and pulled out a scroll, placing it on the table. 'This came from Rome,' he said. 'From Lepidus himself. The emperor is getting impatient. If we don't uncover the truth behind this whole situation soon, we'll be recalled.'

Falco frowned.

'Recalled to Rome?'

Seneca shook his head.

'No. Reassigned. Scattered across the empire. The emperor has made it clear to Lepidus that if we fail, we'll be sent to different legions, different postings.'

The room fell into a heavy silence, the weight of Seneca's words sinking in.

'And what does that mean for the Occultum?' Cassius asked quietly.

'It means we're finished,' Seneca said flatly. 'The Occultum will be disbanded. No more missions, no more freedom. We'll become just another group of soldiers, scattered to the winds to rot in whatever backwater posting the Senate deems fit.'

Falco slammed his fist on the table, his frustration boiling over.

'Damn it, Seneca, we're doing everything we can! What else are we supposed to do? If this priest won't talk…'

'He'll talk,' Seneca interrupted, his tone icy. 'We just need to find the right lever. Everyone has something they fear. Even zealots.'

Falco broke the silence, the scrape of his boots against the wooden floor jarring in the stillness. He stood abruptly, his shoulders rigid with barely contained frustration.

'Where are you going?' asked Seneca.

'To break the bastard's knees,' he said.

'*Falco,*' shouted Seneca, '*Sit down.*'

Falco froze, his fists clenching at his sides. For a long moment, he stared at the door, his broad shoulders heaving with barely suppressed rage. His knuckles whitened as he ground his teeth, his body coiled like a predator ready to strike. The others watched in tense silence, the air in the room thick with unease.

Finally, with a slow, deliberate motion he turned away from the door and crossed the room to drop heavily back into his seat.

Seneca's sharp gaze lingered on him for a moment before he spoke.

'Good. Now sit still and listen.' He turned his attention to Cassius and Decimus. 'You two,' he said, 'tell us again what happened to you in that temple.'

Cassius shifted uncomfortably in his chair, his brow creasing.

'We already told you.'

'Tell us again,' Seneca interrupted. 'We need to be sure we haven't missed anything.'

Cassius shifted uncomfortably in his chair, his hands clasping and unclasping as he tried to gather his thoughts. Decimus sat silently beside him, his pale face cast in shadow, his expression unreadable. Finally, Cassius cleared his throat, his voice strained.

'It was... the mist,' he began, his brow furrowed as he stared at the floor. 'I remember it rising from the scarab. Pale, like smoke, curling and twisting across the floor. He hesitated, glancing briefly at Decimus, before continuing. 'There was fear,' he admitted, his voice quiet. 'Not just mine but everyone else in the coffins, I could see them. They were awake, just like me. Most of them looked terrified, but there were others...' He faltered, his face tightening at the memory. 'Some of them were smiling. Like they wanted to be there. Like they... expected something.'

The words sent a shiver through the room, but Seneca's sharp gaze remained fixed on Cassius.

'What else?' he prompted.

Cassius rubbed his temples.

'There was a sound. Someone crying. A man, in one of the coffins nearby. He wasn't screaming, just weeping quietly. The room was silent except for that. I don't know why, but it made everything worse. Like it was pulling at my nerves, and then... the priests came.'

'The priests?' asked Lepidus.

'They were dressed in black,' continued Cassius, 'like shadows. Each of them carried a bowl. I thought they might be offerings, but...' He trailed off, shaking his head.

'Go on,' Seneca urged.

'Each priest went to a coffin,' said Cassius. 'They didn't speak. They just stood there, waiting. Then a gong sounded, loud, like it came from deep within the earth. And that's when they removed the lids, lifting the bowls up to our faces.'

'What was inside them?'

Cassius swallowed hard, his face creasing in discomfort.

'Burning wads of something,' he said. 'Tiny bundles of plants that gave off small wisps of smoke. I tried to turn my head away but couldn't and was forced to breathe it in. We all were. The smell hit me first. Sweet, so sweet it was almost sickly. I could feel it in my lungs, in my head. It wasn't like smoke, it was... heavier, thicker, somehow.'

Falco shifted in his seat, his brow furrowing, but he said nothing.

'The priests stayed only a few moments,' Cassius continued. 'They replaced the lids, as though they didn't want to breathe it themselves, and then they left. Every last one of them, just... gone. And after that...' He hesitated, his voice trailing off as he searched for the words.

'After that?' Seneca prompted.

'I don't know,' Cassius admitted with a sigh. 'The smell, the mist, it made everything blurry. My thoughts... I couldn't hold onto them. I felt sleepy, like I was floating, and then...' He gestured helplessly, 'nothing. Just a faint dream, slipping away the more I try to remember it.'

Seneca frowned, his sharp eyes narrowing.

'What kind of dream?'

Cassius shook his head, his frustration evident.

'I don't know. I just remember... darkness...and shapes. That's it, really, and when I woke properly, I was wandering through the streets of Alexandria being held up by you.'

'That's it?' asked Falco from across the table.

'Sorry,' said Cassius, 'that's all I have.' He fell silent, his eyes downcast, as all attention shifted to Decimus, who had yet to speak.

'Decimus,' Seneca said, 'what about you?'

Decimus's head tilted slightly, his face partially obscured by shadow, but his trembling hands betrayed him. He didn't answer immediately, and when he finally looked up, the haunted look in his eyes was unmistakable. Cassius turned to him, his brow creasing in concern.

'Decimus?'

Decimus's lips parted as though he were about to speak, but no words came. The silence in the room thickened, the weight of whatever he had seen pressing heavily on everyone. Seneca leaned forward, his tone softening slightly but still insistent.

'Decimus. What did you see?'

Decimus's trembling hands clenched into fists as he stared at the floor, his shoulders hunched as if bearing a weight no one else could see. The room held its breath, the tension thick as the others waited for him to speak.

'Cassius is right, he said eventually. 'The mist, the smell, the priests... all of it. But...' he faltered, his eyes darting to Cassius and then to Seneca. 'My dream... it was different.'

Seneca leaned in slightly.

'Different how?'

Decimus swallowed hard, his Adam's apple bobbing visibly. He didn't answer immediately, his breathing uneven as he forced himself to relive whatever horror lingered in his mind.

'The room,' he began. 'got darker. I don't know if it was real or just the fumes, but the light from the torches, it faded. Everything felt... heavy. The air, the darkness. And then the sound started.'

'The sound?' Falco prompted, his tone uncharacteristically cautious.

Decimus nodded.

'A terrible sound. Like... like the earth groaning. Low and deep, but growing louder, sharper. It felt like it was coming from everywhere at once, shaking the walls, rattling my skull.'

Cassius shifted uneasily in his chair, his brow furrowing.

'I don't remember any sound,' he muttered.

Decimus ignored him, his voice growing more strained.

'I was scared. More scared than I've ever been. And then...' He paused, his hands gripping his knees so tightly that his knuckles turned white. 'Then they appeared.'

'Who?' asked Seneca.

Decimus raised his gaze, and the haunted look in his eyes sent a shiver through the room. Cassius stiffened, Falco leaned forward slightly, and even Sica lowered his gaze from the ceiling to stare at Decimus with rapt attention.

'The creatures,' Decimus said flatly, his eyes glazed and staring at nothing. 'Horrible, deformed things. They crawled out from beneath the scarab, through the cracks in the stone. At first, they were just shapes in the mist, but then... then they took form.' He shuddered, his breath catching.

'What did they look like?' Seneca pressed.

'Human,' Decimus said slowly, his face contorted in revulsion. 'But not human. Their limbs were wrong, too long, too thin. Like spiders. Their movements were jerky, unnatural, as though they didn't belong in this world. Their faces...' He hesitated, his voice faltering. 'Twisted. No eyes, just pits. Mouths that were too wide, full of teeth. They weren't... they weren't alive. They couldn't be.'

The room was silent, save for the faint creak of Decimus's chair as he shifted, his body tense.

'What happened next?' Seneca asked.

'They came closer,' Decimus continued, his words tumbling out now as though he needed to purge the memory.

'They moved through the mist, crawling, slithering, floating, whatever it was. And then they... they started to climb into the coffins.'

Cassius's face twisted in disbelief.

'What do you mean, 'into' the coffins?'

Decimus turned to him, his eyes wide.

'I mean they went into them. Into the prisoners. They wrapped around them, like smoke, but thicker, like they had weight. They poured into their mouths, their noses, their eyes. The other men... I could see them. Some were crying, some screaming, but others... others looked like they welcomed it. Like they wanted it.'

Falco muttered a prayer under his breath, his hand gripping the edge of the table as if to steady himself. Decimus's voice grew quieter, his words trembling.

'I couldn't move, but I could see it. The way the creatures... consumed them. And then...then it got worse.'

'Worse? gasped Falco. 'How?'

Decimus nodded slowly, his voice barely audible.

'More things appeared from the very air itself. The mist seemed to tear apart, like it was being ripped open, and from *they* came.'

'What are you talking about?' hissed Falco.

Decimus raised his head, his face pale as a corpse, his eyes glinting with something that might have been fear, or reverence. He looked directly at Falco, then at Seneca, his voice hollow as he spoke.

'The gods,' he said simply. 'The Egyptian gods.'

The room fell silent again, waiting for Decimus to continue, not sure what horror would leave his lips next.

'They weren't just statues or carvings,' Decimus began, 'they were alive. The gods of Egypt, floating around the room, moving through the mist. The crocodile came first,' he continued, his voice trembling. 'Sobek, I think they call him. His head, it was massive, with teeth like knives, but his body was… human, thick, muscular, and covered in scales. Its jaws snapped as it moved, and I could hear the sound, the crunch of bone, the tearing of flesh. It was everywhere, in my ears, in my mind.'

Cassius shifted in his chair, his brow furrowed deeply, but he said nothing. Decimus's words seemed to hold them all captive.

'And then came Anubis,' Decimus said, his voice dropping lower. 'He was worse. His head was a jackal, but his eyes… his eyes weren't like an animal's. They were glowing, yellow, like fire, but empty, soulless. He moved so slowly, like he was taking his time, like he wanted us to feel the weight of his gaze. His claws…' Decimus trailed off, swallowing hard. 'They were like knives, stained red, and every time he passed a coffin, the mist seemed to thicken, like it was alive and reacting to him.'

The others exchanged uneasy glances, but Decimus didn't stop.

'They weren't alone,' he said. 'I saw others. Thoth, he had the head of an ibis, but his beak was too long, too sharp, and when he moved, it was silent, like he wasn't even there. And Sekhmet… I could feel her heat from across the room. Her lion's head seemed too large for her body, and her mouth was open, her fangs glinting like they were ready to tear into someone. She circled the coffins, her eyes burning like embers, and everywhere she passed, the mist seemed to burn away.'

Falco shifted uncomfortably, his fists tightening on the table.

'Dreams can twist things, Decimus,' he said, 'that's all this was.'

Decimus ignored him, his voice dropping to a whisper as he continued.

'But then, finally,' he said. 'she appeared. Ammit.'

The name hung in the air like a curse.

'Ammit?' Falco asked, his voice tinged with unease.

'The devourer,' Decimus said, his hands trembling. 'The one who eats the hearts of the unworthy. Her head was that of a crocodile, massive and jagged, her teeth stained with blood. Her body was part lion and part hippopotamus, massive and hulking, her muscles rippling as she moved. But it was her eyes...' He trailed off, shuddering. 'Her eyes glowed, like fire burning in the pits of a swamp. She moved through the room with this... purpose, like she knew exactly where she was going.'

The men stared at him, their faces pale.

'She came toward me,' Decimus continued, his voice breaking slightly. 'Slowly at first, her claws scraping across the floor. I tried to move, but I couldn't. I could only watch as she came closer. Her jaws opened, so wide, and I could see the blood, the torn flesh, still clinging to her teeth.' He swallowed hard, his voice trembling. 'She stared into my eyes, and it felt like she was looking into my soul. I knew what she was there for. She was there for me.'

Falco exhaled sharply, breaking the silence.

'It was just a dream, Decimus,' he said again, 'a nightmare, nothing more.'

'No,' Decimus snapped, his voice stronger now. 'It wasn't just a dream. I could feel her claws on my chest, the weight of her body as she pressed down. I could hear the sound of my ribs breaking, the wet snap as her jaws... as her jaws reached into me.'

Cassius flinched, but Decimus didn't stop.

'She tore it out,' he shouted, making them jump. 'My heart. She ripped it out with her jaws. I saw it. I felt it. Beating, dripping with blood, clenched between her teeth.' He looked up, his haunted eyes locking on Seneca. 'And she was smiling.'

The room was silent as everyone stared in horror. Finally, Seneca broke the silence.

'It wasn't real, Decimus. Just a dream. The fumes, the

mist, it played tricks on your mind,'

'No,' Decimus said firmly, shaking his head. 'It wasn't a dream. Maybe the creatures, the gods, maybe they were, but the heart...' He hesitated, his voice dropping. 'The Egyptians believe that after death, a soul's heart is weighed against a feather. If the heart is impure, Ammit devours it. That's how they judge the dead.'

The others exchanged uneasy glances. Decimus looked up again, his face pale but resolute.

'Dream or not, it's clear to me now. My past has caught up with me and when I die, there will be no weighing, no mercy. I'll just be judged unworthy, and she'll take it. Just like she did in that chamber. The Roman gods have deserted me, Seneca, and my soul now belongs to Ammit.'

----

## Chapter Thirty-Three

## The Nile

The Nile stretched endlessly on either side of the Baris, its slow-moving waters gleaming under the late afternoon sun. For ten days, Marcus had watched the world drift past, endless stretches of reeds and palms, the occasional fishing boat, and the great stone temples that loomed over the riverbanks like silent sentinels of history. The journey from Syene to Alexandria was long, but it had its own rhythm. Passengers came and went at the river ports, their faces blending into the background of the voyage.

Yet two men had remained constant since Marcus had boarded, two fellow Romans who had, despite their vastly different stations, become his closest companions on the journey.

One was Lucius Aelius Scapula, a wounded Tribunus Laticlavius, the son of a senator back in Rome. He was a young but proud man, hardened by battle, though now worn down by pain. The other was Titus Cornelius Merula, a Medicus, assigned to tend to the Tribune's wounds and escort him back to Rome.

The three had formed an easy camaraderie over the past days, finding solace in shared experience and the slow passage of time on the river. They spent most of their waking hours together, whether drinking watered wine beneath the shade of the sail, sharing stories of their campaigns, or simply watching the sun sink behind the palm-lined banks. Unable to tell the truth, Marcus had spun a tale about being redeployed to Britannia, due to his experience fighting the Celts in Gaul.

'They'll need more than experience,' Scapula muttered, shifting painfully on his makeshift cot near the stern. 'The Celts fight like wolves. A single Centurion won't make much difference.'

Marcus had merely shrugged.

'Rome doesn't care for such warnings, he said, 'only for

victories.'

Scapula had laughed at that, though the sound had quickly turned into a painful cough. Marcus watched him now, reclining under the shade of the sail. The man was pale, his once-strong features hollowed by fever. His injury, deep wounds along his ribs, poorly healed, were slowly poisoning him. The medicus fussed over him again, checking the wrappings with an air of resigned frustration.

'You shouldn't even be awake, Tribune,' he muttered. 'You need rest, not more of your damned speeches.'

Scapula waved him off.

'Rest,' he scoffed. 'I'll have plenty of time to rest when we reach Alexandria. And more still when my father drags me back to Rome like a wounded dog.' His expression darkened. 'Damn him. I should be with my men, not lying here like a dying old man.'

Marcus studied him carefully.

'How did it happen?'

'The wound?' asked Scapula. 'Carelessness, overconfidence. A bit of both I suppose. I led a charge against a group of rebels in Numidia. They set a trap, and I took a spear to the side.' He glanced at Marcus. 'I killed the bastard who did it, but that didn't help when I was bleeding out in the sand.'

'You should be grateful your father had the influence to pull you out of that mess,' said Merula.

'He had no right,' said Scapula. 'My place is with my men.'

'You'd rather die in Numidia?'

'The choice was taken from me,' said Scapula. 'And now I'll be paraded through Rome like some tragic hero.'

Marcus exchanged a glance with Merula. The medicus said nothing, but there was an unspoken agreement between them. Scapula might even not make it to Rome at all. The wound was festering and despite Merula's best efforts, the infection was winning.

Marcus leaned back against the rail, watching as the sun dipped lower, the sky turning crimson over the Nile. The wind caught the sail, pushing them steadily northward, but for Scapula, Marcus wasn't sure how much time was left.

----

Two days later, Scapula's fever worsened, and the entire boat seemed to fall under a heavy, silent watchfulness. Merula, had tried everything, ointments, boiled herbs, wine mixed with crushed bark, but nothing had worked.

Scapula lay sprawled on his cot near the stern, his body shivering despite the humid night air. His skin had turned a ghastly shade of yellow, his lips cracked, and his breath came in shallow, uneven rasps. His fevered murmurs had long since dissolved into incoherent ramblings, the words spilling from his lips like the babbling of a madman.

The small gathering of passengers watched in quiet resignation. Some shook their heads, others whispered amongst themselves, but none could offer anything more than murmured condolences. Death was a familiar spectre on these long journeys. It had claimed men before, and it would claim Scapula soon enough.

A few of the older men muttered suggestions, cooler water, different herbs, prayers to their gods, but their voices were laced with the same helplessness that clung to them all.

Marcus stood at the edge of the group. He had seen many men die before, but something about this, about Scapula's slow, helpless descent, felt particularly cruel. He had been a warrior, a leader. It wasn't right that he should slip away, drenched in sweat, delirious and raving like some forgotten wretch. The moment stretched, heavy and unbearable, until a quiet voice broke the silence.

'I can help.'

The words were spoken softly, yet they cut through the murmurs like a blade. The gathered passengers turned in unison, their eyes falling on the speaker.

A small, hooded man, clad in black, stood behind them, his posture rigid, his face partially hidden beneath the deep folds of his cowl.

Marcus stared. The man had boarded the boat two days earlier, stepping aboard with quiet steps and speaking to no one. From the moment he arrived, the others had avoided him, edging away as if his very presence was cursed. Marcus had noticed, but he had not questioned it. Egypt was full of strange priests, strange gods. This one had been no different, until now.

The others hesitated, exchanging wary glances.

Merula, kneeling beside Scapula, wiped his brow and looked up, frowning.

'How?' he asked bluntly.

The priest slowly raised his hands and lowered his hood.

Muted gasps rippled through the gathered passengers and even Marcus felt a flicker of unease as his gaze settled on the tattoo of a beetle, inked in deep black on the center of the man's forehead.

The word image struck him like a hammer to the chest. Yet again, the scarab had become a feature in his life. It had appeared too many times, too many places. First in Aquae Tarbellicae when Lepidus had first mentioned a tenuous link, then in Pselchis mentioned by the servant and now here, on this boat, floating down the Nile under the silent watch of the gods.

He looked around as even the hardened sailors stepped back, some making the sign of protection against evil. A woman in the group whispered a quiet prayer, her eyes darting toward the priest as if expecting him to bring forth some terrible curse.

Marcus recovered quickly. Every instinct cried out not to

trust this man, but he had no one else to turn to. Scapula was dying.

'Can you save him?' he asked.

'I have potions that can ease his pain,' said the priest. 'They may not save his life, but they might keep him alive until Alexandria. Perhaps Rome has physicians there that can save him."

Silence fell over the deck once more as Marcus considered the priest's words. Had he detected a hint of sarcasm, mockery perhaps? Either way, he knew he had no other choice. With a short nod, he gestured toward the priest.

'Do it.'

The murmurs among the gathered passengers grew louder, uncertain, but Marcus silenced them with a single glare.

'Give him space,' he ordered, and one by one, they stepped back as the priest lowered himself to the deck, crossing his legs with practiced ease. His movements were unhurried, deliberate and he reached into the folds of his robes to withdraw a tightly rolled leather pouch, placing it carefully on the wooden planks beside him. A shallow clay bowl followed, along with a slender mixing stick, both of which he arranged with quiet reverence.

Marcus felt his patience fray at the man's agonizingly slow pace. Every moment lost was another step closer to death for Scapula. He shifted uneasily, but the priest gave no sign that he noticed or cared, until at last, he unrolled the leather pouch.

Inside, neatly arranged in tiny pockets, were several small clay bottles, their surfaces marked with faded symbols that Marcus did not recognize. The dim lantern light flickered over them, casting long shadows across the priest's fingers as he ran them lightly over each container, as if searching for something specific.

But it wasn't the bottles that caught Marcus's attention. It was the dried flowers tucked carefully into a larger pocket to one side of the pouch.

He caught his breath, his pulse quickening. He knew those flowers. The shape of the petals, the faded purple hue, the way the stems twisted together like woven thread…because he had his own bundle, hidden beneath his cloak, the ones he had stolen from the caravan.

A chill ran down his spine as his fingers instinctively brushed the hidden flowers at his side. Coincidence? Or something else? For the first time, Marcus felt a flicker of doubt. Who was this man? And what did he truly intend to do?

----

The priest's fingers hovered over the small clay bottles, his touch as delicate as a scribe selecting ink for a sacred text. He murmured something under his breath, words too quiet for Marcus to catch, before selecting three vials. With the same methodical patience that tested Marcus's nerves, the priest uncorked each bottle, carefully pouring the contents into the shallow clay bowl before reaching for a nearby water jug, tilting it slowly until the clear liquid joined the strange concoction, dark tendrils swirling as the powders dissolved.

Marcus shifted impatiently, but the priest gave no sign of haste. Taking up the wooden mixing stick, he stirred the liquid in slow, deliberate circles, the motion hypnotic.

Then, without warning, he lifted the bowl high, his hood falling slightly as his lips moved in a low, rhythmic chant. The language was ancient, the syllables curling and twisting like the river's current, unfamiliar and unsettling. The passengers, already wary of him, stepped back even farther, some muttering prayers of their own. Even Merula, the pragmatic medicus, cast Marcus a questioning glance.

Marcus said nothing. He simply watched.

The priest's chant grew softer, until the last whispered word faded into the night. Lowering the bowl, he gave a single nod to Merula.

'It is ready.'

Marcus crouched beside the cot as the medicus and another passenger carefully sat Scapula upright, his fevered body slack against their grip. The priest moved closer, placing the rim of the bowl against Scapula's cracked lips.

'Drink,' he murmured.

At first, the Tribune did not react, his head lolling to the side. But then the liquid touched his tongue, and his body jerked. He coughed, spluttered, trying to turn away, but the priest held firm, his voice low but commanding.

'Drink.'

Somehow, Scapula swallowed, his throat working sluggishly. More of the potion spilled onto his chin than made it down his throat, but he managed to take in enough before his body sagged back down onto the cot, exhausted. The crowd watched in uneasy silence, their faces tight with uncertainty.

'What happens now?' asked Marcus.

The hooded man studied Scapula's pale, fever-slick face, then met Marcus's gaze with dark, unreadable eyes.

'He will sleep,' the priest said simply. 'He will dream. He will fight. And by morning, there will be relief.'

Marcus frowned.

'Relief?'

The priest's lips pressed into a thin line.

'Either he will wake... or he will be dead.'

A murmur ran through the gathered passengers, but the priest did not linger to answer questions. Without another word, he turned away, pulling his hood back over his head, his form retreating into shadows.

He moved to the corner of the deck he had claimed as his own, settling himself among the stacked crates, his back against the hull. With a quiet sigh, he pulled the folds of his cloak tighter, concealing himself from the prying eyes of the others.

Marcus watched him for a moment longer, his thoughts troubled, and as the riverboat drifted onward through the black waters of the Nile, all he could think about was that black tattoo engraved onto the priest's forehead. The Scarab.

----

Morning crept over the Nile in soft gold and muted blue, the river still and glasslike beneath the first light of dawn. The wind was low, the water smooth, and the faint cries of distant birds echoed along the banks as the sailboat drifted northward toward Alexandria.

Marcus had barely slept and sat near Scapula's cot, watching, waiting. At last, the fever had broken, and the Tribune's chest rose and fell in a steady rhythm, his breathing no longer laboured, his face no longer twisted in pain. His skin, once burning to the touch, had cooled.

But Marcus was not at ease. His mind raced, and he turned his focus to the hooded man sitting alone, curled among the cargo crates at the far end of the deck. He had not moved since dawn, neither eating or drinking, seemingly oblivious to the world around him.

Marcus studied him for a long moment, then rose and strode toward him.

'He is stable,' he said. 'I thought you should know.'

'Alive, dead,' said the priest, 'ultimately it is all the same.'

Marcus took a step closer.

'What exactly did you give him?'

'Why does it matter?' asked the priest. 'You would not understand anyway.'

'Because,' said Marcus, 'I have seen some of those drugs before and would learn more of their capabilities.'

The priest sat motionless for a few moments before, turning his head slightly, just enough for Marcus to glimpse the lower half of his face.

'Be careful what you seek, soldier. Take your friend home to die amongst friends and forget what you saw here. The truth is not for the likes of you.'

Marcus felt a ripple of unease crawl down his spine but knowing he would get no more, he walked back towards the stern.

He was only halfway when a rough voice stopped him in his tracks.

'I'd stay clear of that one, if I was you.'

Marcus turned to find the captain standing near the mast, his weathered face creased with a look that was half caution, half warning.

Marcus took a step closer.

'Why?'

The captain shook his head.

'It doesn't matter what he did last night. The priests of the Scarab are not good people.'

Marcus narrowed his eyes.

'You say that with certainty.'

'That's because I know.' He glanced toward the priest's unmoving form before lowering his voice further. 'I carry him, and others like him, often. Always alone. Always quiet. But the same destination, every time.'

Marcus frowned.

'Where?'

'Saqqara. An ancient place for only the evil and the dead.'

Marcus felt his pulse quicken.

'We'll reach it in two days,' the captain continued. 'Just before the full moon.'

'What do they do there?'

The captain's gaze darkened.

'I don't ask. And neither should you.'

Marcus looked past him toward the priest, still motionless

277

in his corner. His fingers brushed the hidden bundle of dried flowers beneath his cloak. The same flowers the priest had carried. It may be nothing, but his instincts had not let him down so far. Eventually he turned back to the captain.

'Do you have parchment and a quill on board?

'I do,' said the captain. 'Why?'

I need to write a message to someone very important,' said Marcus. 'And I want you to deliver it.'

----

## Chapter Thirty-Four

### Alexandria

Seneca walked in silence down the alley, his cloak drawn tight against the filth clinging to the walls, his boots careful to avoid the slick patches of decay.

Ahead, Decimus navigated the ruins with ease and as they passed the skeletal remains of a building long since gutted by fire, Seneca exhaled sharply through his nose.

'How did you find this place?' he muttered.

'Cross enough palms with silver and you can learn anything,' said Decimus.

They reached the charred remnants of a doorway, its blackened beams stretching toward the sky like the ribs of a long-dead beast. The entrance gaped open before them, a hollow ruin leading into the husk of what had once been a home.

They stepped over the threshold and headed to a cluster of fallen timbers near the far corner and though they seemed haphazardly placed, their careful arrangement became clear as Decimus uncovered the heavy cellar door beneath.

He paused, glancing over his shoulder, his eyes narrowing as he checked the alley behind them. Satisfied, he pulled a candle from his belt, struck a flint, and touched the flickering flame to the wick. The dim light barely cut through the darkness as he reached down, grasped the handle, and heaved the door open. The hinges groaned in protest, the scent of stale air and damp earth rushing up to greet them both.

Decimus descended into the gloom, the candlelight casting shifting shadows against the stone walls. Seneca followed, his hand resting lightly on the hilt of his gladius as the weight of the underground pressed in around them. The steps led to a narrow passage, the walls damp and uneven, worn by time and neglect.

Water dripped from the ceiling, the soft plip-plip of droplets striking stone the only sound beyond their footfalls.

At the end of the corridor stood another door, this one heavy, reinforced with rusted iron bands. Decimus set the candle on a ledge, retrieved a key from his belt, and slid it into the lock. The mechanism clicked, and the door swung inward.

The small chamber was bare save for a single torch bracketed to the wall, its weak flame casting uneven light over the room's lone occupant. The priest was slumped against the far wall, his hands bound before him, his mouth gagged with a strip of coarse cloth. His robe was torn and stained, but his posture remained eerily composed despite the clear discomfort of his captivity.

Decimus untied the gag and withdrew a small flask from his belt, tipping it to the priest's lips. The priest drunk greedily as Decimus reached into his satchel and produced a chunk of hard cheese, placing it in the priest's hands.

The man ate in silence, his sunken eyes flickering between them, unreadable in the dim light. Seneca and Decimus sat back against the opposite wall, watching him, waiting.

The silence stretched between them, thick with unspoken tension.

'My name is Seneca,' said Seneca eventually, his tone almost conversational. 'I know you've refused to speak, and I can understand why. But I'm not here to waste your time, nor mine. I want to make a deal.'

The priest continued to chew slowly, his hollowed eyes fixed on Seneca with an unreadable expression. He swallowed, wiped the corner of his mouth with his wrist, then exhaled softly through his nose.

'A deal implies I have something you want,' the priest murmured. 'But I have nothing. I know nothing. I am just a servant of the gods. I do as I am told, and I ask no questions.'

Seneca leaned forward slightly, resting his forearms on his knees.

'Who tells you what to do?' he asked.

The priest shook his head.

'I do not know. I watch those who come to pray. I collect the offerings. That is my role. Sometimes, one of the priests in black comes to give instructions, but that is all.'

'And these priests?' Seneca pressed. 'Who are they? Where do they come from?'

The priest's bony shoulders lifted in a slow, resigned shrug.

'I have never asked. They appear, they speak, and then they are gone. That is all I know.'

Seneca studied him for a long moment, then leaned back with a slow, deliberate breath.

'Two of my men want to hurt you,' he said. 'It is all I can do to hold them back.'

The priest regarded him without reaction. Then, slowly, a faint smile ghosted across his lips.

'I do not fear pain,' he said simply. 'It does not concern me. Hurt me if you wish. It will make no difference. I cannot tell what I do not know.'

Seneca sat in thoughtful silence, his fingers steepled beneath his chin. The priest had been unmoved by threats, immune to the fear of pain, and indifferent to his own captivity. But everyone wanted something. He shifted his approach.

'Have you ever seen what happens to the men inside the inner sanctuary?' he asked, his tone lighter now, almost curious.

The priest's expression flickered, just for a moment. A hint of longing, a touch of something deeper than mere curiosity. He shook his head.

'No,' he admitted. 'I am not yet worthy.'

Seneca's eyes narrowed slightly.

'Not worthy?'

'Only those chosen by the gods may witness the enlightenment,' he said. 'Those who enter never speak of it, not even to us. All I know is that it changes them.' His gaze grew distant, his voice almost reverent. 'It is the greatest gift of all. To be remade. To see beyond the veil of this world.'

Seneca exchanged a brief glance with Decimus, a silent conversation passing between them. Then, turning back to the priest, he spoke carefully.

'My friend here has seen what lies within. He remembers it. Every detail. He could tell you, if you so require. Just give me something, anything useful, and he will reveal everything he knows.'

The priest's lips parted as if to speak, but no words came. He looked down, his fingers twitching against the stone floor as he searched his thoughts. Seconds stretched into silence.

With a sigh, Seneca stood and turned toward the door.

'Tie him up again,' he said.

But just as Decimus moved, the priest jolted upright.

'Wait,' he blurted. 'I remember something. It is not much, but… I think it is important.'

Seneca turned back.

'What is it?'

The priest swallowed hard and turned to Decimus.

'First, you must swear that you will tell me everything.'

Decimus hesitated. Then, with clear reluctance, he gave a slow nod.

'I swear.'

The priest licked his lips, his voice barely above a whisper.

'Sabratha.'

Seneca and Decimus stared at the priest, the name hanging between them like a weight. It meant nothing. Seneca frowned.

'Sabratha. That's a name?'

The priest nodded.

'I have heard it many times. It is important to the priests in black, though I do not know why.'

Seneca leaned in slightly.

'Is it a man or a woman? Roman or Egyptian? A priest, a noble, a merchant? Think. Anything you can remember.'

The priest pursed his lips, his brow furrowed as he searched his thoughts. His fingers twitched slightly, betraying his frustration as silence stretched between them, broken only by the distant dripping of water somewhere in the passage beyond. Finally, he exhaled, shaking his head.

'All I know,' he said slowly, 'is that somehow, the one called Sabratha is responsible for the smoke that brings the dreams.'

Decimus tensed, his fingers curling into fists against his knees. Even now, the memory of that thick, cloying smoke lingered in his mind, its taste still bitter on the back of his throat. He could feel it again, seeping into his lungs, wrapping around his senses, twisting reality into something unnatural, something wrong. The priest turned his gaze to him, eyes dark with expectation.

'Now,' he said, his voice eerily steady, 'you must honour your promise. Tell me what you saw.'

Decimus hesitated. He turned to Seneca, uncertainty flickering in his eyes. Seneca held his gaze for a moment, weighing something unspoken before giving the smallest nod.

'Get what you can from him,' he said, 'and see if you can find out more about this Sabratha. I'll be outside.'

He turned and pulled the door open. The hinges groaned, the torchlight flickering against the walls in the sudden draft. Decimus watched him go, his heartbeat drumming in his ears. Then, with a quiet thud, the door closed, sealing him alone with the priest.

The silence was suffocating. Decimus sat opposite the priest, legs stretched before him. The priest tilted his head, watching him with quiet curiosity.

'Well?' he murmured. 'Tell me.'

Decimus exhaled through his nose, steeling himself. He had faced battle, seen men gutted on the end of a sword, had watched life bleed from their eyes as they died in the mud. And yet, nothing had unsettled him quite like what he had experienced in that temple. The darkness. The voices. The gods.

He swallowed, closing his eyes for a brief moment as the memories stirred again, crawling back from the depths of his mind like creeping fingers dragging themselves up from the abyss. Then, voice hollow, quiet, and filled with a distant dread, he began to speak.

----

Seneca climbed the last few steps out of the ruined building, the night air cool against his skin after the damp weight of the cellar. He exhaled slowly, rolling his shoulders, his mind already moving ahead to their next step. Then he looked up and stopped dead.

A line of palace guards stood waiting for him, blocking the narrow street, their spears levelled in a bristling wall of steel. No one spoke. The air was thick with tension, the only sound the distant murmur of Alexandria beyond the alley.

Seneca's hand twitched toward the gladius at his side, but he didn't draw it. He was outnumbered and had no chance against so many men.

The line of guards shifted, their disciplined ranks parting with precise coordination and a figure emerged through the gap, stepping forward into the torchlight. Governor Postumus.

His robes were immaculate as ever, but his expression was dark with restrained fury. His sandals crunched against the dirt as he strode forward, stopping a few paces from Seneca. He did not speak immediately, letting the weight of his presence settle over the moment.

'Tell me, Tribune,' he said at last, his voice low and edged with steel, 'why are you holding a priest in captivity?'

Seneca did not answer.

The governor's eyes narrowed, and with a sharp gesture, he signalled to his men.

'Find him,' he ordered.

Two guards stepped forward, their spears lowering slightly as they moved past Seneca and into the building.

'What are you doing here?' asked Seneca.

'There are reports that a priest has been killed,' replied Postumus. 'And another taken captive. The culprits? A group of Romans, including a giant of a man.'

Seneca felt his stomach tighten. It didn't take much to guess who the 'giant' referred to.

The governor continued, his voice heavy with accusation.

'It wasn't difficult to piece things together, Tribune. And as fortune would have it, we found an informer who was very eager to tell us exactly where to find your men.'

Seneca glanced over at a beggar lurking in the shadows. The same man who Falco had given his ring. He turned his attention back to Postumus.

'Where are my men?' he asked.

'They are in custody,' said Postumus. 'And are totally safe… for now.'

'What do you mean?' asked Seneca. 'What's going on?'

'You have questions to answer, Tribune,' said the governor. 'And I suggest you start thinking about your answers carefully.' With a flick of his hand, he gestured to his guards. 'Take him away.'

Before Seneca could react, rough hands seized his arms, twisting them behind his back. Coarse rope tightened around his wrists, binding them tightly, then, with a hard shove, they dragged him forward, pulling him through the darkened streets toward the governor's palace.

----

## Chapter Thirty-Five

## Saqqara

The boat rocked gently against the dock as the gangplank thudded onto the worn wooden pier. The morning heat was already rising, casting rippling waves of distortion over the sands beyond the settlement. Saqqara loomed ahead, its ancient monuments barely visible through the haze of dust and sunlight.

One by one, the passengers disembarked, some eager to stretch their legs, others gathering their belongings with quiet resignation. Among them, the hooded priest moved with purpose, his black robes trailing like shadows behind him. He did not speak, did not look back, simply stepped off the boat and melted into the narrow streets beyond.

Marcus watched him go and picked up his pack to follow. The gangplank creaked beneath his boots as he stepped onto solid ground. The air was thick with the scent of spice and the ever-present dust of Egypt. Merchants called out in sharp, accented Greek, waving wares from shaded stalls, while donkeys and camels shuffled through the winding streets, their handlers guiding them with weary patience.

Ahead, the captain had already begun haggling with a local trader over a crate of dried dates and fresh bread, but as Marcus approached, the captain caught sight of him and abruptly broke off the exchange. He stepped forward, his expression dark with concern.

'Don't do this,' he said in a low voice. 'You have no idea what you're walking into.'

'Then tell me what you know,' said Marcus.

The captain exhaled sharply and motioned to the trader. The man hesitated but approached, his weathered face wary. He and the captain exchanged hurried words in the thick dialect of the region before the captain turned back to Marcus.

'The priests in black,' he said, his voice quieter now. 'They are dangerous. Every full moon, people disappear from this place. No one knows why, but it always happens on those nights, when the priests are here.'

Marcus glanced toward the dusty streets, where the priest had already vanished.

'Do they know where they go?'

'Yes,' the captain said grimly.

'But no man should follow.'

'Where?' asked Marcus. 'I need to know.'

The trader swallowed, his throat bobbing. Then, after a long pause, he whispered something under his breath and abruptly turned away, disappearing into the market. The captain looked back at Marcus.

'The City of the Dead,' he said. 'Now you know.'

Marcus stiffened. He had heard whispers of it before, Saqqara's vast necropolis, the ancient resting place of kings and priests, stretching into the desert like a labyrinth of stone.

He turned back to the captain and reached into his cloak, withdrawing a pouch. Inside was the folded message he had written the night before and the flowers and powder he had taken from the caravan. He pressed it into the man's hand.

'Take this to the governor's palace in Alexandria, he said. 'Find a man named Seneca. Tell him everything you just told me.'

The captain hesitated, placed the pouch beneath his Thawb.

'I'll see it done.'

'Thank you,' said Marcus and with a curt nod, turned on his heel and strode into the town, his path set, his destination clear. Behind him, the captain watched him go, then shook his head and turned back toward his boat.

----

Marcus moved quickly through the winding streets of Saqqara, his thawb shielding him from unwanted attention. He kept his distance, never lingering too long in the open, never walking too fast nor too slow. The priest never looked back, seemingly unaware of the silent shadow following him.

Beyond the town, the land sloped upward, shifting from cracked streets to barren, rocky ground. The plateau that separated the fertile Nile Valley from the endless sands of the Sahara loomed ahead, its rocky slopes burned orange by the fading sunlight. It was a stark divide, on one side, life and water: on the other, desolation and dust.

Halfway up the escarpment, the first remnants of the necropolis emerged and even from a league away, Marcus could see its vast sprawl. The city of the dead, ancient even before Rome's first stones were laid and a sacred burial ground for the rulers of Egypt's earliest dynasties. It was an expanse of crumbling mastabas, towering stone pillars, and deep-cut burial shafts, all scattered among the shifting dunes. Some tombs stood open to the sky, their inner chambers exposed like wounds, while others remained hidden beneath the sand, their entrances sealed by time and secrecy.

The most imposing of them all was the Step Pyramid of Djoser, rising in the distance like a great, tiered monolith. It was a place of whispers, where the past refused to die, where the spirits of the long-dead lingered in the shifting winds.

Ahead, the priest stopped at the edge of the town, where a small cluster of market stalls catered to late-day travellers. He exchanged a few coins for a loaf of flatbread and a handful of dried dates, then moved to a shaded corner near a low wall, settling himself on the ground to eat. His posture was relaxed, but his eyes, dark and watchful, stayed fixed on the setting sun as it dipped behind the plateau, casting long shadows over the necropolis.

Marcus followed suit, choosing a different establishment, one that offered a shaded view of the street. He ordered nothing, simply settling himself against a wooden post, his gaze locked firmly on the priest.

The sun bled across the sky, turning the world gold and crimson as the first hints of night crept over the desert. The air grew still, but Marcus did not move. He waited.

Night tightened its grip on the desert, the heat of the day slowly bleeding away as a ghostly chill settled over the landscape. Overhead, the moon hung swollen and bright, casting a pale glow over the necropolis, its silvered light stretching long, spidery shadows between the broken ruins and sunken tombs.

Finally, the priest got to his feet, his black robes flowing around him as he left the town behind. He never faltered, never paused to check his surroundings. He knew precisely where he was going.

Marcus followed, his body tense. Instincts honed from years of survival warned him that this was not an ordinary chase. The moment they had stepped beyond the last of the mudbrick homes, the sounds of the town had vanished, swallowed by the vast silence of the desert. No voices, no music, no distant bray of donkeys or the cries of merchants haggling over their wares, only the soft whisper of the wind stirring through the sand and the distant hoot of an unseen owl.

He kept his distance, his movements careful. The thawb he wore helped him blend with the night, but it was his experience that kept him unseen. He moved from shadow to shadow, mirroring the priest's steady gait, his eyes locked onto the dark figure ahead.

The land began to rise, the ground shifting from packed dirt to uneven rock as they neared the plateau. Here, the necropolis began, stretching up the escarpment in a silent, sprawling maze of the dead. Even from a distance, it was overwhelming.

Marcus felt the weight of history pressing in. This was a place of kings and priests, of gods and forgotten rituals. Even the air tasted different here, drier, thinner, tinged with something ancient. And yet, the priest moved without hesitation.

Marcus frowned. Most men would glance around at least once when walking into a graveyard at night, even the bravest feared the dead. But this man never hesitated. He did not check for pursuers, did not even appear cautious. He walked as if he belonged here.

A cold unease settled in Marcus's gut. He quickened his pace, careful to keep to the deeper shadows. The priest was becoming harder to follow, slipping behind the tombs, his dark robes melding into the ruins like smoke.

Marcus cursed under his breath. He needed to get closer. The ground sloped upward, leading toward the rocky escarpment that marked the boundary between the necropolis and the deeper desert beyond. The terrain grew harsher, jagged boulders jutted from the sand, the pathways twisting unpredictably between crumbling mausoleums. The priest's movements grew more fluid here, as if he had walked this path a hundred times before.

Marcus caught one last glimpse of him, then suddenly, he was gone. Marcus stopped dead, his eyes sweeping the landscape. Nothing. No sound, no flicker of movement. One moment, the priest had been there, silhouetted against the pale rock, the next, he had vanished.

He took a step forward, then another, his pulse quickening. The land ahead was open, there was no cover large enough to fully conceal a man, no passage or cave that he could see. He hurried forward, his fingers twitching toward the dagger hidden beneath his thawb. Where in Hades had the bastard gone? The silence pressed in. His every step felt deafening now, his boots crunching against the loose gravel, his breath sharp in his ears.

The wind had died completely. Marcus swallowed. Something wasn't right. A prickle of unease crawled up his spine, slow and deliberate, like a spider skittering over bare skin. His instincts screamed at him, leave, turn back, this is not your place. He ignored them.

He scanned the area once more, his fingers gripping the dagger's hilt. He took another step forward, Then he heard it, a soft sound, just behind him. His muscles tensed, his body moving on instinct. He whirled, hand flashing toward his weapon but he was too slow, and a heavy blow crashed against the side his skull. White-hot pain exploded through his vision, his knees buckled, and the world tilted violently as his body gave way beneath him.

The last thing he saw was the moon, huge and luminous, watching from above like the eye of an indifferent god, and then… the darkness swallowed him whole.

----

## Chapter Thirty-Six

### Alexandria

Seneca sat alone in the dimly lit antechamber. The room was sparse, stone walls, a single narrow window that let in a sliver of daylight, and a wooden writing desk that had seen better years. A jug of watered wine sat untouched on a side table, but he had no appetite for it.

He exhaled slowly, staring at the wall opposite, though his mind was far from still. He was at his wits' end. Weeks had passed, and he was no closer to the truth than when he first set foot in Alexandria. The crisis gripping Egypt, the dwindling grain shipments, the growing unrest, the whispered fears that something unnatural was at play, remained an enigma. He had found threads, yes, but none had yet woven into something tangible. Every answer led only to more questions.

And now, his mission stood on the brink of failure. His men, his Occultum, were imprisoned beneath the palace, held in cramped cells like common criminals. He had no idea how they were faring, whether they were being mistreated, whether they still held hope or if doubt had begun to fester among them. He had tried to demand answers, but the governor had allowed no contact.

And then there was Marcus. Weeks had passed without a single word from him. No reports, no messengers bearing his seal. Had he failed? Had he been captured? Or worse? Seneca's gut twisted at the possibilities. Marcus was one of the best among them, experienced, disciplined, unshakable. If he had vanished, it did not bode well. And yet… despite it all, Seneca knew they were close.

The name, the one word given by the priest in the cellar, Sabratha. It had to mean something. He had turned it over in his mind endlessly, searching for some connection, some hidden meaning, but nothing fit. Still, the priest had been certain. That was the key to it all. He could feel it. But was it enough? No matter how close they were, none of it would matter if they were recalled. The Occultum would be disbanded, its men scattered to postings across the empire, swallowed by the legions like grains of sand in the desert. If that happened, the truth, whatever it was, would be lost forever.

A sharp knock on the heavy wooden door jolted him from his thoughts. The iron latch clicked, and the door creaked open to reveal a Decurion standing in the threshold. He was an ever-present face in the palace, a trusted man, and over the previous weeks, had become quite friendly with Seneca, often playing dice with him in the small hours when Seneca couldn't sleep.

For the briefest of moment's Seneca entertained the possibility of bribing him, but as quickly as the thought came, it disappeared. Despite his friendliness, the Decurion was a professional soldier and obviously loyal.

'Tribune Seneca,' he said, 'you need to come with me. The governor demands your attendance.'

'Thank you Decurio,' said Seneca with a sigh, before following the guard into the corridor.

----

Several minutes later, Seneca stepped into the chamber, the heavy door closing behind him with a dull thud. The room was dimly lit, the air thick with the scent of parchment, oil lamps, and the faint traces of incense.

At the far end, behind a broad wooden desk, sat Governor Postumus. His expression was unreadable, his fingers steepled as he regarded Seneca with a gaze that carried both expectation and quiet authority. But Seneca's attention was quickly drawn elsewhere.

On this side of the desk, seated with her back to him, was

a woman. Her presence was unexpected, out of place in this room of politics and power and for a moment, confusion flickered through him, his mind scrambling for an explanation. Then the scent reached him. Soft, unmistakable, familiar. He knew that fragrance, a scent that had lingered in his memory longer than he cared to admit.

His steps slowed as he neared the desk. Then, as if sensing his presence, she turned to face him. The Lady Callista. Seneca stared at her, his mind struggling to make sense of her presence. What in Hades was she doing here?

Memories surged unbidden, the warmth of her skin beneath his hands, the way she had whispered his name in the dim light of the oil lamp, the scent of salt and jasmine clinging to her as they lay tangled together on that tiny offshore island. A night that had felt like it belonged to another life. A moment stolen from the chaos of his duty. He turned sharply toward Postumus.

'What is going on?' he demanded. 'Why is she… '

'Sit down, Seneca!' the governor snapped, his patience already thin.

Seneca hesitated, his eyes flicking once more to Callista, searching her face for some clue, some unspoken message. But she gave away nothing. With a slow breath, he lowered himself into the chair opposite the governor's desk, his body tense.

Postumus stared at him coldly. His next words were cold and clipped getting straight to the point.

'Why did your men murder a priest and kidnap another?'

Seneca exhaled through his nose, pausing before answering. His instincts screamed that this was a trap, a carefully laid snare meant to force his hand before he could understand what game was being played. Instead of answering, he turned again to Callista.

'Why are you here?' he asked, his voice quieter now, but edged with something he couldn't quite hide.

Her lips parted slightly, as if she meant to speak, but before she could answer, Postumus cut across them both.

'I asked you a question, Tribune,' the snapped, 'answer it. Now.'

Seneca sighed, leaning back in his chair. He knew better than to antagonize a governor in his own palace. He considered lying to protect his men, but the fact that they were here on the emperor's business held a lot of weight, and sometimes, when things went wrong, men died. It was as simple as that.

'Two of my men were taken,' he said evenly. 'Drugged and tied up inside the temple by the priests. We had to get them out before they were,' he hesitated, searching for the right words, 'before anything lethal could happen to them.'

Postumus said nothing, his expression unreadable.

'In the process of getting them out,' continued Seneca, 'one of the priests was killed. It was… unavoidable.' He let the word hang in the air, careful not to sound either too remorseful or too indifferent. 'The other we took alive, hoping to find out what was happening in that temple.' He met the governor's gaze evenly. 'That's the truth.'

Silence in the chamber stretched thick and heavy, and then, at last, Callista spoke. Her voice was just as he remembered, soft and as smooth as flowing water. It stirred something in him, something he thought he had buried in the weeks since she had left.

'Did you know your men paid to enter the temple?' she asked.

Seneca frowned.

'Why does that matter?'

Callista didn't answer immediately. Instead, she reached into the folds of her robe and withdrew a small object, setting it gently on the polished wood of the governor's desk. A golden scarab.

The lamplight caught the edges, making it gleam, a tiny, perfect thing, carved with intricate markings.

'Because,' she said simply. 'This was handed over by one of your men in exchange for enlightenment.'

Seneca stared at the scarab, then at her.

'They may have used it to gain access,' he admitted. 'But that doesn't change what happened. They were drugged in some kind of mist and then tied into coffins.'

He expected shock, disbelief, maybe even amusement, but Callista's face remained calm. When she finally spoke, her voice was quieter, almost reverent.

'Yes,' she said. 'They were. That was what they paid for.'

A chill crept into Seneca's spine.

Callista leaned forward slightly, her gaze unwavering.

'It is part of the ritual, Seneca. People pay a great deal to experience the full ceremony. To go through the first encounter with the mist and everything that follows. Whether their experience is joyous or terrifying, it is what they seek.'

The chamber felt colder now, the weight of her words pressing down on him.

'It is a sacred journey,' she finished, 'revered by many people in this city. And you, and your men have dishonoured it.'

Seneca felt the ground shift beneath him, not physically, but in his mind, in the foundation of everything he thought he understood. They *paid* for it?

The words rattled through his skull, colliding with logic, with instinct, with the undeniable truth of what he had seen in that temple. He had thought them victims, helpless men drugged and bound in the dark, prisoners of a twisted ritual. But Callista spoke as if it had been a privilege, as if those men had gone willingly into the mist and the coffins, eager to surrender themselves to whatever nightmare awaited beyond. His pulse hammered in his throat. No. It made no sense.

He forced himself to focus, to latch onto something solid in the storm of his thoughts. His gaze flicked to the scarab still resting on the table.

'And this?' he asked, his voice sharper than he intended. 'What does this mean? What does a scarab have to do with any of this?'

Callista shook her head in frustration.

'You still don't understand…'

'I understand the scarab means something,' snapped Seneca. 'It's all connected. There is a sect, one that is controlling Egypt, manipulating its people. The dwindling harvests, the low crop returns, it's all part of something larger.'

Callista's expression darkened, her amusement vanishing in an instant.

'You think the scarab is a sign of corruption?' she gasped, 'of conspiracy?' She shook her head slowly. 'You see the surface of things, Seneca, but not the depth.'

She reached forward and picked up the golden scarab from the table, holding it delicately between her fingers, the lamplight dancing along its polished back.

'The scarab,' she continued, 'is one of the most sacred symbols in all of Egypt. It represents Khepri, the god of the rising sun. We believe the sun is reborn each morning, rolling across the sky just as the dung beetle rolls its sphere of earth. It is a symbol of life, of renewal, of transformation.' She turned the scarab slowly, letting Seneca watch as it caught the light. 'But more than that, it is a sign of the unseen. Of the forces that work beneath the surface, shaping the world in ways we do not always understand.' Her eyes flicked up to meet his. 'It is not a symbol of power, but of faith. And faith, Seneca, is not something you can control.'

Seneca's gaze remained locked on the small golden scarab.

'Then explain the sects,' he said quietly. 'Why do they operate in the shadows instead of the open?'

Callista sighed, placing the scarab back onto the desk.

'There are hundreds of groups across Egypt who hold the scarab sacred. Some are simple devotees, worshippers who honour the old ways. Others seek enlightenment, believing the scarab holds the key to rebirth, not just of the sun, but of the soul.' She hesitated. 'And yes, some take it further. Some twist its meaning into something darker.'

Seneca frowned.

'So, you admit there are those who use it for their own gain?'

'As there are in every faith,' said Callista eventually, 'but do not mistake belief for corruption, Seneca. Not all who follow the scarab are evil.'

She moved the collar of her gown and pulled on a chain around her neck to withdraw a pendant and Seneca was momentarily stunned into silence. It was a crystal scarab. He swallowed hard, the implications sinking in like a stone thrown into deep waters.

'If your theory is correct,' she said, 'then what does that make *me*?'

Seneca lifted his gaze, meeting hers, but he found no answers there, only a challenge. A silent demand for him to *say it*. To call her what his accusations implied. A conspirator? A criminal? A murderer? But he couldn't. His mind, usually so quick to find patterns, to see the invisible strings of a larger game had failed him.

Callista exhaled softly and replaced the pendant.

'You are mistaken, Seneca,' she said. 'And your mistake has cost a priest his life.'

'I've heard enough,' said Postumus, interrupting. 'Your time here is over, Tribune. You and your men will be sent back to Rome and will probably be tried for murder. Until then, you are confined to the palace until further notice. If you run, then be assured, your men will pay the price. Now, begone.'

Seneca stood slowly. His movements felt distant, like they belonged to someone else. He turned toward the door, but something inside him resisted, one last ember of defiance.

'One more thing,' he said, turning to face Callista. 'Does the name Sabratha mean anything to you?'

A flicker of frustration crossed Callista's face. She exhaled sharply, shaking her head.

'I know nobody called Sabratha,' she said. 'You're chasing ghosts, Seneca. Running down blind alleys. You need to let this go.'

Seneca stared for a few more moments before nodding slowly and stepping out, the heavy door shutting behind him.

----

The corridor was dimly lit, the air thick with the scent of burning oil from the torches lining the walls. The Decurion walked beside him, back toward his chamber.

'I heard the conversation,' he said, 'that name you said in there... Sabratha?'

'What about it?'

'I've heard it before.'

Seneca's pulse quickened. 'Go on.'

The guard exhaled, his brow furrowing as if pulling the memory from the depths of his mind.

'It's not a person,' he said at last. 'It's a place. A port city on the coast west of Carthage in the province of Africa Proconsularis.

'Isn't that near Leptis Magna?' asked Seneca.

The Decurion nodded.

'It is and it is a very long way from here.'

----

## Chapter Thirty-Seven

### Alexandria

Seneca lay on the narrow cot, staring at the cracked plaster of the ceiling, his hands resting on his chest. His thoughts circled the same frustrations, his men, locked away beyond his reach, their fate hanging in uncertainty. Every request he had made to see them had been denied, every effort to assert his authority, dismissed. He was no longer a Tribune here; he was a man in a gilded cage, waiting for judgment.

A servant arrived in the morning with a wooden tray, laying it carefully on the small table by the window. Bread, dates, watered wine, enough to break his fast, but he found he had no appetite. The servant lingered only a moment, glancing at him as if expecting some command, then departed in silence.

The day stretched on, the heat pressing against the walls of his chamber, thick and unmoving. Outside, the city lived, voices drifted through the window, merchants calling, donkeys braying in the streets below, but within these walls, time felt stagnant.

It was only when the sun began to dip toward the horizon that the door opened once more, and the Decurion stepped inside.

'There's someone to see you,' he said.

Seneca sat up.

'Who?'

The Decurion didn't answer, only gestured for him to follow.

He rose, smoothing the creases from his tunic, and fell into step beside the guard. They walked in silence, their footsteps echoing through the stone corridors but instead of leading him outside, the Decurion stopped at a door off the main hall, pushing it open to reveal a dimly lit antechamber. A man stood waiting inside.

Seneca slowed, his eyes narrowing as he took in the stranger, tall, broad-shouldered, draped in a cloak that had seen better days.

The Decurion stepped back, pulling the door shut behind him, leaving Seneca and the stranger alone. The man shifted his weight, adjusting the folds of his worn cloak. His skin was tanned from years on the river, his voice rough, like a man accustomed to shouting orders over wind and water

'I'm a captain,' he said simply. 'My ship runs the Nile, from Alexandria to Syene and back again.' He reached into his belt and withdrew a pouch. 'A few days ago, I took on a passenger. He left my boat a few days ago but before he went, he asked me to deliver this.'

Seneca frowned but took the pouch, opening it to see a folded parchment inside. He glanced at the seal, it had been pressed hastily, the imprint barely discernible. He unwrapped it, his fingers tracing the familiar, sharp strokes of the handwriting. Marcus.

He read the words once, then again, slower this time, as if the meaning might change upon second reading. But it did not. He looked up at the captain, his mind racing.

'Where is he now?'

'Last I saw him, he was heading for the Necropolis in Saqqara.'

Seneca exhaled sharply, glancing at the words on the parchment once more. Saqqara, the city of the dead, an ancient necropolis older than Rome itself. Temples, tombs, secrets buried beneath the shifting sands of time. And now, Marcus. His pulse quickened.

'When was this?'

'Three days ago.' The captain hesitated. 'But there's something else.'

Seneca narrowed his eyes.

'What?'

'When I was at the docks in Saqqara, I spoke with a trader. He told me your friend should never have followed the priest, that he was in mortal danger.' The captain's expression darkened. 'And that if he is caught, whatever fate awaits him… it will happen on the last day of the full moon.'

Seneca's breath caught.

'How long do we have?'

The captain met his gaze.

'Two days.'

Seneca folded the parchment carefully, slipping it into the belt at his waist. His mind snapped back into focus. He had been trapped in this palace for too long, playing a game he did not understand. Now, he had direction. A path forward. He met the captain's gaze.

'If I needed passage up the Nile to Saqqara, how quickly could you arrange it?'

'My boat is already waiting,' he said, 'but you need to move quickly,' and with that, he left the room and headed down the corridor, closing the door behind him.

Seneca stood alone in the dimly lit chamber, the weight of urgency pressing against his ribs. He began pacing, his thoughts clawing through the scattered pieces of information, trying to force them into some kind of order. But there were still too many gaps, and every second wasted was another step closer to disaster.

Frustration surged through him until suddenly, he turned and banged his fist against the door, the impact sending a dull echo through the stone.

'Decurion,' he shouted, 'open this door!'

A moment later the door swung open, and the realization hit Seneca like a hammer. *I have no choice. I have to trust him.*

'Listen to me,' he said. 'I need to speak to my men.'

The Decurion's expression remained stony.

'That's not possible, Tribune.'

'It has to be,' Seneca pressed, stepping forward. 'I have new information… information that could change everything. But I need to ask my men something first.'

The Decurion hesitated.

'You know my orders, Seneca. I can't do that.'

'Damn the orders,' snapped Seneca. 'If I'm right, the future of Rome is at risk.' He let the words hang, watching as the Decurion's brow furrowed ever so slightly.

'You and I both serve Rome,' he said. 'We have both fought for her, bled for her. I swear to you, this is bigger than any one of us. But if we move now, if we act together, we might have a chance, not just to stop whatever is happening across Egypt but also to save a fellow legionary from certain death.'

The silence between them stretched, thick with unspoken weight, until finally the Decurion's took a deep breath and exhaled slowly.

'Follow me.'

----

## Chapter Thirty-Eight

### Alexandria

The Decurion led him through the torch-lit corridors before stopping before a locked wooden door. The Decurion reached into his belt, withdrawing a key. As he fit it into the lock, he turned to Seneca.

'Be quick.'

Seneca gave a sharp nod. Inside, the chamber was small, the walls bare. A single torch burned in an iron sconce, casting long shadows over the four men seated against the wall, Falco, Decimus, Sica, and Cassius.

Falco pushed himself up, stretching stiff limbs, his sharp eyes locking onto Seneca with something between relief and impatience.

'About time,' he muttered. 'Are we getting out of here?'

'Not yet,' said Seneca. 'First, I need some answers. Fast.'

'Answers about what?'

Seneca turned sharply, his gaze locking onto Sica.

'Think back,' he said. 'At the dinner in the royal palace, after the gladiatorial fight, what did you eat?'

Sica blinked, caught off guard.

'Why?'

'It doesn't matter why,' Seneca pressed. 'Just think. What did you eat?'

Sica hesitated, his brow furrowing as he tried to recall.

'Uh... there was roasted lamb, I think. Some olives. A dish with honey and dates and some fish.'

Seneca turned to Falco.

'And you?'

Falco frowned.

'Same as him, more or less. Lamb, olives, bread, and

wine.' He rubbed his jaw. 'Why does this matter?'

Seneca ignored the question. He studied them carefully before asking,

'That night, did either of you experience the dreams?'

Sica looked confused.

'Dreams? No.'

Falco shifted, his expression changing.

'I did. But it wasn't too bad. Just flashes, but nothing like Decimus experienced in the temple.'

Seneca nodded slowly, his mind racing. He turned to Cassius.

'And you? Have you ever had the dreams?'

Cassius shook his head without hesitation.

'Never.'

Seneca exhaled sharply, the pieces clicking into place. He turned back towards the door.

'I have to see the governor.'

'Seneca,' Falco started, but Seneca cut him off.

'I'll be back as soon as possible,' he said, 'so be ready… we are getting out of here.'

----

Seneca strode out of the chamber, the Decurion falling into step beside him. Their boots echoed against the stone floor, the flickering torches casting restless shadows along the corridor walls.

Neither man spoke as they moved through the palace's labyrinthine passageways, but Seneca's mind churned. Two days. That was all the time he had. He had been too cautious, too patient. That ended now.

At the next turning, Seneca suddenly stopped. Instead of following the usual route back to his quarters, he turned sharply down a different passage.

'Where are you going?' asked the Decurion, following.

'To see Postumus.'

'The governor is in a meeting.'

Seneca didn't slow his pace.

'This won't wait.'

The Decurion stepped in front of him, blocking his path.

'You know I can't let you do that.'

Seneca met his gaze, his expression hardening. His voice was calm, but there was a dangerous edge to it now.

'Listen to me my friend. We are the same, you and I, loyal servants of Rome. I really do not want to hurt you but one way or another, I'm going to see the governor. Whether you allow it or not.'

The words hung between them like a drawn blade.

The Decurion's hand twitched toward the hilt of his gladius—not in threat, but in instinct. He wasn't afraid, that much was clear. But he wasn't a fool either. He could see it now—the shift in Seneca's posture, the sheer determination in his eyes. The Tribune was done waiting.

He glanced once down the hall, then back at Seneca, weighing his choices. Finally, with a quiet sigh, he gave a single nod.

'Fine,' he muttered. 'Follow me.'

Without another word, he turned and led the way, taking them up through the palace levels. When they reached the heavy doors of the audience chamber, the Decurion held up a hand.

'Wait here,' he said before stepping inside and pulling the door shut behind him.

Moments later, he re-emerged. His expression was unreadable, but the answer was already in his eyes.

'The governor is busy,' he said.

Seneca stared at the man for a long moment, then exhaled, seemingly defeated. He turned away, but without warning, spun back around and drove his fist into the side of the guard's jaw.

The Decurion stumbled back, catching himself against the stone wall, his hand flying to the hilt of his gladius but by the time he regained his footing, it was already too late, Seneca had slammed his shoulder into the door and burst inside.

----

The chamber was warm, filled with the scent of perfumed oil and spiced wine. The air was not tense with business or politics but something else entirely, a quiet, intimate charge.

At the far end of the room, Postumus sat reclining in his cushioned chair, a goblet of wine in his hand. But it was Callista who drew Seneca's full attention.

She sat close to the governor, almost too close, her body angled toward him, her lips curved slightly at something he had just said. There was no tension in her shoulders, no urgency in her posture, only ease, familiarity, and something dangerously close to flirtation.

Postumus and Callista stood quickly his feet, the governor's face dark with fury.

'What is the meaning of this?' he bellowed.

Before Seneca could answer, the doors crashed open again, and the Decurion stumbled inside, his gladius drawn, his mouth streaked with blood from Seneca's blow.

Seneca barely spared him a glance. Instead, he strode forward, his focus locked onto the governor.

'You need to listen,' he said, 'I know what's going on.'

Callista had already moved, stepping back from Postumus, her earlier ease vanishing. For the first time, she looked unsure.

Postumus' lips curled in anger.

'You're finished, Seneca! Guard! *Seize him!*'

The Decurion took a step forward, his grip tightening on the hilt of his sword. Seneca turned to face him. His eyes locked onto the soldier's, cold and unwavering.

'If you come any closer with that blade,' he said evenly, 'I will have to kill you. And I really do not want to do that.'

A flicker of uncertainty crossed the Decurion's face. His breathing slowed. His grip on the gladius remained firm, but he did not move. He had seen men like Seneca before—men who did not bluff. Silence fell over the room and his gaze flickered to the governor, awaiting his command.

Postumus hesitated, weighing his options. Finally, he exhaled sharply and gave a single, curt nod.

'Two minutes, Seneca. Then you submit, or I'll have you dragged out.'

Seneca stepped forward, his gaze flicking between Postumus and Callista.

'You were right,' he said settling on Callista. 'I made a mistake. The priest at the temple… he died for nothing. I thought I understood what was happening, but I didn't. Not fully.' He straightened, his voice growing stronger. 'You were also right about the Scarab. There are many who follow it, many sects, many beliefs. Some are devoted to the old gods, harmless in their worship, but there is another faction, a larger one. More organized. More dangerous. Its reach extends across all of Egypt, and by association, Rome.'

'You're speaking in riddles, Tribune,' said Postumus. 'Get to the point.'

'You already know about the hallucinations,' said Seneca, 'the visions and nightmares that are keeping the workers from the fields. I think that a group that worships the Scarab is working around the edges of society, poisoning their minds and bodies, causing them to abandon their duties in fear of retribution of the old gods. By doing so, the quotas fall, and Rome suffers.'

Postumus frowned in confusion.

'So, you expect me to believe that all this is the working of some cult and that they have some supernatural power to slip into the minds of men and fill them with terror?'

'Not with supernatural powers,' said Seneca, 'with mind altering substances. Potions that make the person taking them susceptible to suggestion.'

Postumus stared at him. His earlier anger had faded, replaced by exasperation and disbelief.

'Do you not think we have already explored the possibility of such things?' he said. 'The problem is so widespread, across such a diverse cross section of the population, any potion would be impossible to administer without being noticed by someone.'

'Not if it was ingested voluntarily,' said Seneca, 'and could not be tasted.'

'How?' sighed Postumus. 'It can't be the food as not everyone is affected and tampering with grain or produce on such a scale would be impossible, it comes from so many different sources.' He gestured vaguely with one hand. 'It can't be the water, either. The entire province drinks from the Nile, yet not everyone suffers these hallucinations.'

'There is a way,' said Seneca. 'And at last, I know how.' He reached beneath his tunic and pulled out the small leather pouch, tossing it onto the table between them. The soft thud echoed in the silence. 'This,' he said, 'is the problem.

Postumus loosened the pouch's bindings and overturned it, spilling its contents onto the polished wood of the table, some dried flowers and a small pile of white powder. He frowned, prodding one of the dried petals with the tip of his finger. The flowers were blue, their colour faded but still vibrant enough to be recognizable. The powder clung to them, coating them in a pale film. He shrugged, unimpressed, and turned to Callista. 'Do you recognise any of this?'

She stepped forward and leaned over the table. Her fingers brushed lightly over the dried stems, rolling one between her thumb and forefinger. Then she dipped a fingertip into the powder, rubbing it against her skin.

'Blue lotus,' she said eventually. 'And... henbane. Both are well known here. The blue lotus is sacred to the gods, it's used in rituals to bring enlightenment.' She took a deep breath before continuing. 'As for the henbane, it's more dangerous. It can also cause visions, yes, but in the wrong hands... it brings madness.'

'And in large quantities?' interrupted Seneca.

Callista hesitated.

'Enough of it,' she admitted, 'could strip a man's mind of reason entirely. It would turn dreams into nightmares, but it is rarely made and even then, in small quantities only.

'What if I was to tell you,' interrupted Seneca, 'that one of my men saw many wagons full of this stuff, all heavily guarded, all headed in the same direction.'

'What man?' asked Postumus looking up. 'They are all in custody.'

'Not all of them,' said Seneca. 'I still have one working with the legions in Pselchis near the Nubian border. While there, he saw a caravan, heavily guarded, heading northeast. It stood out because it obviously wasn't an ordinary supply convoy. They avoided the usual trade routes, as if they didn't want to be seen, and also attacked some of his men when they got too close.'

Postumus narrowed his eyes.

'And this man of yours... what did he do?'

'He did what he was trained to do,' said Seneca. 'He infiltrated them and managed to steal a portion of their cargo.' He nodded to the drugs on the table.

The governor paused, his mind racing.

'I don't know, Seneca,' he said at last. 'Even if his report is accurate and they do indeed have wagons full of this stuff, they could be going anywhere. Egypt is full of caravans, full of traders. How do you know this one is any different?'

'Do you have a map?'

The governor's eyes flickered with intrigue now, despite his scepticism. He gestured toward a large wooden table on the far side of the room.

'Over there.'

Without another word, Seneca strode toward it, Callista and Postumus following close behind. The map was spread across the table, weighed down by polished stones at the corners. Seneca scanned it quickly before planting a finger on a location deep in the south.

'Pselchis,' he said. 'The caravan was last seen here, moving north-east.' He traced a straight line with his finger, dragging it steadily across the parchment, following the direction Marcus had reported. 'If they continued on this course,' he continued, 'they would arrive here.' He looked up as his finger reached the coastline.

Postumus and Callista both leaned closer. A name was printed along the shore, marking a port town on the edge of the empire.

*Sabratha!*

----

Postumus frowned, staring at the map as if the name would somehow reveal its secrets.

'You mentioned this name before,' he said. 'Why is it important?'

'Sabratha is a merchant city,' said Seneca. 'A port that feeds half of Africa's trade routes. Ships sail from there to Carthage, Alexandria, even as far as Rome itself, but it is more than just a port, it's a supplier. A place where goods from the interior are refined and sent across the empire. Grains, oils, rare spices… But there's one product in particular—one that Sabratha is famous for—and it isn't for the common man.'

Postumus narrowed his eyes.

'Go on.'

Seneca didn't answer immediately. Instead, his gaze turned to the lavish spread of food on the table nearby, roasted lamb glazed with honey, bowls of figs, olives glistening in golden oil. And there, amongst the food, sat the answer he was looking for. Slowly, he walked over, reaching down and wrapping his fingers around an unremarkable ceramic jug. He lifted it, turning back to Postumus and Callista.

'This, he said, 'is the problem,' and without breaking his gaze, slowly poured the contents onto the floor.'

----

Postumus blinked.

'Garum?' he said, shaking his head. 'But half the empire eats garum. What makes this type so different?'

'Because,' said Seneca, 'This garum is made only for the Roman administrators and soldiers based in Egypt. If I'm right, someone is mixing those two drugs together and adding it to the Garum stills in Sabratha. Once it is bottled, it is brought to Alexandria before being distributed around all the Roman administrative centres and barracks in Egypt. That's why our own people are affected so badly.'

'That doesn't explain the workers,' said Postumus.

'You know as well as I that there is a huge hidden market for Roman garum' said Seneca. 'Those responsible would know exactly what cargo the affected Garum was in and could ensure that when the ships arrived here in Alexandria they stole or bought enough to distribute amongst the workers.'

'It's too tenuous,' said Postumus. 'I need more proof.'

Seneca turned from the table, pacing slightly as he pieced it all together aloud.

'After the feast at the palace a few weeks ago,' he said, 'one of my men, Falco, experienced the dreams. Sica did not.' He glanced at Postumus. 'Sica does not eat garum.' Seneca pressed on. 'And Cassius has never had the dreams. Not once. And yet he eats the same food, drinks the same wine as the rest of us. The only difference? He hates garum.' Seneca exhaled through his nose, pacing a few steps closer before turning to face them fully.

'As for myself,' he said, his voice quieter now, 'I've had the dreams more than any of my men. And each time, always after a meal. I like garum, Governor. I eat it regularly. But the worst— the most vivid, most terrifying dreams—came after just one particular night.' He let the words hang for a moment, then slowly turned his gaze to Callista. 'The night I spent with you. We had a wonderful meal,' Seneca continued, 'exquisite, but heavily seasoned with garum.' His breath slowed. 'At least... mine was.'

Postumus' eyes flicked toward Callista. Her posture remained poised, controlled, but there was a new tension in her shoulders.

'You did not have any,' said Seneca. 'Was it because you knew what was in it?'

Callista frowned.

'It is true that I never had the garum,' she said, 'but that is because I do not like the taste of rotting fish. That does not mean I am involved with all this.'

Seneca turned back to Postumus.

'Look,' he said, 'I know that there is a lot to take on trust, and I might be wrong. But surely it is worth sending a messenger to the garrison in Sabratha. Ask them to investigate, to taste the garum intended for Alexandria compared to other shipments. If there are any aftereffects, then we have the answer.'

'And if not?'

'Then I have failed and will face whatever consequences you deem appropriate. There is a lot of evidence here, governor. Surely it is worth investigating?'

Postumus leaned against the table, fingers pressing into the polished wood as he weighed everything Seneca had laid before him. His gaze drifted from the map to the spilled garum to the scattered dried flowers and powder, then back to Seneca. At last, he let out a slow breath.

'Fine,' he said. 'I will send a deposition immediately. The garrison at Sabratha will be ordered to investigate the stills. If they find anything, even the slightest trace of what you claim, the stills will be shut down and those responsible held to account.'

Seneca exhaled, nodding. It was the right call, but Postumus wasn't finished.

'I want you to go with them, Seneca, to make sure...'

Seneca looked up and gave a sharp retort.

'No.'

The response came before the governor had even finished speaking, and it was absolute. Unyielding. Postumus straightened, his brows knitting together.

'This is your investigation, Tribune. You've been fighting to uncover the truth for weeks. I would think you'd want to see it through.'

Seneca's expression darkened.

'My work here is done, Governor,' he said, 'he stills, the supply lines, the shipments, all of that is yours to do with as you wish.' He took a slow step back from the table. 'But I have other matters to attend to and I need your help.'

Postumus studied him carefully, as if searching for something beneath the hardened exterior.

'What exactly do you need?'

'I want my men freed,' said Seneca, 'a hundred legionaries and safe passage out of Alexandria.'

The governor's eyes narrowed.

'To where?'

'Saqqara,' said Seneca, 'and if I don't get there within two days, the man who may have just handed us the keys to this whole thing will be dead before the full moon sets.'

----

## Chapter Thirty-Nine

### Saqqara

Marcus woke to darkness and pain. The air was thick, stale, tainted with the stench of rot, the kind that clung to places meant for the dead. A single candle flickered on a crumbling ledge, its light feeble against the oppressive gloom.

Marcus blinked, forcing his thoughts into order. His head throbbed and his scalp was sticky with blood, the wound pulling painfully as he moved. He remembered the strike, the blunt force against his skull, the world tipping sideways as he collapsed. And now… this place.

He swallowed, throat raw. He had been here for days, left in this black tomb to rot with nothing but his own thoughts and the two others imprisoned with him. He turned his head toward the sound.

Two shapes lay curled in the darkness, barely more than shadows themselves. They breathed, one in short, shallow gasps, the other in slow, measured exhales. The three of them had been locked together in this pit, yet they shared nothing but silence.

They had tried, at first, muttered words in different tongues, gestures, strained attempts to understand, but what was the point? They had no answers for one another. No promises of escape, only time and suffering.

Once a day, the door would scrape open, and a shadowed figure would step inside, face concealed beneath heavy folds of black. Silent. Expressionless. They would set down a wooden tray of stale bread and water, sometimes a handful of dried dates, and then vanish again, locking the door behind them. No questions. No commands. Only waiting.

They weren't starving him, they weren't beating him. They were keeping him alive for something, and that thought unsettled him more than death itself.

----

Just over a league away, the Nile was black as oil, its surface smooth beneath the pale light of the full moon. Two vessels glided silently through the water, their oars slicing through the current in perfect rhythm, one the Baris that had carried the message from Marcus, the other a Roman war boat carrying a hundred men.

The first vessel nudged against the dock, the hull scraping softly against the warped wooden planks. The legionaries disembarked quickly and once they had secured the dock, Falco and the rest of the Occultum followed from the Baris, leaving their sarcinas behind them. Before he joined them, Seneca walked over to the captain

'The last time you saw him, which way was Marcus heading?'

The captain hesitated, then raised a hand, pointing.

'There,' he murmured. 'Up toward the tombs.'

Seneca followed his gaze. The rocky plateau stretched out beneath the moonlight, mastabas and broken temples standing like silent sentinels.

'This is madness,' said the captain. 'You don't understand what's buried there. Men don't go into those tombs to fight, Tribune, they go there to die.'

Seneca turned to him.

'Then it's a good thing we're not just ordinary men,' he said and without another word, stepped ashore to join his comrades.'

----

Moments later, Seneca knelt in the dust, his men gathered around him. Their faces were grim, their eyes sharp.

'The legionaries will go ahead,' said Seneca. 'They'll clear the way, make sure we're not walking into an ambush. We will stay close behind and if they find anything, we move in, fast and quiet. Any questions?'

A cold wind stirred the dust, rattling loose stones against the rock. No one spoke.

'I don't like this,' said Falco eventually.' He glanced toward the silent tombs, their dark doorways like gaping mouths in the earth. 'Old spirits wander these ruins. The dead don't rest here.'

'Then they'll have to move aside,' muttered Sica. But even he couldn't shake the feeling. Seneca could feel it too, all of them could. It wasn't fear, not of men, or the battle ahead, they had walked into a hundred ambushes, fought in streets slick with blood, torn through shields and flesh without a second thought, but this… this was different. It was something in the air, something that watched, something that listened. The weight of the dead pressing down upon them, waiting for them to join their ranks.

'Marcus is up there. somewhere,' said Seneca. 'He's one of us. And we are his last chance. He'd do the same for us so get ready to move.'

One by one, they rose, their hands tightening on their weapons. Ahead, the legionaries moved forward, shields raised, spears glinting in the moonlight. Seneca turned toward the dark necropolis.

'Let's go,' he said, and together, they followed the soldiers out of the small town and into the endless maze of tombs, mastabas, and crumbling mausoleums.

----

For the next few hours, the legionaries moved in disciplined silence, searching the graveyard with methodical precision. They checked every doorway, every tomb, every opening that could be used as a meeting place or a hidden passage.

Eventually, the Centurion in charge broke away from the ranks and walked toward Seneca. He dropped to one knee, resting his forearm on his thigh.

'The search has revealed nothing,' he said quietly. 'No sign of movement. No hidden passages. No gathering places. It's empty.'

Seneca exhaled slowly. They had come all this way, risked everything, and yet… nothing. No hidden chambers, no gathering places, no sign of Marcus. For the first time, doubt crept in.

'What are your orders, Tribune?' asked the Centurion.

Seneca inhaled sharply, pushing aside his doubts. This wasn't over… not yet.

'Search again,' he ordered. 'Every tomb, every shadow. We're missing something.'

The Occultum spread out again, moving with the same methodical precision as the legionaries. Sica ran his hands along the edges of tomb doors, testing for false openings. Cassius climbed atop a collapsed wall, scanning the necropolis from above while Decimus rapped his knuckles against slabs of stone, listening for echoes.

The night dragged on and Falco muttered a curse under his breath. He had no patience for tombs, spirits, or riddles carved in stone. Grumbling, he strode toward a small crag on the edge of the ruins, where a slab of rock jutted out, featureless, empty. It was as lifeless as the rest of this damned place.

He sighed and dropped onto the stone, pulling a small flask from his belt and taking a long drink. The wine burned his throat, and for a moment, he let himself breathe. He stared out over the graveyard, his eyes drifting across the broken landscape. Nothing but tombs, stone and shadows. He glanced over to his left and just at the edge of his vision, along the side of the rock, he saw a shadow, darker than the rest.

His brow furrowed. He stood slowly, setting the flask aside, and took a careful step towards it. His fingers brushed the rock, until suddenly, his fingers disappeared into a void behind it, and his pulse quickened. It was a narrow gap in the rock.

He turned his head, back towards the graves.

'Seneca,' he hissed. 'I've found something.'

----

## Chapter Forty

## The Necropolis

Marcus sat upright, his back pressed against the cold stone wall, his breath coming in short, controlled exhales. His eyes were wide, scanning the darkened chamber, but there was nothing to see. Only shadows. Only fear.

The very air in the tomb seemed to hum, a vibration just at the edge of hearing. Distant whispers, chanting. It was barely audible, yet it crawled beneath his skin, just enough to let him know that something was happening. Something was coming.

The sound of a bolt sliding back made him jump and the door creaked open, a sliver of candlelight spilling into the chamber. Two hooded figures entered, their robes brushing against the stone floor, their faces hidden beneath deep folds of black cloth. They moved without hesitation, their hands reaching for one of the prisoners... the woman.

She woke with a sharp inhale as their fingers curled around her arms and for a heartbeat, she was too stunned to react but as they dragged her to the door, she started to struggle, her voice breaking as she screamed for help. Marcus lunged forward, pulling at his binds with everything he had but it was no use, they were just too tight.

'Leave her!' he shouted, his voice shaking with fury. 'You bastards, let her go!'

The hooded men said nothing and dragged her backward, her heels scraping against the stone as she bucked and twisted, her eyes wild with panic.

Moments later, the door slammed shut and her screams faded into the distance.

Marcus sat there, chest heaving, his pulse hammering in his throat. The other prisoner, the broken man who had long since given up, didn't even move.

Eventually, the tomb fell deathly still. A silence so deep, so absolute, it felt as though the entire world had ceased to breathe. Marcus closed his eyes, seeking the respite from the fear that sleep brought, but suddenly, a deafening scream tore through the darkness, terrified, and soul breaking. Not of resistance, not of struggle, this was a scream of something worse, of pure and blood-curdling horror.

----

Marcus sat motionless, his heart pounding like a war drum. Across from him, the remaining prisoner stared back. Neither spoke, they didn't need to. Fear was a language all men understood.

Almost in unison, they began struggling against their binds again, desperate, reckless. The ropes burned against their skin, digging deeper into the flesh of their wrists, but neither stopped. There was no other choice.

The door creaked again, and Marcus froze as the hooded figures returned and reached for the other prisoner. The man let out a strangled whimper, shaking his head violently. He thrashed violently, trying to throw himself backward, but the hands of the priests were firm, and as he was dragged from the chamber, the door slammed shut again leaving Marcus truly alone.

He sat in the darkness his body trembling with dread, knowing what to expect. It could have been minutes, it could have been hours, he had no way of telling but eventually it came. The scream… and it was worse than before.

Marcus closed his eyes, swallowing hard. He was next. He had fought all his life, for Rome, for his men, for his own survival but here, in this gods-forsaken tomb, there was no fight left to win, and for the first time in years, he lowered his head and prayed. Not for salvation, not for mercy, but for the strength to die well.

----

Outside, the night was deathly still. Seneca ran his fingers over the rough stone, tracing the outline of the aperture Falco had discovered. At first glance, the rock face seemed uninterrupted, a solid slab of limestone just like the others. But now, up close, the difference was clear. Sometime in some ancient age, the slab had broken away and slid down the rock face, leaving behind the slightest gap, barely wide enough for a man to slip through sideways. Behind it was an opening, carved into the hill by countless hands over thousands of years.

The Occultum waited in tense silence, their expressions unreadable in the flickering moonlight. Behind them, the Centurion and his legionaries stood in disciplined rows, their helmets and short swords gleaming dully in the dim light.

'This must be it,' said Seneca.

A few of the men exchanged uneasy glances. The very air around them felt charged, unnatural. Even hardened soldiers could feel when something wasn't right.

Falco let out a breath.

'Then let's get this over with.'

'What's the matter, Falco?' asked Sica without looking up, his gaze examining the edge of his knife. 'Afraid of ghosts?'

Falco shot him a look.

'No. I'm afraid of dying in a tomb with your ugly face as the last thing I see.'

'Then don't die,' muttered Sica.

Seneca ignored them and turned to the Centurion.

'You will take ten men in first to clear the way. We will follow and another dozen legionaries will bring up the rear. The rest of your men stay are to stay outside as back up in case things go wrong.'

The Centurion nodded.

'Understood.'

'Remember, we don't fight to hold ground, we fight to

move forward. Stay together and keep your eyes open. We don't know what's waiting for us in there.'

A few moments later, the first ten legionaries slipped into the crack, disappearing one by one into the darkness, as if the world itself had sealed them inside.

----

The tunnel pressed down on them, the air thick with the scent of dust, damp stone, and something older—something rotten and cloying. It was the smell of a place untouched by sunlight, of things buried and long forgotten. Faint candles burned in deep-set crevices along the walls, their flames flickering in the stale air. The light barely reached the edges of the tunnel with thick shadows clinging stubbornly to the rock. The candles were both a relief and a warning. Someone had been here recently.

At the head of the column, the Centurion moved cautiously, his gladius held firm, its edge gleaming in the candlelight. The Occultum followed close behind, their own weapons drawn, their bodies tense with anticipation. Every step was careful, every breath measured. The tunnel descended sharply, winding deeper beneath the necropolis, its walls narrowing, pressing inward like a tomb tightening around them.

Seneca moved near the center of the formation, his instincts gnawing at him. This was not the silence of an abandoned place, this was something else. A held breath, a watching presence, and yet, he knew, there was no turning back.

The tunnel suddenly widened into a cavern, the ceiling arching high above them, lost in the gloom. More candles flickered along the walls, casting long, shifting shadows.

It was empty, but on the far side, a darkened opening yawned like a wound in the rock, leading even deeper under the necropolis. Seneca scanned the chamber, his fingers tightening around the leather-wrapped hilt of his sword. Something felt wrong.

'Careful,' he whispered, almost afraid to break the silence.

The legionaries stepped forward, spreading out across the cavern floor. Their shields were raised, their blades steady. They had done this before, entered hostile ground, moved through enemy strongholds in the dead of night, and yet, despite their discipline, there was an unease hanging in the air.

They made it halfway across when a roar shattered the silence and from the darkness along the walls, a figure burst forward, plunging a dagger deep into one of the legionary's throat. A spray of hot blood misted the air, catching the candlelight and as the soldier crumpled to the ground, the cavern erupted into chaos.

More black-robed figures surged from the shadows, moving with unnatural speed, their curved blades flashing in the candlelight, fanatics who knew no fear, who cared nothing for their own survival.

The legionaries met them head-on, their discipline turning what could have been a slaughter into a vicious, grinding battle. The air filled with the sickening sounds of metal biting into flesh, of screams cut short, of boots skidding across slick, bloodied stone.

A soldier to Seneca's left fell, his throat ripped open by a wickedly curved blade. Another died with a dagger lodged between his ribs, crumpling against the cavern wall, but the Romans pushed forward, shields locked, stabbing outward with ruthless precision.

A gap opened in the line, and more legionaries rushed past Seneca into the melee, their eyes sharp with the cold focus of men trained for war.

Seneca turned sharply, seeing Falco drawing his gladius, ready to throw himself into the fight.

'No!' shouted Seneca.

Falco hesitated, blade still raised, his breath coming fast. 'But they need...'

'The soldiers can fight,' said Seneca, staring across at the dark opening beyond the cavern. 'We continue.'

He made his way across the cavern, weaving through the madness. The others followed, stepping over the dead and dying. Behind them, the cavern roared with battle, but Seneca barely heard it now, his focus was on the darkness ahead, and Marcus… if he was still alive.

----

## Chapter Forty-One

## Saqqara

Marcus opened his eyes as the door creaked open for the last time. The two hooded figures entered, moving with the same unnerving silence as before, their hands reaching for him, fingers working at the knots that secured him to the wall. His mind screamed at him to fight, to run, to do something, but deep down, he knew... it was pointless.

The men dragged him up from the cold floor. His legs shook beneath him, weak from days of captivity, exhaustion and fear, but they forced him forward, out of the chamber, into the waiting darkness of the corridor beyond.

A few minutes later, the corridor opened into a vast, breathtaking chamber, carved out of the living rock and lit by hundreds of candles. The air was stifling, thick with the scent of wax, smoke, and dried blood. And then he saw them, the dead.

All along the chamber walls, dozens of ancient sarcophagi stood open, their lids removed, and inside, the fleshless remains of the dead, their hollow sockets seemingly turned toward the center of the chamber as if bearing witness.

Marcus felt his heart hammering against his ribs, a raw, primal terror seeping into his bones. At the center of the chamber, raised slightly on a carved platform, was a flat stone slab, its surface etched with ancient symbols, hieroglyphs older than Rome itself, many obscured by blood.

Some of it was fresh, glistening under the candlelight, still dripping from the edges to pool onto the stone floor below.

Marcus's stomach turned. At the far end of the slab, three short stone pillars had been arranged in a row. The first held the severed head of the woman prisoner, her lifeless eyes staring forward, her mouth locked in a frozen scream.

The second held the head of the second prisoner, his dark hair still matted with blood, his face twisted in an expression of pure horror. The third was empty, as if still waiting for its prize.

One of the priests approached with a bowl containing a liquid and forced him to drink. He tried turning away but his captors held him tight until he swallowed. Once done, they placed him on the slab and tied him down. Marcus could feel his thoughts getting unclear as the drug started its work and finally realised that this was it. His time had come.

----

In the tunnel, Seneca and the Occultum raced forward, their boots striking the stone with dull, muted thuds. At the head of the charge, Falco was a force of nature. His breath was ragged, his grip tight on his gladius, his eyes alight with the savage thrill of battle. A dark shape lunged from an alcove, but Falco drove his shoulder into the attacker, sending him sprawling, cutting his throat before the man could recover.

Another figure emerged, curved dagger raised high, but Falco didn't hesitate, slashing low, severing the man's tendons. The cultist collapsed screaming, and Falco drove his boot into his chest, crushing the last breath from his lungs.

Behind him, Sica and Cassius followed like reapers, dispatching any enemy that still clung to life. A dying man reached for his weapon, but Sica silenced him with a quick thrust to the heart. Another crawled away, dragging himself through the dust until Cassius knelt beside him and opened his throat with a practiced stroke.

Seneca barely noticed the corpses littering the ground, and as the last of the defenders fell, the tunnel opened up and they burst into the chamber. And stopped dead in their tracks, shocked at the scene before them.

----

The moment Decimus stepped into the cavern, he froze, his breath catching in his throat. His gaze swept across the chamber, the candles, the altar, the dozens of open coffins lining the walls, and for a moment, it was as if he had been dragged back to the temple in
Alexandria.

That other chamber, hidden beneath the temple, carved from the same ancient rock, also had coffins lining the walls, filled not with corpses but acolytes, lying in death-like trances, their faces twisted in rapture or terror, seeking 'enlightenment.' He had thought it was hell then, but this... This was worse, these weren't seekers, these were the dead.

His hands began to shake, the weight of the memory crashing down upon him as he felt the same cold fear crawling up his spine, the one that had haunted him since that day in Alexandria. His vision blurred. The walls felt as though they were closing in, the faces of the dead mocking him, and all he wanted to do was turn and run until a sharp voice snapped him out of the spiral.

'Decimus.'

His head jerked toward Seneca, whose hand gripped his shoulder hard, grounding him in reality.

'Focus,' Seneca hissed. 'Stay with me.'

Decimus swallowed hard, forcing air into his lungs, and nodded. His hands were still trembling, but he gripped the hilt of his sword, anchoring himself. The fear didn't leave him, it wouldn't, but now, it wouldn't control him. Seneca let go and turned back toward the altar, his gladius gleaming, and as he stepped forward, Decimus followed, though the dead watched him every step of the way.

----

The cavern was vast, carved into the very bones of the earth, its ceiling lost in darkness. At its center lay the altar, and

Marcus was bound to it, his body shaking violently. His eyes were wide, glassy, unfocused, staring into something that wasn't there. Something only he could see.

Seneca gasped and raced down the ramp, followed by his men.

Down below, Marcus let out a strangled gasp, his body arching off the stone as the visions got stronger. They erupted around him, swirling in the flickering candlelight—shadows that should not exist, shapes that defied understanding. A colossal form loomed behind him, its limbs grotesquely elongated, its fingers tapering into endless points, its face a shifting, writhing mass, as though the flesh itself refused to take shape. Another grotesque entity slithered along the cavern floor, its body coiled like a serpent made of human limbs, each arm clawing at the air, its dozens of mouths whispering in a language older than time.

Then, the eyes, too many eyes, blinking into existence within the blackness beyond the chamber walls. Lining the ceiling, the floor, the altar itself.

Marcus let out a shuddering scream, but it was not his own voice. Something else spoke through him, something vast, something beyond the comprehension of mortal men. He had been dragged into another place, another realm where mortals did not belong. And it was killing him.

----

## Chapter Forty-Two

## Saqqara

Seneca took in the scene in a heartbeat—the flickering candles, the grotesque altar, Marcus writhing in agony, his body bucking against his restraints. This place was a temple to madness, a nightmare carved into stone.

More black-robed figures stepped from the shadows, their curved blades gleaming in the candlelight. They did not shout, did not call for their brothers. They simply moved, silent, swift, deadly.

Falco was the first to meet the threat, his gladius flashing as he parried a downward strike, stepping in close and slamming his pommel into the robed man's temple. The cultist staggered, but Falco did not give him a chance to recover. He pivoted, driving his sword through the man's gut, twisting viciously before tearing it free.

Sica was already past him, his dagger a blur in the dim light. He ducked under a wild swing, grabbed the attacker's wrist, and plunged his blade into the soft flesh beneath the ribs.

Decimus and Cassius joined Seneca to cut a path toward the altar. Seneca sidestepped a thrust, catching his opponent's arm and twisting hard, the snap of bone lost in the din. He reversed his grip and slammed his gladius through the man's throat, ripping it free in one brutal motion.

Behind them, the rest of the legionaries poured into the cavern to join the fight, forcing the cultists back against the cavern wall until finally, the fighting stopped with both groups of men staring at each other in the gloom.

Seneca turned to Cassius and Decimus.

'You two, get Marcus. I'm going to see if I can get some answers.'

He walked over to the remaining cultists, now trapped against the cavern wall.

'Do any of you understand me?' he asked.

One man stepped forward and returned Seneca's stare. 'I do.'

'Tell me what this place is.' said Seneca. 'Who are you, and why are you sacrificing those people?'

The priest paused for a moment but when he spoke, his voice was quiet, but the weight of his words filled the cavern.

'You are the invaders,' the priest said, his gaze unwavering. 'Barbarians who trample upon the old ways. You think you understand this land, but you do not. You never will.'

Seneca narrowed his eyes. The calmness of the priests unnerved him. He had expected defiance, even fear. But not this. He stepped forward, his eyes narrowing as he studied the priest standing before him. The man's expression was eerily calm, as if he had foreseen this moment long before it had arrived. He stood with his hands loosely at his sides, unconcerned by the armed men surrounding him.

'You will answer me,' Seneca said, his voice edged with steel. 'Who are you and what is your purpose here?'

The priest did not flinch. Instead, he regarded Seneca with something that resembled pity.

'You already know the answer, Roman,' he murmured. 'You simply refuse to see it.'

Seneca stared back in silence for a moment before responding.

'It matters not if you stay silent,' said Seneca. 'Postumus will extract the truth from you, and he is far less patient than I.'

A slow smile crept across the priest's lips.

'There will be no interrogations, Roman,' he said quietly, 'no revelations, no confessions.' He paused before adding, 'after all... dead men cannot reveal their secrets.'

Before Seneca could process the meaning of the words, a ripple of motion spread through the gathered priests and each one of them reached into their robes to retrieve a lethal skinning knife.

Marcus and his men reacted instantly, drawing their own weapons in preparation for an attack, but the strike never came. Instead, each priest turned their weapon inward and without hesitation… slit their own throats.

The wet sound of steel biting flesh filled the cavern. Blood sprayed in crimson arcs, painting the floor and dripping down their ceremonial robes. One by one, they collapsed, their lifeless bodies crumpling into the spreading pools of their own sacrifice.

Seneca stood amidst the carnage, his face pale with shock and fury. Blood seeped into the cracks of the stone floor, its scent thick in the air. He had seen men die before, by sword, by poison, by the slow decay of sickness, but never like this. Never in blind, willing sacrifice.

He turned his gaze back to the last priest, still standing untouched by the massacre, his eyes now dark pits of contempt.

Seneca took a step forward, his voice rising in the darkness.

'Why,' he shouted, 'Explain this madness.'

The priest smirked.

'Madness? Is that what you call it, Roman?' His voice was quiet yet laced with venom. 'And what would you call your own empire? Your conquests? You slaughter thousands in the name of your so-called civilization. You nail men to crosses for sport. And you dare judge us?'

'We do not slaughter our own people for the sake of superstition,' said Seneca.

The priest let out a sharp breath, almost a laugh.

'No, you slaughter others. You steal land, destroy temples, defile the gods of those you conquer. And now you come here, to the heart of Aegyptus, demanding explanations like a child who does not understand the world.'

'This is not the world. This is just butchery.'

The priest took a step closer, his voice lowering to a growl.

'This is faith. It is devotion. Something no Roman will ever understand. You kneel before your emperors, call them gods, and yet you mock us? Hypocrites, every last one of you.'

Seneca's eyes narrowed.

'It seems you worship nothing but death.'

'We don't worship it, Roman, we embrace it,' the priest snapped. His calm was unravelling, his tone growing sharp, furious. 'You think yourself above us, but you are nothing. An insect in a foreign land, pretending to be a man of wisdom. Rome is a parasite, a gluttonous beast that feasts on the gods of others and spits them out when they are no longer useful. You stand here demanding answers? You deserve none.'

Seneca held his ground as the priest took another step, his dark eyes burning with scorn.

'This is Aegyptus, Roman. Our land, our gods, and what we do is no concern of yours. You are nothing but flea on the hide of a dying jackal and when Rome is dust, when your legions are bones scattered in the sands, our gods will still remain.'

Seneca's hand twitched toward the hilt of his dagger, his patience at its limit. The priest saw it and sneered.

'Does the Roman tremble? Does the hand of the emperor feel fear?'

'Enough,' Seneca said sharply, raising his hand, and turned to Sica. 'I am wasting my time here, tie him up and send him back to Alexandria.'

Sica and Falco stepped towards the priest, but before they could reach him, he exhaled slowly, almost in relief.

'You will never understand,' he whispered and without another word, lifted the blade to his own throat.

Seneca's breath caught as the priest dragged the knife

across his flesh, parting skin and muscle in a single brutal stroke. Blood erupted from the wound, spilling down his chest in thick, pulsing waves. He dropped to his knees, his body swaying, yet his eyes never left Seneca's, and even as the life drained from him, his gaze burned with something ancient, something unreadable. Seneca wanted to look away, but he couldn't, until finally, the priest tilted forward, collapsing onto the stone floor with a dull, wet thud. His fingers twitched, his body shuddered once… twice… and then, finally, he was still.

----

A thick silence settled over the chamber. Blood pooled across the stone floor, dark and glistening in the torchlight. The chamber seemed to hold its breath, the only sound, the slow, steady drip of blood pooling into the cracks of the stone.

Seneca felt the weight of the cavern pressing down on him, suffocating. He had always believed himself immune to the effects of battle, but standing here, surrounded by death and devotion beyond reason, he felt something he had not known in years. Fear.

----

## Chapter Forty-Three

## The Necropolis

The first light of dawn crept over the horizon, casting long shadows across the necropolis. The air was still fresh and cool, as though the chaos of the night had never happened. The Occultum sat scattered amongst the tombs, their backs against ancient headstones, drinking water from their flasks. Their faces were drawn, hollow-eyed from exhaustion, but their wounds were minor—scrapes, bruises, nothing more. Legionaries carried their dead from the underground chamber, determined to give their comrades the burials they deserved.

Cassius knelt beside Marcus, who stirred at last, blinking against the harsh glare of the morning sun. He groaned, shifting against the cold stone, his mind sluggish as the effects of the drug slowly ebbed away.

'Easy,' Cassius murmured, offering him a waterskin. 'You've been out for a while.'

Marcus took it with trembling fingers, drinking greedily before wiping his mouth. His eyes darted around the necropolis, his confusion deepening. 'Where…?'

'You're safe,' Cassius assured him. 'We got you out.'

Footsteps approached as Seneca emerged from the scattering of men, his robe smeared with dirt and dried blood. He lowered himself onto a fallen headstone, exhaling as he studied his friend.

Marcus swallowed hard.
'Seneca?'
A small smirk tugged at the edge of Seneca's mouth.
'You look like you've been to Hades and back.'
Marcus let out a weak chuckle, then winced.

'I feel like it.' He ran a hand over his face, his mind still swimming with half-formed memories. 'Tell me what happened. I don't understand.'

Seneca glanced around at the rest of his men, at the exhausted legionaries, and at the bodies that would never see another sunrise.

'It's a long story,' he said, 'and I'm still not sure I understand it myself.'

Marcus met his gaze.

'Then tell me what you have,' said Marcus. 'I need to understand.'

Seneca leaned forward, elbows on his knees, his face illuminated by the rising sun.

'For weeks, we were chasing shadows,' he said. 'Clues that led nowhere. We followed whispers in the marketplaces, questioned informants, bribed merchants, but it was always the same, dead ends and blind alleyways.' He shook his head. 'But through it all, one thing remained constant. The followers of the Scarab.'

Marcus frowned.

'A cult?'

'Not all of them,' Seneca corrected. 'Most of them harmless, people clinging to the old gods, to traditions long since buried by Rome. But one group—one in particular—was responsible for something far worse.'

Marcus rubbed his temples.

'The drug,' he murmured. 'They were using it to influence people.'

Seneca nodded.

'At first, we couldn't see the pattern. Small amounts of the drug appearing in different places, people claiming visions, priests gaining influence, but no clear source, no single explanation. Then your note arrived.' He fixed Marcus with a measured look. 'That changed everything.'

Marcus shook his head.

'I barely remember what I wrote.'

'You wrote enough,' Seneca assured him. 'Enough for me to realize that this cult, whoever they are, had found a way to harvest the drug in great quantities. And more than that, they had found a way to distribute it.'

'How?'

'Garum,' Seneca said flatly.

'The fish sauce?'

'The very same.' Seneca leaned back against the headstone. 'We think they infiltrated the largest supplier of garum to the Romans in Egypt, a place in Sabratha, and poisoned the vats. Not enough to kill, not enough to be obvious, but enough to make men see things. To make them doubt, to make them fear.'

Marcus exhaled sharply.

'By the gods…'

'It was genius, in a way,' Seneca admitted. 'The Romans in Egypt were affected first, not everyone, of course, as not everyone likes the sauce, but that's what made the cause difficult to identify. But it soon spread to local villages as well, affecting anyone who managed to get their hands on the Sabratha Garum. And there were many as it is the best in Africa. Soon they began to experience the same visions, the same paranoia. Fear spread like wildfire, and with it, the influence of those who still worship the old gods.'

Marcus frowned, trying to process it all.

'So that's why everything was falling apart.'

Seneca nodded.

'It was never just about faith. It was about control.'

Marcus let out a bitter laugh.

'And I led myself straight into their hands.'

Seneca's expression softened.

'You found the source, Marcus. Without you, we might never have uncovered it.'

Marcus shook his head, still grappling with the weight of it all.

'And the cult? The ones responsible?'

Seneca's gaze darkened.

'Many are dead, but I suspect they are spread far wider than we imagine.'

Marcus sat up straighter, ignoring the aching in his limbs.

'Then we're not done.'

Seneca allowed himself a small smirk.

'There is much more to do, my friend,' he said, 'but Postumus has to step up now, and prove why he holds one of the most important roles in the empire. Our work here is done, Cassius. Tomorrow, we go back to Alexandria.'

'What then?' asked Marcus.

'We get as drunk as it is possible to get,' shouted Falco from a nearby gravestone, 'and send the bill to Claudius.'

Seneca laughed and turned back to Cassius.

'Do you know what?' he said, 'for once in his life, I think Falco has come up with a perfect plan.

----

## Chapter Forty-Four

## The Port of Ostia

The docks were alive with the familiar clamour of the empire's beating heart. Sailors shouted over the crash of waves, dockworkers hauled amphorae and crates, and the scent of brine, fish, and sweat filled the air. Seagulls cawed overhead, circling the mast of a newly arrived merchant vessel, while the steady hum of trade and travel wove through the morning like an unbroken thread.

Seneca sat outside a weather-worn taberna, shaded beneath a tattered awning. He adjusted the sarcina at his feet, shifting its weight before leaning back against the rough wooden chair. He reached for his cup of wine, rolling the clay between his fingers before taking a slow sip, the bitterness settling on his tongue like an old friend.

It had been a long journey but at last, he was back in Rome, and it felt…right. After leaving Saqqara, they had returned to Alexandria under heavy escort, confined to a villa on the outskirts of the city under house arrest. For a month, they had waited, uncertain of their fate, the weight of failure pressing against their chests. Seneca had been sure they would be punished—exiled, imprisoned, perhaps even executed, but when the summons finally came, the governor's words had surprised them all.

The vats in Sabratha had indeed been poisoned. The drug had spread through the garum supply exactly as Seneca had predicted, and the evidence was undeniable. The cult's influence had been deeper than anyone had suspected, stretching across Egypt like a hidden web. Many cultists had been captured, their network dismantled piece by piece. The campaign to find the rest continued, but the worst of the damage had been contained so they had been freed to return to Rome. Now, after crossing the Mare Nostrum, he had returned to Rome's gateway. The Occultum had dispersed upon arrival, fading into the crowds, and only he remained, waiting for their handler.

Seneca took another sip of wine, staring out at the horizon where the sea met the sky, reflecting on all that had transpired. The blood, the secrets, the sacrifices had all taken its toll, but at last, it was over.

The murmur of the dockside faded beneath the measured sound of approaching footsteps and Seneca looked up from his wine as a familiar figure emerged from the shifting crowds. Senator Lepidus, his longtime friend and founder of the Occultum.

Lepidus was dressed plainly, his senator's toga replaced by a simple tunic and travel-worn cloak, but even in disguise, he carried himself with the authority of a man who moved the pieces of the empire from behind the curtain. He met Seneca's gaze with a knowing smile before grasping his wrist in the firm clasp of friendship.

'It's been too long,' Lepidus said as he slid into the seat opposite. He picked up the untouched cup of wine waiting for him, swirling the liquid before taking a sip. 'I see you still prefer this dockside swill.'

Seneca smirked.

'It's honest wine, at least.'

They exchanged a few pleasantries, discussing the voyage, the state of the city, the usual complaints about Roman politics. But soon enough, the conversation turned. It always did.

Lepidus leaned forward, his expression sharpening.

'You did well in Egypt. You all did'

Seneca exhaled and looked up.

'It took too long, and mistakes were made. We were lucky to get back alive.'

'The poisoned vats in Sabratha were real, Seneca. Many cultists were captured and the conspiracy exposed.' He gestured with his cup. 'That is a victory, my friend.'

Seneca frowned.

'Not a complete one. What about the innocent man we killed?'

Lepidus sighed, already anticipating the questions.

'His death was compensated with a sizable donation to the temple.'

'And the cavern?'

'Destroyed. The doorway sealed.'

Seneca stared into his wine. Hesitating before looking up again to ask the question.

'What about Callista. Is she involved in all this?'

Lepidus took a deep breath, He had been briefed about Seneca's liaison and knew it was a tricky subject.

'No proof, one way or another,' he said. 'She was close to the cult, but being part of the royal family makes her untouchable. No one is pursuing it.'

Seneca stared into Lepidus's eyes. It wasn't the answer he wanted, but it was the one he expected.

'And what about the emperor? Is he satisfied?'

Lepidus let out a soft chuckle.

'Satisfied, yes. But of course, Postumus has taken all the credit and glory.'

Seneca smirked.

'Naturally.'

Lepidus set his cup down and glanced around.

'Where are your men?'

'They've all been paid,' said Seneca. 'Sica and Decimus have gone back to the Hornless Bull in Aquae Tarbellicae. Marcus has gone to find the wife and children of a Tribune who died in Pselchis and Cassius is somewhere in Rome, getting drunk.'

Lepidus chuckled but then glanced at Seneca with curiosity.

'You didn't mention Falco.'

Seneca laughed and took another drink before replying.

'Falco is still in Alexandria. The last time we saw him, he was half drunk scouring the bars around the royal palace. Something to do with a dancer he needed to find.' He looked up at Lepidus. 'Why are you so interested?'

Lepidus took a deep breath, then leaned forward.

'Because we have a new assignment, Seneca. We need them back in Rome within a month.'

Seneca held his gaze for a moment, then gave a slow nod.

'That's doable. What's the mission?'

'It's the most straightforward mission you have had so far, yet it is also probably the hardest.'

'Stop stalling,' said Seneca. 'Just spit it out.'

'It's an assassination,' said Lepidus. 'Just one man… but he is deep in the heart of Britannia.'

A gull shrieked overhead, the waves slapped against the dock and the city of Rome's greatest port churned with life. But for Seneca, the world had gone still. He reached for his cup, turned it once between his fingers, then drained the wine in a single pull before setting it down with finality.

'Tell me everything,' he said and as Rome continued its daily life around them, Seneca and Lepidus discussed the death of a man on the very edge of the empire.

----

# Epilogue

## Britannia

It had been several weeks since the journey south, and Veteranus had begun to settle into the rhythms of village life. The days passed in quiet routine, his concerns less pressing with each sunrise. He spent his time with Raven, learning the ways of the settlement, how the people lived, how they worshipped, how they fought. It was a world apart from the Roman legions he had once marched with, and yet, he found himself adapting.

What had once felt foreign was now familiar. Evenings were spent around the central fire, sharing food and stories with Mordred, the druid leader. The man was an enigma, calm, deliberate, his gaze always searching for meaning in the smallest of things. Veteranus had no illusions that he was truly one of them, but Mordred never treated him as an outsider. That, perhaps, was what unsettled him most.

Still, the questions lingered. What was his place here? He was Roman, and across the other side of Britannia, the legions of Claudius were tearing through the Celtic tribes like a relentless storm. It was an odd conflict of interests, one he wrestled with in the quiet of the night. He owed Rome nothing, he had left that life behind. And yet, the pull of his past remained, a whisper in the back of his mind that refused to be silenced.

----

The village was quieter than usual, though the evening was bright under the full moon. An air of unease lingered, woven into the hushed whispers of the women as they moved about their homes, avoiding the gaze of their men. There was something unspoken in their silence, something they did not wish to acknowledge.

Veteranus noticed it immediately. He had spent enough

time in tense camps and restless garrisons to recognize when men prepared for something weighty, something that carried consequence. He asked one of the elders what was happening, but the man only shook his head and turned away. A few minutes later, Raven appeared at the edge of the firelight, his dark eyes unreadable.

'Come with me,' he said and turned away without waiting for an answer.

Veteranus stood and followed Raven out of the village, away from the warmth of the fires, deeper into the forest than he had ever gone before. The trees thickened, their gnarled limbs twisting toward the sky, casting jagged shadows in the moon's glow. The night was alive with the distant sounds of creatures stirring in the undergrowth, but the path they walked was unnervingly still.

After what felt like an hour, they reached a clearing. It was unlike anything Veteranus had seen before. A ring of towering standing stones encircled the space, their rough surfaces etched with symbols worn by time. In the center of the stones was a pit, deeper than a man was tall, surrounded by a low wooden wall.

The warriors of the tribe were already there, gathered around the pit, staring down in solemn silence. As Veteranus stepped closer, he saw what lay at the bottom, two heavy wooden crates, their slatted doors reinforced with iron. Thick ropes were attached to the top of each door, coiled at the edge of the pit, ready to be pulled up.

Understanding dawned on Veteranus. There was to be some sort of contest. A fight, perhaps. He had seen such things in the arenas of Rome—bears against wolves, men against beasts. It was nothing to be concerned about. He had witnessed far worse.

But as he looked around, he noticed something else. Many of the men now wore the dark cloaks of the druid warriors, their faces painted in pale markings that seemed almost spectral under the moonlight. Their lips moved in unison, low and rhythmic. A chant.

It began as a whisper, a murmur barely louder than the rustling leaves. Then it grew, voices blending into something primal, something ancient.

A cup was passed around, filled with the familiar white liquid. When it reached Veteranus, he hesitated only briefly before drinking. The bitterness spread across his tongue, and soon the light-headed warmth followed, familiar now, almost comforting.

The chanting swelled, a rhythmic hum that seemed to vibrate through the very ground. A single drumbeat sounded, deep and resonant, like the heartbeat of the earth itself. Another followed. Then another. The men around the pit moved in slow, deliberate motions, their eyes fixed downward, their breath coming in measured anticipation.

Then Mordred arrived.

He moved through the gathering like a spectre, his cloak of raven feathers catching the moonlight, making him appear almost otherworldly. His face was streaked with woad, intricate patterns curling along his skin like the markings of a forgotten god. His eyes, dark and piercing, flicked over the assembled warriors before settling on the pit.

Veteranus could not look away. The drug had taken hold, dulling the edges of his thoughts, heightening his senses in strange and unsettling ways. He felt the moment in his bones, as if the very air was alive, as if the night itself was watching.

Mordred raised his staff, and the chanting ceased instantly. Silence fell over the clearing and all eyes turned downward.

A warrior stepped forward, gripping one of the thick ropes. With slow, deliberate movements, he pulled, lifting the door of the first crate. The wood groaned as it rose, revealing only darkness within.

For a moment, nothing happened, then, slowly, hesitantly,

a figure emerged from the shadows. A boy... the same boy they had taken from the Ordovices.

His steps were uncertain, his bare feet moving cautiously across the dirt. The flickering torchlight cast long shadows across his face, his expression a mixture of confusion and growing fear. His eyes looked up at the gathered men, then back to the other crate.

Veteranus felt a cold dread coil in his stomach. This was no mere contest. Something else was happening here, something far older, something far darker. A sacrifice. The realization clawed its way into his thoughts, cold and unrelenting.

He looked around, searching for some sign that he was mistaken, that this wasn't what it seemed but the expressions of the warriors, the way they stared into the pit with unblinking devotion, told him otherwise.

This was real. This was happening.

His chest tightened. He wanted to speak, to voice his horror, to demand an end to this madness, but before he could open his mouth, the chanting started again. It was louder now, frenzied, a wall of sound that wrapped around the clearing like a vice.

All eyes remained fixed on the pit.

Another warrior stepped forward, took hold of the second rope, and pulled. The wooden door lifted with a slow, deliberate groan.

For a moment there was nothing. Then the boy turned and stared into the shadows of the second crate.

Veteranus saw the change instantly, the way his body stiffened, the way the look on his face changed to one of pure horror... the way his breath caught in his throat before erupting into a piercing scream.

----

The sound cut through the night like a blade, raw and full

of unrestrained terror. He stumbled backward, his small hands reaching blindly behind him, trying to escape. His cries were swallowed by the thunderous chanting above, but the sheer desperation in his voice sent a shiver down Veteranus' spine.

Something was in there. Something worse than a wild animal. Worse than anything he had ever seen in the arenas of Rome. The air felt thick, suffocating, pressing down on him as the thing in the crate finally moved.

The torchlight barely touched it at first, revealing only furtive movements and shifting shadows until finally, it stepped fully into the light, and Veteranus felt his stomach drop. He couldn't move… he couldn't breathe.

The thing that emerged from the crate was wrong, terrifying, almost unreal and, as the watchers roared in approval, the slaughter began.

----

Veteranus had seen men torn apart in the Colosseum, had waded through the blood-soaked fields of Rome's conquests. But this—this was something else. This was not battle, this this was something ancient, something beyond reason. He turned sharply, bile rising in his throat, his heart hammering against his ribs. He grabbed Raven's arm, his voice tight with horror.

'What is that thing?'

Raven didn't look at him. His expression was unreadable, his dark eyes reflecting the torchlight from below.

'That, my friend,' he said, his voice disturbingly calm, 'is a wraith.'

He finally turned to meet Veteranus' gaze, a slow, knowing smile curling at the edge of his lips.

'And we are going to get to know it very well…Very well indeed.'

**The End**

## Author's Notes

### Alexandria

In AD 43, Alexandria was a vital Roman provincial capital, renowned for its wealth, culture, and strategic importance. Governed by a Roman prefect, the city was the empire's primary supplier of grain, earning its title as 'Rome's breadbasket,' and was heavily guarded by Roman troops to protect its resources.

Dominating the city's skyline was the Pharos Lighthouse, a towering beacon and one of the Seven Wonders of the Ancient World, symbolizing Alexandria's maritime prominence. Though the Library of Alexandria had diminished over time, it remained a center for scholarship and intellectual life, attracting philosophers and scientists.

The bustling Canopic Way, a grand colonnaded boulevard, served as the city's main artery, linking its vibrant markets and cultural landmarks. Its two major harbours facilitated extensive trade across the Mediterranean, making Alexandria a hub for goods from Africa, the Near East, and beyond.

Despite its Roman rule, the city retained a distinctive character shaped by its Greek heritage and Egyptian traditions, making it a unique cultural and economic jewel of the empire.

### Nomes

The nomes of ancient Egypt were administrative divisions, similar to provinces, established as early as the Old Kingdom (c. 2686–2181 BC) and continuing through the Roman period. Egypt was divided into 42 nomes: 22 in Upper Egypt (the south) and 20 in Lower Egypt (the north). Each nome had a central city, often with temples dedicated to local gods, and was governed by a nomarch, who oversaw taxation, irrigation, and law enforcement.

The nomes were essential to Egypt's economy, as they provided resources like grain and livestock, relying heavily on the annual flooding of the Nile to ensure productivity. Many nomes were also religiously significant, tied to specific gods, for example, Thebes (the 4th nome of Upper Egypt) was sacred to Amun, Crocodilopolis (Faiyum) to Sobek, and Heliopolis (in Lower Egypt) to Ra.

During the Roman period, the nomes remained key for administration, especially in supplying grain to Rome, but local governance was overseen by Roman officials under the authority of the prefect in Alexandria. While their autonomy diminished under Roman rule, the nomes remained central to Egypt's agricultural and cultural identity, blending ancient traditions with Greek and Roman influences.

### The Scarab

The scarab beetle, associated with the dung beetle, was a profound symbol in Egyptian mythology, representing creation, rebirth, and protection. It was closely tied to Khepri, a solar deity depicted as a scarab-headed man or a scarab beetle, who was believed to roll the sun across the sky, mirroring the beetle's behaviour of rolling dung balls.

The Egyptians linked the scarab's life cycle, emerging from the dung ball as if from nothing to themes of renewal and transformation. This association with rebirth made scarabs integral to burial practices; heart scarabs were placed over the deceased to ensure protection and rebirth in the afterlife.

Scarab amulets, jewellery, and seals were common, inscribed with prayers or magical spells for protection and good fortune. The scarab also symbolized Maat, the Egyptian concept of cosmic order, and was linked to the sun's cyclical journey.

Scarab motifs adorned temples, tombs, and personal items, reflecting its significance in life and death. Large scarab statues, like those at Karnak, served as focal points for offerings and prayers. Its connection to Ra and creation reinforced its spiritual importance.

The scarab became a symbol of eternal cycles, divine protection, and cosmic balance, influencing both religious practices and daily life. It remains one of the most iconic symbols of ancient Egypt, embodying their understanding of life, death, and renewal.

### Nilometers

A nilometer was an essential ancient Egyptian structure designed to measure the Nile River's water levels during its annual flood. These measurements were crucial for predicting agricultural yields and determining tax assessments, as the river's floodwaters directly influenced the fertility of the surrounding farmland.

Functionally, a nilometer often doubled as a well. Typically located near the riverbank or within a temple complex, it featured a shaft or staircase descending to the water level. These structures were calibrated with precise markings to monitor the rise and fall of the river. When the Nile receded, the water trapped within the Nilometers shaft remained accessible, providing a clean, reliable source of water for drinking, cooking, and irrigation.

Examples of Nilometers include the stepped well on Elephantine Island and the cylindrical nilometer on Rhoda Island in Cairo. These structures were both practical and sacred, embodying the Egyptians' deep respect for the Nile and its life-sustaining role in their civilization.

## The Blue Lotus

The Blue Lotus (Nymphaea caerulea) was revered not only for its beauty but also for its psychoactive effects. It contains compounds such as apomorphine and nuciferine, which can induce mild euphoria and altered states of consciousness. These properties led to its use in religious rituals and as a symbol of life, creation, and rebirth.

Depictions of the Blue Lotus are prevalent in ancient Egyptian art and artifacts, underscoring its importance in their culture. The flower was often associated with the sun and the concept of resurrection, as it blooms during the day and closes at night, mirroring the sun's cycle.

## Henbane

Henbane (Hyoscyamus niger) is a toxic plant that has been known since ancient times for its potent psychoactive and medicinal properties. Native to Europe, North Africa, and parts of Asia, henbane was historically used in rituals, medicine, and occasionally for more nefarious purposes due to its hallucinogenic effects.

Henbane is a tall, bushy plant with pale yellow flowers veined in purple and sticky, hairy leaves. Its unpleasant odour is another defining feature.

The plant's psychoactive properties made it a common ingredient in magical or spiritual rites. It was sometimes used to induce visions or communicate with the divine.

Henbane was often intertwined with mysticism and medicine, used both for its therapeutic potential and its ability to bring on altered states. It was known to the ancient Greeks and Romans, as well as in medieval Europe, and it often found its way into both remedies and darker practices.

**The Scarab Potion**

For the purposes of this novel, I researched a concept that would combine the two drugs to achieve a mixture highly potent and deadly hallucinogenic. The idea was to combine the effects of the Blue Lotus with the extreme toxicity and mind-altering effects of Henbane. This would then be crafted in high quantities to poison food or water sources and result in a mixture that causes both vivid hallucinations and disorientation, along with potentially lethal outcomes depending on the dosage.

The mixture's effects would make victims highly suggestible, creating chaos as their perception of reality crumbles. Survivors might emerge permanently damaged, haunted by lingering hallucinations or psychosis.

In theory this could possibly work so please do not try this at home. ☺

**Baris**

The baris was a versatile and iconic vessel of ancient Egypt, designed specifically for navigating the Nile River's unique conditions. Constructed primarily from local acacia wood or imported cedar for durability, its hull featured a broad, rounded shape with a flat bottom, ideal for traversing the shallow waters and shifting sandbanks of the Nile.

The baris typically carried a single square sail made of linen, which caught the steady winds to propel the ship downstream. When heading against the current, the crew would employ long oars or poles for propulsion, making it effective in either direction. This combination of wind power and human effort gave the baris impressive versatility for both speed and cargo capacity.

## Sabratha

By 43 AD, Sabratha was a growing Roman port city in Tripolitania (modern Libya), integrated into the province of Africa Proconsularis under Emperor Claudius (r. 41–54 AD). Originally a Punic settlement, it had been under Roman control since 46 BC and was developing into a key trade hub.

The city was a major garum-producing centre, exporting high-quality fermented fish sauce across the Mediterranean, along with olive oil, grain, and wild animals for Roman arenas. In return, it imported wine, pottery, and luxury goods from Rome and the eastern Mediterranean.

Sabratha was connected by Roman roads to Leptis Magna and Oea, forming part of the Tripolitanian trade network. The city's infrastructure was expanding, featuring a forum, temples, bathhouses, and an early theatre, with later Roman improvements to come. Its population was a mix of Romans, Punic descendants, Berbers, and Greeks, speaking Latin, Punic, and Berber languages. Religion blended Roman gods with Punic deities like Baal Hammon and Tanit, reflecting its diverse heritage.

Daily life centred around commerce, markets, public baths, and entertainment, including gladiatorial games and theatre. By this time, Sabratha was on its way to becoming one of North Africa's most important Romanised cities.

## Garum

Garum was a highly prized fermented fish sauce in the Roman world, used as a seasoning in everything from stews and meats to bread and wine. Made by layering fish (often mackerel, anchovies, or tuna) with salt and leaving it to ferment in the sun for several months, the resulting liquid was strained and bottled for sale.

The best quality garum, known as garum sociorum, was a luxury product, while cheaper varieties were widely consumed by the lower classes. North Africa, Spain, and Gaul were major production centres, with cities like Sabratha, Leptis Magna, and Neapolis (Tunisia) mass-producing it for export.

Factories lined the coasts, taking advantage of abundant fish stocks and warm climates ideal for fermentation. Garum was not just a flavour enhancer, it was also believed to have medicinal benefits, used as a remedy for digestive issues and even as an aphrodisiac.

The sauce was so valuable that it was often taxed and traded like fine wine. Despite its strong smell, garum was a staple of Roman cuisine, found in the homes of both commoners and emperors, and its production remained a key industry throughout the empire.

----

Order the Next Book in this Stunning New Series

**Dark Eagle V**

THE WRAITH!

**Book V in the Exploratores Series**

## The Occultum Faces a Foe Unlike Anything They have Ever Seen Before

As Rome tightens its iron grip on Britannia, the *Occultum* are summoned to apply their unique skills once more. Their mission is clear: infiltrate enemy territory, cross the shadowed forests and sacred hills, and assassinate the most powerful Druid in Britannia.

The mission is perilous, a near-suicidal undertaking, and as the truth unravels, a devastating revelation shatters their resolve. Rome has made a fatal mistake: they've targeted the wrong man.

Bound by an unyielding duty to the Empire and an unbreakable loyalty to one another, the Occultum now stand on the brink of their greatest test, a confrontation with an enemy unlike any they've faced before, one that claws at the deepest recesses of their fears.

As the line between betrayal and obedience dissolves into shadows, they are forced toward a harrowing decision, one that threatens not only their lives but the very foundations of everything they have fought to protect.

In this gripping continuation of the Dark Eagle saga, the Occultum face their deadliest mission yet, a harrowing trial of courage, loyalty, and humanity that will change their fates forever.

## Subscribe

If you want to be informed the moment the next book is ready, just go to **KMAshman.com** and hit the subscribe button.

## Also Available

Printed in Dunstable, United Kingdom